THE MIDDLE EAST: AN ANTHROPOLOGICAL PERSPECTIVE

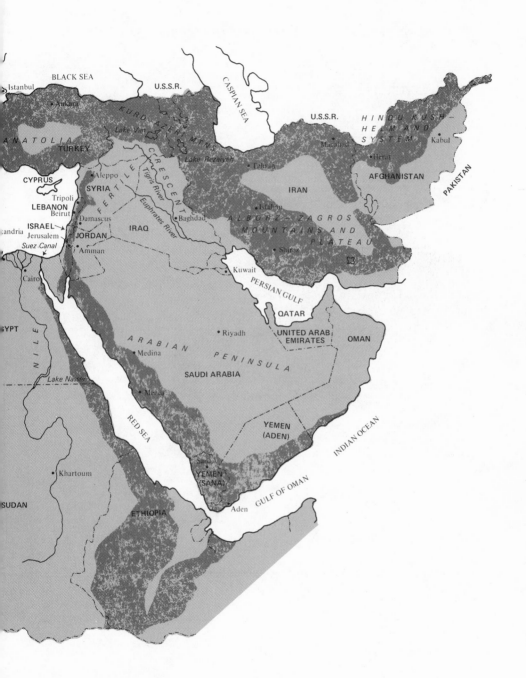

GOODYEAR REGIONAL ANTHROPOLOGY SERIES

Edward Norbeck, Editor

ANTHROPOLOGICAL PERSPECTIVES OF:

MODERN EUROPE
Robert T. Anderson

INDIA
Stephen A. Tyler

INDONESIA
James L. Peacock

CIRCUMPOLAR PEOPLES
Nelson H. H. Graburn and B. Stephen Strong

NORTH AMERICAN INDIANS
William W. Newcomb, Jr.

MAINLAND SOUTHEAST ASIA
Ronald Provencher

CHINA
Leon E. Stover and Takeko Kawai Stover

THE MIDDLE EAST
John Gulick

THE MIDDLE EAST: AN ANTHROPOLOGICAL PERSPECTIVE

John Gulick
University of North Carolina at Chapel Hill

GOODYEAR PUBLISHING COMPANY, INC.
Pacific Palisades, California

Library of Congress Cataloging in Publication Data

Gulick, John, 1924–
   The Middle East.

   (Goodyear regional anthropology series)
   Includes bibliographies and index.
   1. Near East—Social life and customs.
I. Title.
DS57.G84   956   75-26052
ISBN 0–87620–578–3
ISBN 0–87620–577–5 pbk.

Copyright © 1976 by

GOODYEAR PUBLISHING COMPANY, INC.
Pacific Palisades, California

Library of Congress Catalog Card Number: 75-26052

Current Printing (last digit):
10 9 8 7 6 5 4 3 2 1

ISBN: 0–87620–577–5 (Paper)
      0–87620–578–3 (Cloth)

Y–5775–5 (P)
Y–5783–9 (C)

Maps by: A. Marshall Licht

Printed in the United States of America

CONTENTS

PREFACE

This book grows out of a course that I have taught regularly at the University of North Carolina since 1955. The table of contents is basically the same as the syllabus of the course in 1976 but differs radically from the syllabus of 1955. The changes represent many developments in my thinking and knowledge that came about as the result of my own field research and of the increasingly rich literature on the area. The number of professional anthropologists doing field research in the Middle East has increased greatly; their concepts have become more sophisticated and their methods more effective. Scanty and deficient when I first began serious study of the Middle East, the literature has, accordingly, grown to the point where it is now difficult even for the specialist to read everything. By the time this book is published, additional publications will doubtless have appeared too late for use in the present book. I am not dismayed by this prospect, for much good material is now available, and my goals do not include reaching any final or dogmatic conclusions.

My interest in the Middle East began early in 1943 when, as a member of a group of volunteer ambulance drivers of the American Field Service, I was landed at Suez on the Red Sea. We were removed from the ship in lighters flying the flag of the kingdom of Egypt and taken to a camp devoid of any vegetation. Our first assignment was to drive a convoy of trucks from Cairo to Baghdad—across the Sinai desert, up the coastal plain of Palestine, across the Jordan and the desert to the Euphrates and the Tigris Rivers, bordered by groves of dusty date palms. We went from one horn of the Fertile Crescent to the other. From Baghdad we returned to the Mediterranean coast as passengers in the backs of open-bodied trucks driven by members of the Imperial Indian Army, a trip that took five days. This episode was not much of an adventure as adventures go, but it left indelible impressions: the short-lived springtime verdure surrounded by deserts; the sweet scent of the blossoming orange trees that surrounded the fortified stations of the Palestine Police, whose grim faces expressed the already bitter situation in which they were living and presaged more bitterness in the future; the meaninglessness of the political boundaries, for we crossed them all without let or hindrance; and the vulnerability of human existence in the oases as well as the desert. Today it takes one hour to fly by jet from Baghdad to Beirut, and the traveler remains oblivious to all that lies below.

The ensuing six months were spent in Lebanon, Syria, Egypt, and Libya. Attached to units of the British army and wearing military uniforms, we were not, on the whole, able to become well acquainted with the inhabitants, and, indeed, fascinated as I had become by the area, my thoughts, as we left Tripoli (Libya) for the beachhead at Salerno, were that I would like to return someday—as an archeologist.

When I returned to college in 1946 and decided to specialize in the social and cultural anthropology of the Middle East, I was encouraged by Professor Carleton Coon, who was one of only a handful of anthropologists who had done field work there. It was an area virtually unrecognized and certainly unknown by anthropologists generally. Since then, I have done field research on a Lebanese village (1951–1952), a Lebanese city (1961–1962), Baghdad (1965), and Isfahan (1970–1971). In 1972 the membership of the Middle East Studies Association of North America included eighty-six anthropologists, a figure that did not include *all* anthropologists concerned with the area. This book is an expression of my thinking about the Middle East based on my own experiences, feelings, and research, and it is further augmented by the publications of this steadily increasing number of anthropologists and other social scientists who have a similar orientation to Middle Eastern studies.

This orientation is toward understanding the everyday lives of ordinary people as perceived largely by direct observation during extended periods of residence, participating in local life to the extent that the people will permit, doing interviews and surveys, and supplementing data gathered by these means with appropriate documentary materials when they are available. Much of the work I have drawn upon was done by anthropologists, but the contributions of other behavioral scientists—especially sociologists, modern historians, psychologists, political scientists, and geographers—have also been of the utmost value and importance.

The subject of this book is, then, who the people of the Middle East are and what they are like, as perceived mostly during the third quarter of the twentieth century. The perception is largely that of the behavioral sciences, a view that differs considerably from the perceptions of other, mostly older, scholarly fields that are important in the understanding of the nature of the Middle East. Among these other fields are history (with subspecialties such as pre-Islamic, early post-Islamic, and Ottoman history), oriental studies (Middle Eastern languages, literature, and art), religion and philosophy (including Islamic theology and law), national and international economics (including the production and marketing of Middle Eastern petroleum), and international diplomatic relations (including the Arab-Israel conflict). Experts in these subjects are many, and the literature on each subject is enormous. Some of this literature is undoubtedly better known than the behavioral science literature, most of which is recent, and the purpose of this book is certainly not to attempt to supplant general works in these other disciplines but rather to present an account of the Middle East that, depending on one's viewpoint, is supplementary, complementary, or alternative. Readers familiar with some of the non-behavioral science literature on the Middle East may well be startled by what seem to be serious omissions. These, I think, are inevitable, and I hope that compensation will be found in fresh viewpoints and different perspectives.

Six books come readily to mind that are comparable to some degree with the present work in their topical priorities and, to a considerable extent, in their coverage. Three are by anthropologists: Carleton S. Coon's *Caravan: the Story of the Middle East*, revised edition (New York: Holt, 1958); Raphael Patai's *Society, Culture, and Change in the Middle East*, 3rd edition (Philadelphia: University of Pennsylvania Press, 1969); and Joe E. Pierce's *Understanding the Middle East* (Rutland, Vt.: Tuttle, 1971). The other three are by sociologists: Morroe Berger's *The Arab World Today* (Garden City, N.Y.: Doubleday, 1962); Gabriel Baer's *Population and Society in the Arab East* (New York: Praeger, 1964); and C. A. O. van Nieuwenhuijze's *Sociology of the Middle East: A Stocktaking and Interpretation* (Leiden, Netherlands: E. J. Brill, 1971).

Though comparable to these books, this book is also very different from them, and this fact requires further discussion.

The American news media are full of caricatures of Middle Eastern life. Among the stock scenes are flying carpets and slave auctions, harems where the women look either like nuns or like stripteasers, rapacious "oil sheiks" brandishing improbably shaped scimitars, and big flabby Goliath ("Arabs") confronted by heroic little David ("Israel"). These grotesque images express, and at the same time reinforce, the generally distorted, misinformed, and uninformed conceptions that many Americans and other Westerners have of the Middle East.

This book cannot obliterate these images, but it does attempt to counteract the misconceptions with information, much of which has been recently obtained by observers of modern Middle

Eastern life. While this information has now become, as I said earlier, fairly voluminous, it is also still fragmentary and subject to differing, sometimes conflicting, interpretations. The reasons for this state of affairs are many. One of them is that the Middle East is undergoing much change, and this makes the task of identifying norms difficult, if not impossible. And since norms are difficult to identify, it is difficult to make simple, straightforward generalizations. If change didn't complicate matters enough, there is also the increasing awareness among scholars that some of the traditional, "premodern" norms of Middle Eastern life (many of which still persist) may have been seriously misunderstood by earlier observers and therefore must be reconsidered at the same time that ongoing changes are being observed and analyzed.

An important case in point is the traditional role of women in the Middle East. There was a time, not very long ago, when everyone, it seems, knew what this was; it was apparently all settled and we could concentrate our attention on the *changing* role of women. The truth is that it is not all settled, that there is considerable controversy about it, and that the distinctions between traditional and modern that seemed so clear to some people are not so clear after all.

In the long run such complications will, I believe, lead to understandings and depictions of the Middle East that are more accurate, more humane, and more interesting than what we have had heretofore. Meanwhile, however, the difficulty of depicting the realities of Middle Eastern life, from an anthropological perspective, is considerable. Our new knowledge takes us beyond the mere repetition of shopworn generalizations like "Middle Eastern people are family oriented." Yet our new knowledge is fragmentary, subject to differing interpretations, and therefore problematic. There is some consensus, but there is also much controversy. In order to depict the reality as I perceive it, I must take account of, and put together, as many of the fragments as I can, in the end producing something analogous to an incomplete jigsaw puzzle with an indefinite number of missing pieces. The text is replete with references to, and comments on, many publications, together with references to works in which more details can be found. This mode of presentation has its faults, but I have tried to mitigate them by periodic statements of conclusions, however tentative they must be.

I am particularly concerned that those who read this book as their introduction to the Middle East get some clear understandings of what the whole forest is like. I am convinced, however, that in order to do this I must lead them through the trees and the underbrush, rather than skirting around them. In this way the book will also, I hope, be useful for Middle Eastern specialists whose main interests are in new growth—and perhaps some new species—in the trees and the underbrush. Readers who seek some sort of "briefing" on the modern Middle East may find this book more difficult than they had anticipated. It is not intended to be a briefing but rather a guide to those who want to understand the Middle East better by thinking about it more.

The organization of the book is phased and cumulative. Phase one consists of the first two chapters, which in different ways set forth some of the features that make the Middle East distinctive. Chapter One discusses the system of multiple desert-oasis environments that is the land of the Middle East, and it outlines important historical events that took place on this land. The present culture of the Middle East results from these events having taken place in this particular system of environments. Chapter Two states, and elaborates upon, a hypothesis about Middle Eastern people in general. This hypothesis is that they—more than many other people in the world—are highly conscious of the perils inherent in human relationships and that while there are perceived refuges from peril in those relationships, none is a complete refuge. The refuges themselves are perilous. This hypothesis is based on a great variety of comments by many other observers of the Middle East. It is not a scientific model or paradigm. It is not the book's "conclusion" (perversely presented near the beginning). Nor is it the organizing principle of the book; many details presented later would have to be forced into it if it were to serve that purpose. What is it, then? It is simply the broadest generalization in the book. It is presented early because I have found that students prefer it that way; they find it helpful in their efforts to make more sense of some of the important material that comes later.

Phase two comprises Chapters Three and Four. Where do Middle Eastern people actually live, and what are the characteristics of the places and settlements in which they live? The importance of this obviously fundamental matter is accentuated in the Middle East by the constrictions, perils, and challenges of the desert-oasis environments of the region. In the literature there is an abundance of clichés about nomads, villagers, and city dwellers. Chapters Three and Four counteract these clichés by amassing ideas and data that show the complexity and variety of pastoralism, village life, and city life. Much of the material in these chapters is drawn from very recent studies. Sometimes these studies revise previously held views of past or traditional conditions, and sometimes they focus on the conspicuous changes taking place today. Both approaches are reflected in Chapters Three and Four.

Phase three is Chapter Five and consists of a summary and synthesis of the major sociocultural aggregates of the Middle East: linguistic, religious, national, and ecological. This material could be introduced at the beginning of the book, but instead I have placed it near the middle. It brings together many of the things discussed in previous chapters, and it also describes the larger contexts in which Middle Eastern individuals carry on their immediate, everyday lives. In this fashion Chapter Five serves as a bridge between the earlier material that emphasizes aggregates and the last three chapters (phase four), in which individual or microcosmic perspectives are more prominent.

In phase four a number of major concerns of everyday life are discussed. As before, recent findings are used to replace worn-out clichés wherever possible. Important points in the individual's life cycle and the individual's involvement in important institutions are systematically treated. However, they are often dealt with in ways that the reader may, because of convention, expect to be treated differently. For example, there is no chapter entitled "Kinship and Marriage" or "The Family," yet sex and gender and alliances among relatives are given the very serious attention that they require.

A book that deals with gut issues of life and death, as this one does, is likely to be shaped by the author's emotional biases as well as by his scholarship. In what follows, my scholarship should, for better or worse, be evident. My biases, however, might remain hidden, or they might obtrude in unwelcome ways, if I did not make some of them explicit at this point.

Human beings cannot, for many reasons, survive without other human beings. Yet much of the misery that people must endure in life is caused by other human beings. I do not see anything necessary or inevitable in this seeming paradox. As far as I know, it is a phase in human evolution and is therefore subject to change and modification. The paradox has been greatly aggravated by all the rationalizations that people have thought up, or been sold on, that purport to explain why it is not subject to change, why human beings are not responsible for it, why it is, in fact, justified. These rationalizations consist essentially of presumptions about what human nature is, reinforced by presumptions about what God is. These are not merely autosuggested reassurances of ultimate certainties in a very uncertain existence. They have also been used repeatedly to justify self-serving policies and the denigration and exploitation of others.

I think that a major purpose of social science should be to challenge these conventional wisdoms and thereby to help human beings everywhere see and realize new choices and alternatives. Yet even within social science itself the conventional wisdoms have their rationalizers. Racism and ethnocentrism persist, though often in subtle guises. The Naked Ape hypothesis gets a ready reception among many social scientists; it "explains all" in terms of the inevitability of hostile aggression, war, territorialism, and male dominance/female submission. Claiming genetic determinism—without much genetic evidence—one version of Naked Apism invokes Original Sin for good measure. It also claims that the Fall occurred when Man the Noble Hunter (the Naked Ape's descendant) turned into a farmer, thereby condemning himself to perpetual frustration and perversion of his noble-hunter instincts. Since modern hunting-and-gathering cultures do not in fact give much ethnographic support to the Naked Ape-Noble Hunter image, this ingenious gambit preserves the hypothesis, but it makes it more tenuous than ever, for the evolution of farming, which first occurred in the Middle East, was just as "natural" an adaptation as was some people's retention of hunting and gathering.

The constrictions imposed by these rationalizations are nowhere more apparent than in what is currently called sexism. Anatomical femaleness and maleness are genetically determined, and in all cultures there are customary recognitions of the obvious differences between the two. Sexism is the carrying of these customary recognitions to extremes. Thus, it is concluded, men and women have totally different behavioral natures, and these are predetermined, not being subject to modification or adaptable to changing conditions. Individuals who do not fit the ideal male and female personality types involved are ipso facto defective persons. No more cruel a conformist strait jacket was ever devised. It is not merely folklore; it, too, has been reinforced by various social scientists bent on the fixation of conventional wisdoms.

Sexism is also directly pertinent to the Middle East, for this is one of the areas of the world where the customary distinctions between female and male (distinctions of gender as opposed to anatomical distinctions of sex) are particularly sharply drawn. Of this there is no doubt. There is also no doubt that, as new options for change open for Middle Eastern people, their customary gender definitions are being consciously subjected to critical scrutiny. This is what one would expect if one looks upon gender definitions as adaptational systems rather than as eternal, immutable verities.

In the portrayal of the modern Middle East that follows, I consciously reject the Naked Ape-Noble Hunter-sexist views of humankind. I regard them as pernicious, and particularly so in this case, as it would be very easy to interpret the Middle Eastern scene in terms of them. Having said this, I will say little more on the subject except at the beginning of Chapter Seven, nor will I use the text that follows as a battle ground in the dispute. I refer readers who may want to pursue the subject further to Alexander Alland's *The Human Imperative* (New York: Columbia University Press, 1972) and to Elaine Morgan's very funny and readable parody of Naked Apism, *The Descent of Woman* (New York: Bantam, 1972).

If the inhumanities that people inflict on each other are not predetermined, what *are* they caused by, and what *can* anyone do about them? I do not pretend to have any definite answer, and I doubt that there is any single or simple one. I do think that one of the root causes is probably that a substantial number of people in every generation have been unwanted by their parents, have been made to feel unwanted (but with the reason usually disguised), and have taken fearful, polymorphous revenge thereafter. There is ample and varied evidence for the high frequency of unwanted pregnancies, but there are many people who passionately reject even the thought of unwanted pregnancies. Why, and why the passion? Instinct for survival aggressively asserting itself? Try to prove it! Where is the instinct for survival among those who strenuously oppose the legalization of abortion but express no matching opposition to the indiscriminate slaughter wrought by modern warfare? Where is the instinct for survival among those who feel sure that portrayals of the pleasures of sexuality are far more harmful to the onlooker than portrayals of mayhem and murder? Whence come these strong feelings? I think they come from the dreadful sense of unwantedness. The fact is, though, that large numbers of unwanted people are not necessary or inevitable. The average human being is overendowed with physiological reproductive capacity. The ability to choose whether to reproduce is clearly present in our nature, but such choices are difficult, and most cultural traditions have made careful decision in this matter painful, if not impossible. I think the time has come when, for the sake of survival, human beings are ready to evolve new customs that allow reproduction and nonreproduction to be genuine, viable, equal alternatives. However, this evolution will require replacement of many of the old rationalizations about what human nature is and about what is natural for females and males, with radically new viewpoints and social arrangements. Such innovations will be resisted, and what the outcome will be no one knows. In any case this is what the population problem means, equally as much as it means overload on the carrying capacity of the Earth, and several of the Middle Eastern governments are at least talking about the population problem, whatever the depth of their perceptions of it may be. So much for the biases of the author.

The anthropological perspective of this book emphasizes Middle Eastern mental sets, emotions, motivations, and behavior, as well as criticism of many stereotypic misconceptions concerning these subjects. By the end of Chapter One it should become apparent that this emphasis is informed by important ecological and material considerations. Nevertheless, the material aspects of Middle Eastern culture per se are not dealt with in any great detail. Subjects such as farming and building techniques, tools, clothing styles, crafts, and the fine arts may seem to some readers to be neglected. This is a matter of priorities. I have much to say that I think needs saying on the subjects that are emphasized. I do not have much to say about material culture per se, even though it happens, actually, that Middle Eastern architecture, calligraphy, and some musical modes are important sources of pleasure for me. In any case, material and sensory aspects of Middle Eastern culture are treated splendidly in other, readily available books, and I refer the reader to them on numerous occasions.

An important aspect of Middle Eastern culture that I do not attempt to convey any particular sense of is the distinctive sounds of Middle Eastern languages. One way that this can be attempted is by rendering Middle Eastern words in precise phonetic transliteration. However, this involves expensive and troublesome typesetting complications that do not seem warranted, given the fact that this is not a philological book. My spelling of these words is as simple as possible consistent with clarity, and it is not intended to accurately represent correct pronunciations. Sounds that cannot be easily approximated by ordinary English letters (such as the glottal stop and the Arabic pharyngeal phonemes) are disregarded. It is important—but sufficient—that all readers, Middle Eastern specialists and nonspecialists alike, be aware that the use of simple, inaccurate transliteration in this book is the result of deliberate decisions, not of carelessness or ignorance.

ACKNOWLEDGMENTS

Professor L. Carl Brown of Princeton University and Professor Edward Norbeck of Rice University read the first draft of this book and offered many careful comments, criticisms, and suggestions. As a result, I made extensive changes in the manuscript. I believe that the book is better than it would have been without the benefit of their ideas, but I remain responsible for the shortcomings of the book in its final form.

My wife, Margaret Gulick, also made specific, helpful comments. Beyond them, her patience and support were steadfast throughout the trials and stresses of writing and revising the manuscript.

THE MIDDLE EAST: AN ANTHROPOLOGICAL PERSPECTIVE

ONE

THE EVOLVING ECOLOGY

THE OASIS CONCEPT

Oasis is a word that conjures up a clear image: a grove of trees and other vegetation completely surrounded by hot desert as far as the eye can see. As the scene of action in countless books and movies, this oasis means life-renewing shade and relief from thirst and hunger; and depending on who its inhabitants are, it may mean help and hospitality, extortion in return for safe passage, or, if survival is granted at all, being held as a hostage in some power game. The oasis may be an armed camp—a rebel hideout or an army outpost—or its inhabitants may be the subdued subjects of the power of others. Though remote and difficult of access, the oasis is not, in fact, really isolated.

This is just one type of oasis. There are several others: a river running through a desertic plain, its banks consisting intermittently of desert and strips and enclaves of vegetation between the water and the desert; high mountain meadows, often snow-covered in winter, grassy in summer, contrasted with the desiccated slopes and plains below; mountain streams, large and small, tumbling down through gorges and treeless slopes, passing through intermittent clumps of trees and bushes where the gradient is slight and there is bottom land, and ending in a green delta where the river disappears into the desert or the ocean; hillsides with open stands of small pines and oaks, with no ground cover except grass and wild flowers in the spring; open plains, sometimes traversed by water courses, green with grasses or crops in spring but parched and desertlike by midsummer; spring sites in mountain valleys or in cirques—bowls of vegetation encircled by treeless slopes.

These are some of the more common habitable environments that recur, in a wide variety of sizes and juxtapositions, from Morocco in the west to Pakistan in the east and from Turkey in the north to south Yemen. Their recurrences are combined with recurrences of desert that vary greatly in size, shape, and topography.

It is more realistic to think of the Middle East as an area where such oases are scattered among deserts than as an area divided neatly into desert and nondesert areas, each of considerable size. The latter impression is conveyed by conventional maps that show the enormous expanses of the Sahara and the Arabian Desert, both of which seem to contrast neatly with the adjoining relatively densely inhabited areas of Northwest Africa and the Fertile Crescent.

The neat, block-type image is misleading for a number of reasons: (1) The major deserts are not uniform but varied in nature, as mentioned above, and one of the major variables is precipitation and associated flora, ranging from areas with none of either to areas with enough to provide resources for moving pastoralists and their herds on a short-term basis. (2) The interfaces between maximum, major deserts and areas of maximum water supply are intricate and complex—sometimes abrupt, sometimes gradual—as suggested by the oasis images that have just been presented. There is not in fact the smooth uniformity of transition that is conveyed by the isotherms and isohyets drawn on climatological maps. Some of the most densely populated and socially complex locations in the Middle East (for example, the cities of Cairo, Damascus, and Isfahan) immediately adjoin minimally habitable deserts. (3) There are other substantial desert or dry-steppe areas besides the Sahara and Arabian Desert. For example, extensive desertic and semidesertic regions exist in central Turkey and central and eastern Iran, two of the most populous countries of the area. (4) Even in the areas most favored in precipitation, the predominantly hot and dry nature of the Middle East is very evident. Among such areas are the northwestern plains of Morocco, lying between the Atlas Mountains and the Atlantic coast, and the western slopes and small plains of Lebanon and Israel. Here about twenty inches of rain and snow can be expected in the winter, enough for field crops, orchards, and vineyards on location and enough for runoff into adjacent rain-shadow areas to make agriculture possible there, too. Yet even in these places, as the long dry summer proceeds and the heat intensifies, desiccation becomes evident everywhere except along permanent watercourses and where there are irrigation systems. By early fall these areas are like minioases in minideserts. Furthermore, while the inhabitants can look forward to cooler weather and rainfall in winter, they cannot rely on equally abundant precipitation every year, for in fact it varies considerably from year to year to the degree of 100 percent variation from one year to the next.

Middle Eastern food production consists basically of wheat and barley agriculture, various kinds of arboriculture, and animal husbandry (mainly sheep and goats but also cattle and camels). For reasons that should by now be evident, these production activities are everywhere precarious. In the face of this precariousness human beings have hedged their bets, as it were, by (1) ingenuity and hard work (for example, multichannel oasis irrigation systems, subterranean aqueducts, and terraced mountain slopes); (2) flexibility (for example, in adjusting dependence on agriculture or animal husbandry to variations in carrying capacity of the land vis-à-vis numbers of consumers, and in changes from food production to wage labor and back again); (3) transfer of food products from one region to another, involving a great variety of exchange processes, institutions, and forms of production; and (4) maximum exploitation of the assorted precarious ecological niches, including the exploitation of various categories of people by others. This last point is intended only to suggest, at this early point in the book, certain realities of human life that will be discussed more fully later on and were suggested in an exaggerated cinema-scenario fashion in the introduction to the oasis concept.

THE DESERT-OASIS ENVIRONMENT

Words alone are insufficient to explain the nature of the Middle Eastern terrain, and the use of an atlas is necessary to understand its distinctive combination of geographical and cultural features. A hydrographic map of the world shows that northern Africa and adjacent southwest Asia together constitute one of the largest of the several major arid zones of the world. No other zone is like this one. Part of two major land masses (Africa and Eurasia), at various points it adjoins two oceans (Atlantic and Indian) and four seas (Mediterranean, Red, Caspian, and Black).

The rain and snow that this area receives falls mostly on the mountains and some of the immediately adjacent plains. Runoff in the form of streams and underground drainage systems carries water into areas that otherwise receive very little precipitation, resulting in many of the oases. Most of these runoff systems are short, but three are long and particularly important: the Nile River, the Euphrates-Tigris Rivers, and the underground flows of water from the highlands of western Arabia to the low-lying shores of eastern Arabia. The Nile originates in the heavy summer rains in the mountains of eastern Equatorial Africa, a region outside the Middle East. The Euphrates-Tigris Rivers originate in the mountains of eastern Turkey. The rains that fall on the escarpments and mountains of southwestern Arabia—south of Mecca and falling most heavily in Yemen—contribute, via underground seepage, to natural oases in eastern Arabia, where the largest petroleum sources also are but where there is very little rain. The natural oases can be, and recently have increasingly been, augmented by wells. The use of wells (and subterranean aqueducts) to tap underground water sources in desertic areas also occurs in many other parts of the Middle East. For example, it makes possible the series of towns on the edge of the Sahara, south of the mountains in Morocco and Algeria, as well as the city of Tehran, Iran, which has grown from a small village to nearly 4 million people in the past 200 years.

The principal mountainous areas are: (1) the Atlas system of Morocco, with extensions into Algeria and Tunisia; (2) the Levantine mountain chain that runs parallel with the Mediterranean shores of Syria, Lebanon, and Israel—actually two parallel chains of mountains with a narrow valley system in between that is 3,000 feet above sea level in Lebanon but below sea level in the Jordan Valley and at the Dead Sea; (3) the mountains and escarpments of western Arabia, running parallel to the Red Sea and culminating in the mountainous node of Yemen; (4) the mountain system of southern and western Turkey (Anatolia), adjoining the Mediterranean Sea; (5) the mountain system of eastern Turkey that runs fairly continuously southeastward through Iranian Azerbaijan and thence in two branches, the Alborz system eastward and the Zagros system southeastward; and (6) the Hindu Kush system of Afghanistan. There are other mountain systems in the Middle East, but they are less significant in terms of the relative abundance of water and its many consequences. Adding to these mountain systems the Nile and Euphrates-Tigris River systems, we complete the list of maximum water-supply areas.

The hydrographic situation just sketched has apparently been essentially the same since the beginning of historical records, at least 4,000 years, and probably longer. This does not mean that ecological (hence social and political) conditions have been constant in each of these areas during all that time—far from it. The element of precariousness has been ever present, with repeated periods of waxing and waning prosperity, creativity, and political hegemony as results. What it does mean, however, is that somewhere in each of the areas there has been a continuous presence and unfolding of concentrated human existence, dependent on the relative abundance of water. In each area certain distinctive cultural patterns have evolved, but important similarities also exist. These similarities are due to the recurrence everywhere of the oasis-desert ecology and to the fact that repeatedly throughout recorded history, and presumably before it, cultural patterns originating in one area have been spread to, or have been imposed upon, other areas. The spread of Islam from the highlands of western Arabia to all of the other areas is probably the single most important event of the many such events that have occurred, at least as far as present-day conditions are concerned.

Having urged the reader to consult an atlas, I must now warn against the misconception, easily gained from atlases or other conventional maps, that each of the areas of relatively abundant water supply is a single, uniformly watered oasis. Oases are more numerous, closer together, more varied, and sometimes larger where water is most abundant. However, even in the areas of relatively abundant water supply, the locations that actually have sufficient water are either discontinuous or sharply differentiated from adjoining deserts, as in the case of the Nile Delta. Consequently, the full ecological variety of the Middle East recurs in each of its major subregions.

CULTURAL-ECOLOGICAL SUBREGIONS

The Middle East consists of nine subregions, which I shall call cultural-ecological subregions since they are based upon a combination of climatological and topographical and cultural features:

1. The Fertile Crescent
2. Anatolia
3. The Kurd-Azeri Mountains
4. The Alborz-Zagros Mountains and Plateau
5. The Hindu Kush-Helmand system
6. The Arabian Peninsula
7. The Nile
8. The Sahara
9. The Maghrib

The list begins with the Fertile Crescent for reasons that will be discussed later, and similarly, there are reasons for discussing the next three subregions in the order presented. The Hindu Kush-Helmand area then follows logically. Having generally moved eastward, we then move generally westward with the last four subregions.

I shall locate the subregions primarily in terms of the modern nations that are involved. It will be immediately apparent, however, that the cultural-ecological subregions do not coincide on a one-to-one basis with the nations, and therefore my presentation may at first seem strange to readers who are accustomed to books on the Middle East organized in terms of nations.

The Fertile Crescent, so called because of its shape and its relative abundance of water, has three main parts: (1) the coastal mountains and associated valleys and plains of Israel, western Jordan, Lebanon, and Syria; (2) the adjacent and continuous plains of northern Syria, southeastern Turkey, and northern Iraq; and (3) the Euphrates-Tigris drainage system, including the Karun River in the lowland plains of Khuzestan, Iran.

Anatolia consists of roughly the western half of Turkey. The Kurd-Azeri Mountains area consists of contiguous mountains in eastern Turkey, northeastern Iraq, and northwestern Iran. The designation refers to the fact that this area has long been the home of two ethnic aggregations, distinct from each other and from the majority of the population of the countries in which they reside. These are the Kurds (Sunni Muslims who speak a language related to Persian, large numbers of whom live in all three of the countries concerned) and the Azeris (Shia Muslims living in Iran who speak

Azeri, a dialect of Turkish). Parts of this area constitute, also, the traditional homeland of the Armenians, who have their own sect of Christianity and speak their own Indo-European language. Very few Armenians now remain in the Turkish part of this area, most of them having emigrated to other parts of the Middle East and the world during the past sixty years.

The Alborz-Zagros Mountains and Plateau area constitutes most of Iran and is dominated in all respects by Persian-speaking Iranians.

The Arabian Peninsula consists of five culturally distinct parts: (1) the western highlands and (2) the central desert (together constituting most of Saudi Arabia); (3) Yemen; (4) the southern shore (South Yemen and Oman); and (5) the Gulf shore settlements divided politically among the United Arab Emirates, Qatar, Bahrain, Saudi Arabia, and Kuwait. As noted before, Yemen and parts of the western highlands are relatively well watered and therefore have supported sustained human activities for a long time. These activities have included the maintenance of trade between Ethiopia and the Fertile Crescent; the development of a complex, distinctive, pre-Islamic culture in Yemen; and the revelation of Islam in the commercial towns of the western highlands. The central desert is the home of the so-called Bedouin, those desert and oasis dwellers on whom one of the most widely known stereotypes of "the typical Arab" has been constructed. The settlements of the southern shore consist mostly of small seaports, with some inland towns, especially toward the west, where they benefit from runoff from the mountains of Yemen. Generally, each town is an oasis, separated from the others by extremely difficult desert terrain, and each until recently having constituted little more than a single city-state. Very much the same has been true of the Gulf shore settlements. However, many of them have recently experienced the discovery of petroleum and its conspicuous consequences. The subject of Arabian oil is being given enormous and vivid publicity in the mass media, eclipsing much of the rest of the Middle East and focusing attention on a subregion that has been less studied by behavioral scientists than probably any of the other major subregions.

The Nile flows northward from the mountains of Ethiopia and the great lakes of east Africa, first through the grasslands of southern Sudan and then to the Mediterranean through the eastern Sahara. It has been realistically likened to a ribbon of water and fertility flowing through a vast arid countryside. The Nile subregion consists of lower (downstream) Egypt, including the Delta, cities such as Alexandria and Cairo, and an extension that includes the settlements along the Suez Canal. Upper Egypt is the upstream portion of the Egyptian Nile. Nubia is a region of some cultural distinctiveness, overlapping the Egyptian-Sudanese boundary and recently greatly affected by the filling of Lake Nasser behind the high dam at Aswan. The Sudanese Nile area includes the city of Khartoum.

The Sahara ("desert" in Arabic) includes the desertic portions of Morocco and Tunisia, the very large desertic portion of Algeria, the entire country of Libya (including the coastal cities), the desertic portions of Egypt and Sudan, and the contiguous desertic areas of Spanish Sahara, Mauritania, Niger, Mali, and Chad, for a rather indeterminate distance southward.

Lastly, the Maghrib ("western" country in Arabic) consists of the relatively well watered coastal areas, mountains, plains, and plateaus of Morocco, Algeria, and Tunisia. The Maghrib is much more frequently referred to in the literature as "North Africa," but I shall not use this term. For one thing it is ambiguous; Libya and Egypt are in north Africa, too, yet they are not customarily included in the designation. Second, it does not discriminate between the well-watered and the Saharan portions of northern Africa. Third, many people have an understandable semantic difficulty in accepting "North Africa" as being part of the "Middle East."

Defining the Middle East in terms of recurrent cultural-ecological phenomena results in deemphasizing many of the national boundaries that are so conspicuous on most maps of the area. I think that there are good anthropological reasons for giving cultural-ecological criteria priority over national identity criteria. National identities will be given some consideration, though, in Chapter Five.

Where does the Middle East "end" and where do other areas "begin"? An obvious way of answering this question would be to include some nations and exclude others, thus giving the Middle East outer political boundaries. This procedure would not, however, be as easy as it might seem, nor would it be consistent with the basic perspectives of this book.

THE MIDDLE EAST ENCOMPASSED

I shall now proceed around the peripheries of the Middle East, explaining why this or that area is to be included or excluded. This will highlight the combinations of cultural and ecological phenomena that are felt to be Middle Eastern. I will begin with the southern Sahara, then move eastward, and then counterclockwise, ending with the Mediterranean coastlands of Europe.

No one, I believe, would quarrel with the idea of including the inhabitants of the Hoggar Mountains (southern Algeria) and Tibesti Mountains (northern Chad) in the Middle East. But how much farther south can one go? There is so little anthropological material on Spanish Sahara and Mauritania that I, at least, would leave the matter open as far as these regions are concerned. From central Mali to central Chad the question becomes more interesting. A study has been done of the town of Timbuktu, the results of which would justify the town's inclusion in the Middle East: It exists because it has been a transshipment point of goods being traded from the Maghrib, across the desert, and thence down the Niger. In connection with this, Timbuktu has an Arab quarter, but it also has quarters identified with cultural groups linked to the distinctive patterns of coastal West Africa that are not Middle Eastern. Farther east there are desert-oasis dwellers who speak one or another of the Berber languages (very important in the central and northern Sahara and in the Maghrib), and I would be inclined to consider them part of the Middle East. Important groups like the Hausa, many of whom live in northern Nigeria, are problematic. They have long been converted to Islam, but, on the other hand, they speak a language that is not otherwise used in the Middle East, and their economic ties are generally toward the south.

The Darfur and Kordofan regions of central Sudan are inhabited by Arabic-speaking Muslims who can hardly be excluded from the Middle East. However, south of them are cultures, such as those of the Dinka and the Nuer, that are not Middle Eastern. They are not Muslims; they do not speak Arabic, Berber, Hebrew, Persian, or Turkish; and they do not have the oasis-desert ecology.

Within Ethiopia's borders are a variety of environments and cultures. The mountainous core of the country is culturally diverse and distinctive. There are various languages, some belonging to the Semitic language family and therefore related to Arabic and Hebrew, while others are related to the Berber languages. The Ethiopian Christian church has ancient ties with the Egyptian Coptic Christian church. However, in general this important segment of Ethiopian culture has a number of unique features that set it apart from all cultures surrounding it, including the Middle Eastern ones. The eastern lowlands of Ethiopia, however, are continuous with the largely desertic area of Somalia, and the little anthropological observation that has been done in Somalia suggests that the pastoral nomadic people there are essentially Middle Eastern.

Farther south, along the Indian Ocean coast of Africa, Arabs from the Middle East have been active as traders for a long time, and they have left their mark in important urban centers such as Zanzibar and Dar es Salaam. But the surrounding hinterlands are not Middle Eastern in language, religion, or ecology.

From the east African peripheries of the Middle East we move to Pakistan, whose western borders are shared with Iran and Afghanistan. A strong case can be made for including Pakistan in the Middle East without any hedging about peripheries. Among the reasons: Pakistan is Islamic; it has definite elements of the desert-oasis ecology, and the Indus River drainage system has many similarities to the major Middle Eastern river systems already mentioned; certain special ethnic groups, for example the Pathans and the Baluch, live partly in Pakistan and partly in Afghanistan and Iran respectively. On the strength of such considerations I shall include some Pakistani data. However, Pakistan is also peripheral to the Middle East because of its many cultural affinities with India. Urdu, the predominant language, though written in the Arabic alphabet, is more similar to certain languages of India than it is to Persian, to which it is distantly related. Pakistan's recent bitter relationships with India to the contrary notwithstanding, political and other cultural ties between the people of the two countries have for a long time been closer than have the Pakistanis' ties with the Islamic countries farther west. It is largely for these reasons that in academic area studies Pakistan is generally considered with India rather than the Middle East.

The Himalayas effectively separate Tibet and Central Asia from Afghanistan and Pakistan, but the dry steppes farther west are inhabited by ethnic groups such as the Muslim Turkmen, who live both in Iran and the Soviet Union and represent the pastoral-oasis ecology of the Middle East. The three cities of Bukhara, Samarkand, and Tashkent are now tourist attractions exploited by the Soviet Union, but they owe their existence to the fact that they were important trading posts linking the Middle East and Central Asia. Their architectural monuments are Persian Islamic in style, and except for their now being heavily influenced by Soviet industrial culture, they are Middle Eastern cities. Farther north and east, however, Islam and the desert-oasis ecology give way to other cultural patterns.

The Caucasus Mountains and the northern shores of the Black Sea are neither culturally nor ecologically Middle Eastern. However, in the Caucasus region immediately south of the mountains and between them and the Soviet borders with Turkey and Iran, Armenian and Iranian influences have been strong.

Finally we come to the Mediterranean area. The sea itself seems clearly to separate the Middle East from Europe so that there apparently need be no further discussion about what is Middle Eastern and what is not. We could indeed leave the matter at this. To do so, however, would be to ignore the many centuries of trans-Mediterranean influences, the generally recognized circum-Mediterranean climate, and certain apparently common cultural themes that may be the long-term results of these connections and natural similarities. A number of behavioral scientists and other observers have reported certain cultural patterns in Spain, southern Italy, and Greece that seem similar to cultural patterns in the Middle East, or that are enlightening concerning them. These may be due to similarities of experience that have prevailed for a long time in similar natural environments, despite very marked differences between Europe and the Middle East in such matters as religion, language, and national identities. These seemingly similar cultural patterns involve some core issues of life, such as relationships between men and women, relationships between the immediate family and outsiders, sense of community (or lack of it), and apparently deep-seated reactions of the individual to other people in general.

One can, of course, label these as circum-Mediterranean cultural patterns that underlie, or are superimposed upon, European and Middle Eastern cultures. The fact is that although Mediterranean Europe and the Mediterranean Middle East are clearly distinct from each other, each is, from the anthropological point of view, important for an understanding of the other.

TIME PERSPECTIVES

The cultural-ecological characteristics of the Middle East have evolved over a long time, and more is known about a longer segment of this Middle Eastern evolution than is known about many other parts of the world.

Fragmentary but very widely distributed evidence indicates that during the Pleistocene geological period, people with paleolithic cultures lived in the Middle East as they also did in Europe and East Asia. These people may have included members of the extinct species called Homo Erectus. They were tool makers, but they had significantly smaller brains than do present-day human beings. Among other early inhabitants of the Middle East were people of the Neanderthal type. Prevailing opinion now is that the Neanderthalers were an early variant of "modern man." They were not only tool makers, they also had brains of "modern" size and had probably developed systems of abstract thought. They lived all over Eurasia, and their presence in the Middle East, as well as the locations of some of their habitations there, suggests that there was regular travel linking the Middle East with other areas even in those late glacial times. Otherwise, however, the data are too fragmentary to allow us to see any clear continuities between those people and later Middle Easterners. Whether occupied by Neanderthalers or other variants of "modern man," the habitations that have been found were evidently the temporary campsites of small bands of people subsisting on the hunting of animals and the gathering of uncultivated vegetable foods. Near the end of the Pleistocene era, approximately 20,000 B.C., these people and all the other people in the world lived in small dispersed bands, subsisting by some form of hunting and gathering.

It was in the Middle East that groups of hunter-gatherers first began domesticating certain animals and plants, gradually developing animal husbandry and agriculture. Parallel sequences of development occurred independently in other parts of the world, but in all cases they were apparently later than in the Middle East. As a consequence, the agricultural village (and a number of other subsequent phenomena) became established earlier in the Middle East than anywhere else.

By approximately 8000–7000 B.C. there were, in the Fertile Crescent, Anatolia, and the Alborz-Zagros Mountains and Plateau, farming villages based on animal husbandry and agriculture and other settlements that may have been fortifications and trading centers. If, as is currently assumed in the absence of contrary evidence, these settlements were developed out of a hunting-and-gathering ecology in this same general location, that development must have taken a long time. Flannery (1970, p. 39) implies a slow developmental period from about 40,000 B.C. to about 10,000 B.C. Since many different discoveries, and presumably experiments and inventions, were involved, the pinpointing of a date of onset of change from hunting-and-gathering is really impossible. However long the developmental process did in fact take, the existence of a variety of settled communities by about 8000–7000 B.C. is indisputable. Inherent in the character of these settlements, furthermore, were three core ecological complexes—agriculture, animal husbandry, and trade—that have constituted the foundation of Middle Eastern subsistence ever since.

It is uncertain why changes away from hunting and gathering were first made in the Fertile Crescent-Anatolia-Zagros region. There has been much speculation about it, but that does not particularly concern us. What is certain is that these developments had very widespread consequences. By 5000 B.C. there were agricultural villages not only in the core area but also along the Nile and the Danube in Europe. Hunter-gatherers continued to live in some parts of Europe for a long time after this, but there is evidence that the animal husbandry-agricultural-trading subsistence system spread gradually from the core area into Europe and other parts of the Middle East.

This diffusion was presumably accomplished both by the migration of people who had the necessary knowledge and skills and by erstwhile hunter-gatherers learning the new skills through contacts with migrants and traders. Evidence of trade between subregions of the core area is very good. Three of the most important natural products involved were obsidian (volcanic glass used for projectile points and various cutting tools), bitumen (natural asphalt used for hafting stone blades), and copper. There is good evidence, in the form of manufactured articles, that trade routes later developed in the Middle East, between the Middle East and Europe, and in Europe.

The earliest agricultural crops were wheat and barley, wild forms of which still grow in parts of the Fertile Crescent. The first groundbreaking tool was a stone-bladed hoe, and it was this hoe agriculture that first spread to other areas. Later the plow (a digging stick drawn by animals) and the wheel (also best used in conjunction with draft animals) were invented, and they in turn diffused. In time copper began to be used for various implements and ornaments. Eventually, techniques for making bronze by mixing copper with tin were invented, and this harder metal was used for a variety of tools and weapons. These products of early metallurgy were also spread to other areas.

By 4000 B.C. towns or small cities—as differentiated from agricultural villages—were well established, at least in the southeastern extremity of the Fertile Crescent (Uruk, near the Euphrates River, for certain) and very probably elsewhere in the core area. Most prehistorians agree that the existence of towns or small cities implies the interrelated existence of an extensive agricultural hinterland, a trading hinterland, occupational specialization, and regional communications patterns. Political controls over, if not beyond, the hinterlands seem likely, but in the absence of written records direct evidence of political controls is difficult to identify.

At this time there still were hunter-gatherers in parts of Europe, and agricultural villages were first being established in relatively remote places like the British Isles. It may be said that the British people of that time lagged far behind their Middle Eastern contemporaries—perhaps 4000 years—in technological development. The British and the Europeans of those and earlier times appear to have been learners of Middle Eastern technological development rather than inventors. For several millennia they were "underdeveloped" compared to the people of the Middle East.

TIME FRAMES

The chronological developments of Middle Eastern culture and ecology need to be set into time frames in order to make them comprehensible. The time frames that I consider most useful for our purposes are:

1. Formative: 8000–2000 B.C.
2. Florescent: 2000 B.C.–A.D. 900
3. Conservative Islamic: A.D. 900–1800
4. Machine-Age Islamic: A.D. 1800–Present

Formative

The term Formative is borrowed from prehistoric archaeology, one of the subfields of anthropology. From 8000 to 2000 B.C. a number of the most important cultural patterns of the Middle East were formed. Among these were the basic ecological adaptations, including settlement patterns, already discussed. As the continental glaciers of Europe receded, progressive desiccation followed, and by 2000 B.C. climatological conditions essentially the same as those of modern times had developed in the Middle East. The many subsequent appearances and reappearances of villages in various desertic areas were apparently not due solely to major, long-term climatic changes but rather depended principally upon changes in social conditions that made exploitation of marginal areas sometimes feasible and sometimes infeasible. Brief climatic fluctuations, such as several years of drought or several years of abundant rain, were undoubtedly also influential.

Other cultural innovations between 8000 and 2000 B.C. characterize the Formative period. One was the development of writing. By 2000 B.C. cuneiform writing, having originated in the eastern Fertile Crescent, was well established, and this essentially ideographic system was later modified by the addition of some phonetic elements. These phonetic elements indicate that by 2000 B.C. a Semitic language was being spoken in the eastern Fertile Crescent. How widely Semitic languages were then being spoken we do not know, but it is highly probable that they were spoken at least in the rest of the Fertile Crescent. As is well known, another ideographic system of writing, Egyptian hieroglyphics, had been developed along the Nile. It is generally assumed that some form or forms of so-called Hamitic language (of which the various Berber languages are representatives today) were spoken along the Nile at that time.

As is also well known, states with city centers had been established along the Euphrates-Tigris and Nile Rivers by 2000 B.C. These were, of course, economically based upon the plant and animal husbandry first developed millennia earlier.

Some information is available about local anthropomorphic deities, the priesthoods serving them, and militaristic, deified kings associated with the urban centers of the Formative states. These data suggest the presence of an elite class and therefore hierarchies of social classes. Several religious phenomena that are generally assumed to have been part of Formative Middle Eastern culture are:

1. Sacred locations imbued with supernatural power.
2. Animal sacrifices, probably human sacrifices, and certainly mutilations of the human body—circumcision being the prime example.
3. Sacramental meals associated with sacrifice.
4. The mythical theme of the death of a god in human form and his resurrection in conjunction with the proliferation of springtime vegetation. Adonis, Osiris, and Tammouz are three of the various names of this god.

5. Anthropomorphic spirits—somewhat susceptible to human wishes—that can cause trouble or be helpful.
6. A major female anthropomorphic deity, usually beneficent in nature.

In various forms and versions, recombinations, interpretations and rationalizations, these symbolic themes have been important in the Middle East ever since the Formative phase of cultural evolution.

Florescent

Florescent is also a term borrowed from archaeology, and it connotes development or elaboration to full potential—or to what appears to be full potential.

The beginning of the Florescent period coincides roughly with the beginning of historical records—made possible, of course, by writing, and greatly facilitated early in the Florescent by the invention of fully phonetic writing.

Whether first invented in Crete or on the mainland, the alphabet seems first to have been used extensively by speakers of Semitic languages in the Fertile Crescent. The letters were simple pictographs, to each of which a different phonemic (meaningful sound) value was assigned. The first two letters were a horned bovine head (alif) that the Greeks eventually turned completely upside down to make *A*, and bayt ("house"), a simple, two-room house plan. These symbols have been preserved in recognizable form in the alphabets that later developed for European languages, which stemmed primarily from the Greek and Roman alphabets. However, the alphabets that were developed for the Semitic languages were changed out of recognition from the original. Apparently, the Semitic speakers very early felt the need for rapid script writing with connected letters, whereas the early needs of the Greeks and Romans seemed to be for separate letters that could be carved on stone. Earlier than the Greeks and Romans, the Semitic speakers' use of their alphabets proliferated into extensive commercial records and sacred texts. Semitic languages *may* have been spoken throughout the Fertile Crescent and the Arabian Peninsula in the Formative period, but alphabetic records make it clear that they were *certainly* spoken there in the Florescent.

Also early in the Florescent, a language (or group of closely related languages) was introduced into the Alborz-Zagros Mountains and Plateau area. This language was ancestral to modern forms of Persian and its close relatives. Supposedly introduced by invaders (the "Aryans"), this linguistic event is not well understood, since neither the invaders nor the inhabitants of the area at the time left any written records that could show what the processes of change were. In any case this episode is believed to have been one of several waves of movement that brought the original Celtic, Germanic, Greek, Italic, and Slavic languages into Europe and the predecessors of Urdu and Hindustani (and others) into Pakistan and India. As far as this book is concerned, the important point is that another one of the distinctive cultural variants of the Middle East was established at this time.

The basic Middle Eastern ecology continued to obtain during the Florescent, most of the people being village dwellers. It was during the Florescent, also, that the present-day pastoral-nomadic ecology (exploiting the minimally watered areas insofar as possible) definitely became widespread. Pastoral nomadism may have first developed in conjunction with animal husbandry, agriculture, and commerce during the Formative, but this is not certain. What is certain is that present-day pastoral nomadism is symbiotic with the agricultural and commercial ecologies of village and city life and is not a survival from pre-Formative hunting-and-gathering times.

Commerce grew greatly in the Florescent, facilitated by extended trade routes and market areas that were established under the auspices of various imperial regimes. It was also facilitated by alphabetic writing, the invention of money, and the new and general use of iron for agricultural tools, for weapons, and for other implements that increased efficiency.

From the small states of the late Formative that were confined to one cultural-ecological subregion, in the Florescent a succession of larger states developed, each of which in its prime exercised centralized political control over one or more cultural-ecological subregions. The inability of these states to maintain such extensive control for long periods is well known and has been attributed to many causes. The difficulty of maintaining communication between different subregions, given the technology of the times, and the cultural differences among the subregions were probably two of the causes.

From the beginning of the Florescent the states of the Tigris-Euphrates and Nile regions repeatedly expanded and contracted, vying for control of the western part of the Fertile Crescent. I will not attempt to summarize the careers of the various Egyptian dynasties or the Babylonian and later Assyrian and Neo-Babylonian Empires. We need to consider the possibility that the effects of the military activities of these states on the ordinary villagers, herdsmen, and town dwellers may have been the beginning of the generally negative attitudes of Middle Eastern people toward government that have subsequently become evident.

About the middle of the second millennium of the Florescent (that is, the first millennium B.C.), Persian speakers in the southeastern extremity of the Fertile Crescent consolidated and extended their power and established what is known as the Persian

Empire. For a brief time it brought under central control more cultural-ecological subregions than any other state had done previously. More lastingly, it established the tradition of a Persian-speaking state structure in the Alborz-Zagros Plateau area. At this time some of the ideas of the Zoroastrian religion, a subject that will be mentioned later, probably spread outside the borders of the Persian Empire.

At about the same time, Semitic speakers from the western Fertile Crescent were establishing colonies in the Maghrib—creating coastal states such as Carthage, which had mountainous hinterlands occupied by Berber-speaking peoples.

Alexander the Great's defeat of the Persian Empire was quickly followed by the division of his own empire into several successor states, encompassing all of the Middle East except the Maghrib, the Sahara, and the southern part of the Arabian Peninsula. The resulting Hellenistic period saw the growth of important new cities such as Alexandria. It also established, for a while, Greek-speaking elites in many of the cities, together with Greek religion and other aspects of culture. This elite Greek culture is important in the historical accounts and the archaeological remains. The many continuities of older, non-Greek, patterns among the villagers and probably many of the city dwellers, too, are generally overlooked. Nevertheless, these rulers must have had an impact on the general populace. The uninterrupted succession of warlike tyrants and dynasts (such as the Ptolemies in Egypt and the Seleucids and Antigonids elsewhere) must have reinforced a set of attitudes toward rulers that may have been present earlier, was certainly present later on, and still is present in the minds of most Middle Eastern people. Rulers in general are understood to be corrupt and corruptible, predatory and self-serving. Government has meant taxes, conscription, and forced labor, though at times with some rudimentary and unreliable protection against invasion or other attacks. Competing rulers have meant war, pillage, extortion, and famine. With occasional charismatic exceptions, such rulers have inspired fear more than loyalty. Evasion and uncooperativeness are the typical defensive tactics to be used against them, reliance on nongovernmental institutions for protection and support is a necessity, and manipulation (when possible) is the chief means of influencing governmental activities. It remains to be seen whether the various *modern* Middle Eastern governments that have explicit goals of service and purposeful social change will be able to implement those goals in such ways that this traditional mental set in regard to rulers and government will be substantially altered.

In the Alborz-Zagros Plateau area Seleucid rule was eliminated, after about a century, by the Parthians. Though invaders, the Parthians adapted themselves to the Hellenistic elite life of the cities, and, as elsewhere, the village-pastoral culture continued, distinct from the foreign cultural patterns of the urban elites.

And so, from the Maghrib to Iran, powerful elites held sway in the cities. They were different from each other, but all had in common the fact that they were culturally alien from the villagers and pastoralists in the hinterlands and from most of the city inhabitants, too. This scenario, with changing casts of characters, has been repeated over and over in the subsequent history of the Middle East. It must be one of the causes of the peril-refuge mentality (see Chapter Two), and it has surely reinforced this mentality at every turn.

Shortly before the beginning of the Christian era, Roman rule, already established in the Maghrib, supplanted that of the Hellenistic rulers, and the Greco-Roman urban elites continued to live very much as the Hellenistic elites had. Many of the most impressive Roman ruins—amphitheaters, forums, temples, and temple complexes—are not in Italy but in the Middle East, scattered all the way from the Maghrib to Anatolia. We must not be deluded into thinking that Greco-Roman culture supplanted the Middle Eastern culture of the great majority of the people. In reality village and herding life went right on. Greek became widely spoken in Anatolia, but Semitic and Berber languages were spoken elsewhere except in elite circles, and Middle Eastern religions remained very much alive.

It was apparently during the Florescent that the concept of a single, generalized supreme deity emerged. Perhaps it grew as an abstraction from more specific single deities such as the patron gods of various cities, or ethnically identified deities like Yahweh of the Hebrews. Some suggest that it may have originated in a universalization of the Egyptian sun deity or in the Iranian deity of fire, sun, and light. In any case it appears to have evolved just as culture in general has. The same is true of the concept of absolute, cosmic good and absolute, cosmic evil as adversaries, the human soul being their battleground and their prize. This was emphasized in the Iranian religion that (like other religions later) is attributed to the revelations of the prophet Zardosht (better known as Zoroaster or Zarathustra), who is supposed to have lived around the middle of the first millennium B.C. Prophets, who claimed special knowledge of monotheistic realities, were another Florescent feature.

Whatever adverse effects the Hellenistic and Roman regimes may have had on the Middle East, travel, trade, and interregional communication were greatly facilitated. It was in this presumably stimulating environment of competing religious concepts, plus political dissidence, that the Christian religion came into being. Some people see Christianity as originally a Jewish sect that soon became Hellenized and was later made imperial within the Roman

Empire. Another explanation of its relatively rapid success is that very early its devotees incorporated into it many of the widespread and ancient religious ideas in the Middle East and the Mediterranean area, thus giving it maximum popular appeal.

After initial persecution, the Christian religion spread rapidly throughout the Roman Empire. But at the same time, centralized Roman rule was being challenged and was headed eventually for dissolution. In Europe the Roman Christian church—modeling its sectarian structure on the empire itself—eventually grew to dominate Western, Central, and Mediterranean Europe. This is why the western image of the early church tends to be of a single body that only much later developed various splinter groups.

From the Middle Eastern perspective, however, it is difficult to see that there was ever, in fact, any single, universal Christian church (whatever contrary theories some theologians may have). A variety of Christian groups existed in the Middle East from very early times, and several of them can be identified with one or another of the cultural-ecological subregions. In other words, early Christian sectarianism was at that time an integral part of the cultural diversity of the Middle Eastern subregions.

There were Christians in the Maghrib, some of whom were opposed as "heretics" by the Roman Catholics. Along the Nile a Christian church was established, with its own structure and distinctive features. In Anatolia the Greek-oriented Byzantine Church had a strong territorial base. It also had members in the Fertile Crescent, where there were also a number of derivative Byzantine sects, many of whose members were Semitic speakers. In the Kurd-Azeri area the Armenians, speaking a distinctive Indo-European language, developed their own Christian church, explicitly different from any other. In addition to these various Christian organizations, Jewish groups lived in various parts of the Middle East, and so-called "pagans" lived in the southern part of the Arabian Peninsula. In the Alborz-Zagros Plateau area Zoroastrianism became the state religion under the Sassanians, a native Iranian dynasty that overthrew the Parthians in the third century A.D.

This is how matters stood in the sixth century A.D. The religious-sectarian situation was diverse, as was the political-military situation, with local potentates ruling in various areas. The main rivals were the Byzantines and the Sassanians competing for control of the Fertile Crescent, neither strong enough to dominate the other and achieve stability. Trade routes to the south connected the Fertile Crescent with the "pagan" Semitic speakers in southern Arabia and the Christians in Ethiopia. About halfway along the western Arabian north-south trade route, at Mecca, Muhammad was born in about A.D. 580.

Mecca was both a commercial town and a pilgrimage center, the chief shrine being the Ka'aba, a cubical structure containing "idols." Muhammad himself belonged to a merchant family. The local language was Arabic, one of the many Semitic languages that were spoken in the Arabian Peninsula and the Fertile Crescent. In about 610 Muhammad let it be known that he was hearing the voice of God through the angel Gabriel. The voice told him that he was the last and greatest of the prophets of the one God, previous prophets having included Noah, Moses, and Jesus, among others. Muhammad received many later revelations until his death in the year 632. These were soon collected in written form (using the Arabic alphabet) and became known as the Quran, meaning "that which is recited." The Quran is the central sacred scripture of Islam, containing sacred myths, a theological system including definitions of the conditions of sin and salvation, and many rules of conduct that together can fairly be regarded as the constitution for a theocratic community.

Details of Islamic belief and practice as seen in the behavior of ordinary Middle Eastern people today will be presented in a later chapter. Here I will simply emphasize that while Muhammad's revelation in itself was unique and had major, far-reaching consequences for the Middle East, its components are largely a resynthesis of religious beliefs already present earlier in the Florescent and the Formative. The one God speaking to Muhammad was acknowledged by him to be the same God that spoke to the Hebrew prophets, and Jesus was included among those prophets, although he was not acknowledged as an incarnation of that God. Sin, salvation, last judgment, angels, the devil, animal sacrifice, pilgrimage to a sacred place imbued with supernatural power, circumcision, prophets, and a sacred and unalterable text are all features of Islam that were derived directly from Judaism or Christianity or from the earlier elementary forms of Middle Eastern religion.

Barbara Aswad has written a short anthropological account and interpretation of the early development of Islam as a sectarian organization (Aswad 1970). She places in a cultural ecological context the initial establishment of Islam at Madina, another West Arabian commercial town, after the hijra ("flight") of Muhammad and his followers from hostile forces in Mecca in 622. Muslim dates begin with that year but are based on a 355-day year (twelve lunar months), so that important Muslim holy days and periods of time occur ten days earlier in each successive solar year—in the long run, therefore, occurring at all seasons of the solar year. Madina was, at the time, called Yathrib. Its name was subsequently changed to Madinat al-Nabi ("city of the Prophet"), commonly shortened simply to Madina. This was where Islam was established as a community by Muhammad, and it was also where the military campaigns were launched that spread Islam to the rest of the Arabian Peninsula and the Fertile Crescent very shortly after the Prophet's death. Aswad's article also sets the stage for these events in a cultural-ecological context. This context, briefly, serves as a corrective to the widespread image of the origin and spread of Islam: inspiration in the desert and the overwhelming of the "civilized world" by hordes of single-minded Bedouins. In fact, the western Arabian highlands were linked to the rest of the Middle East, and Islam was clearly a product of many traditions generalized through linkages. Furthermore, Islam is not a pastoralists' religion. It was developed by townsmen in towns that were, to be sure, surrounded by deserts.

The last part of the Florescent, 632–900 A.D., saw the greatest growth of what is sometimes called the Islamic Empire. The first four caliphs ("successors" of Muhammad as leaders of the Muslim community) ruled in Madina and from there directed the rapid sequence of Muslim victories over non-Muslim armies in adjoining regions.

In 661 the capital of the Islamic state was moved to Damascus, an old city where the full effects of the Greco-Roman and Byzantine cultures had been felt. From 661 to 750 the Umayyad caliphs ruled from Damascus. The Umayyads were succeeded by the Abbasid caliphs, the first of whom moved the capital eastward to the location in the desert where the Tigris and Euphrates Rivers flow closest together. This is north of the marshy delta where they merge. Near the ruins of many earlier cities, a new city, Baghdad, was built especially for the purpose of being the Abbasid capital.

From 661 to about 900 the Umayyads and the early Abbasids held fairly effective control over the Islamic empire, which embraced all of the Middle East except Anatolia, plus the Iberian Peninsula. This empire established Islam as the predominant religion of the Middle East. Quranic codes became the basis for many social norms throughout the area. Also, Arabic became the vernacular language in the Maghrib, the Sahara, the Nile area, the Fertile Crescent, and the Arabian Peninsula.

The spread of Islam and the Arabic language did not coincide everywhere, however. Many Berber speakers in the Maghrib and the Sahara, though converted to Islam, did not adopt Arabic as their vernacular language. Christians who did not convert to Islam, such as the Copts in the Nile area and several sects in the Fertile Crescent, although they eventually adopted Arabic as their vernacular language, must have initially resisted its use. To this day their religious liturgies in many cases are in what was their vernacular language at the time of the beginning of Islam.

Anatolia, though eventually becoming Muslim, never became predominantly Arabic speaking, nor did the Kurd-Azeri, Alborz-

Zagros, Hindu Kush, and Indus basin areas, although the last three were converted early to Islam. However, Arabic vocabulary has influenced the non-Arabic languages of Islamic areas, for the Quran and prayers must be recited in Arabic regardless of what the vernacular language is. Early Islamic scholars in countries such as Iran, for example, wrote in Arabic, much as Medieval European scholars wrote in Latin.

Although the Islamic Empire established and formalized a number of Islamic cultural themes, including art forms, throughout almost all of the Middle East, it did not culturally homogenize the whole area. Arabs migrated to various parts of the Middle East, but they did not on any major scale displace the people already there. In many cases Arabic-speaking urban elites assumed roles similar to those of the earlier Greco-Roman urban elites. Although many Christians, Jews, and Zoroastrians were converted to Islam, not all of them were, and, as just mentioned, non-Arabic languages continued to be spoken widely. The courts of the early caliphs included highly cosmopolitan staffs of experts and specialists representing the wide variety of religious, linguistic, and regional subcultures.

The Florescent ends with the establishment of Islam in the Middle East and also with the disintegration of the empire that made its establishment so widespread. Whether the Umayyad caliphs and the Abbasids, even at the zenith of their power, ever exercised complete centralized control over the entire empire has been questioned. By 900, however, the caliphs had certainly lost control of the Maghrib, Sahara, Nile, and Alborz-Zagros areas and the areas to the east. Though the Abbasid caliphate continued in name until 1258, it ceased by the tenth century to be an empire and was, at best, merely one of many Islamic states centered, as many earlier states had been, in one of the cultural-ecological subregions.

By the time Islam had become the predominant religion in the Middle East, at the end of the Florescent, the major sectarian divisions within it had taken form. Within the authority of the caliphate differing schools of Quranic interpretation developed. Dissident schools of thought, rejecting Umayyad or Abbasid caliphal authority, also developed. The most important of these were the so-called partisans of Ali. Ali was the Prophet's son-in-law and father of the Prophet's only grandchildren. He was the fourth caliph (the last to rule from Madina), but his partisans claimed that he should have been the first caliph and that only his sons and their direct descendants (that is, the direct descendants of the Prophet himself through his daughter Fatima, Ali's wife) were the rightful heirs to the caliphate.

In 680, at Karbala, near the Euphrates River, an army of the Umayyad caliph killed Husayn, one of the sons of Ali and Fatima, together with some relatives and other companions. The partisans of Ali thus acquired their major martyr. Unable directly to overthrow and supplant the caliphate, the partisans of Ali—known as Shias—began recognizing their own succession of religious authorities, the Twelve Imams. The First Imam was Ali; his sons Hassan and Husayn were the Second and Third. The other nine were direct descendants of Husayn. According to the Shias, in 873 the Twelfth Imam did not die but rather entered into a state of suspended animation from which he will return as the Mahdi—Messiah—at the end of the world.

Disputes between the Shias and the Sunnis (followers, originally, of the caliphs) began at the end of the Florescent and have continued ever since. The Shias are further subdivided into various groups, some claiming special adherence to one or another of the Imams. Today Shias are numerous in the Fertile Crescent and overwhelmingly predominant in Iran. From the anthropological perspective the Imams are yet another Islamic resynthesis of older Middle Eastern phenomena. The Imams were and are saints. Holy men in their lifetimes, they were buried in tombs that became shrines, imbued with blessedness (baraka), to which the faithful make pilgrimages. The annual mourning for the martyred Husayn and the great reverence for his mother are highly reminiscent of the ancient myth of the sacrificed deity. Extreme forms of Shia belief—rejected by most Shias themselves—have even claimed reincarnation of God in one or another of the Imams.

Though the Sunnis reject the Shias' emphasis on the holiness of the Imams, they nevertheless recognize descent from Muhammad as the basis for potential special status, provided the individual is otherwise worthy of regard and (of course) is not an imposter. Belief in saints, too, is very widespread among the Sunnis, but as we shall see, descent from the Prophet is not the only, or even a necessary, criterion of sainthood.

Reference to saints and their shrines is not included in the Quran, and worship of them is regarded as heresy by such fundamentalist Muslims as the Wahhabi sectarians currently dominant in Saudi Arabia. Nevertheless, saints and saints' shrines are extremely important to a very large number of faithful Muslims and have been since the end of the Florescent.

Conservative Islamic

I call the time frame extending from A.D. 900 to A.D. 1800 Conservative Islamic for a special reason. It was a highly eventful time, with many drastic occurrences that had far-reaching consequences. However, despite all this, the Islamic cultural patterns established in the Florescent seem to have become relatively fixed thereafter. Islamic law became a standard for continuity rather than a license or plan for change, and Islamic culture was adopted by invaders, such as the Turks, rather than significantly altered by them.

Early in the Conservative Islamic era, Turkish-speaking tribal groups began migrating from northeast of the Caspian Sea into the Middle East. The early Turkish migrants were converted to Islam, adopted other Middle Eastern cultural traits, and conquered various regional rulers, establishing their own dynasties, of which that of the Seljuqs was one of the most important. Once more an alien military elite established itself in the cities, while the Arabic-, Kurdish-, Armenian-, and Persian-speaking villagers, pastoralists, craftsmen, and merchants continued on, as best they could, as before.

An altogether different alien intrusion was the European Crusaders' uneasy occupation of the western Fertile Crescent in the eleventh through the thirteenth centuries. This apparently had two lasting effects on the Middle East. One was an increased European bias among the Christian groups in the Levant, and the other was a heightened defensive and hostile awareness of the Europeans among the Muslims in general.

More invasions from Central Asia, especially those of the Mongols, caused enormous damage and long-lasting disruption of various delicate ecological and political balances. However, these troubles did not prevent the Turks from consolidating their power and influence in Anatolia, establishing the Osmanli dynasty in the fourteenth century, and finally defeating the last remaining forces of the Christian Byzantine Empire by capturing Constantinople in 1453. Turkish became the vernacular language in Anatolia and in much of the Kurd-Azeri area, though many Arabic words were incorporated into it, and the Arabic alphabet was somewhat modified in order to write it.

The Ottoman (Europeanization of Osmanli) Turks went on to capture all of the southern Balkans and, in the sixteenth century, all of the Arabic-speaking Middle East except for Morocco and most of the Arabian Peninsula. Capture meant military garrisons and Turkish-speaking elites in the cities, tribute paid by the local inhabitants, and special semiautonomous status granted to the various non-Muslim groups. The sultan of the Ottoman Empire claimed the caliphate of Islam, but, as with the first caliphates long before, centralized Ottoman control over all its maximum territory was rather short-lived. Ottoman occupation brought Islam to the Balkans, and many Balkan people are still Muslims. In the far west of the Middle East, however, Islam was forced to retreat from the Iberian peninsula. The Muslims, as well as the Jews, were expelled from Spain in 1492, and Spanish military footholds were established in the Maghrib.

In the Alborz-Zagros Plateau area the Safavid dynasty was established at about the same time that the Ottoman Empire reached its maximum extent. The Safavids made Shia Islam the state religion of Iran. Some scholars believe that this was a conscious counteraction to the activities of the Ottoman sultans with their emphasis on orthodox Sunni Islam, and that Ottoman-Safavid competition sharpened and exacerbated the Sunni-Shia division. Be this as it may, the Ottoman sultans and the Safavid shahs were patrons of the arts, and under them many of the greatest master-pieces of Middle Eastern art and architecture were produced. Most of the stylistic themes were, however, not new but consolidations and efflorescences of existing traditions, just as were the Ottoman and Safavid support of the two major Islamic orthodoxies (Sunni and Shia).

Machine-Age Islamic

I call the present time frame of Middle Eastern culture Machine-Age Islamic. Islam continues to be the predominant religion of the area and is very much alive. At the same time, products of the Euramerican "industrial revolution" have become conspicuously present in the Middle East since about 1800, although their points of origin have, of course, changed in the intervening period. There is no doubt about this presence, but there is uncertainty about the extent to which the values, customs, and behavioral patterns of the people have been or are being affected. Most observers would prob-ably say that they are becoming industrialized, westernized, or modernized. I object to these overused terms because they all imply transformation of Middle Eastern culture into some standard form of Euramerican culture. Whether there is, in fact, any such standard culture is an open question that is usually ignored. And transformation—complete alteration—is not the usual way in which entire large-scale cultures change.

The Machine-Age Islamic Middle East is distinguished not only by the introduction of foreign machines and machine-made products but also by the direct political and economic interference in Middle Eastern life of various European nations and the United States. In 1798 Napoleon invaded Egypt, then a vice-regency of the Ottoman Empire, and some observers see this as the beginning of "modernization" in the Middle East. Throughout the nineteenth century certain European nations competed with each other for control of parts of the Middle East either by direct colonization (the French conquest of Algeria in 1830, for example) or, more often, by supporting native rulers against their rivals in return for the opportunity to exercise influence in the area. Spain, France, and Italy were the major rivals in the Maghrib and the Sahara; France and Great Britain in the Nile area—with the British win-ning out rather early. In the Fertile Crescent, where Ottoman controls remained strong until the end of World War I, the French and the British backed different ethnic factions against each other and against the Turks, and the European Zionists established their first colonies. British naval control was maintained around the coasts of Arabia, and the British and the Russians were the chief rivals for control in Iran. With the demise of the Ottoman Empire after World War I, and the restriction of Turkish political influence to the area of Turkey itself, British and French influences were, for a time, even stronger than they had been before.

In the middle third of the twentieth century the decline of the French and British empires increased the opportunities for people in various Middle Eastern areas to establish independent governments. Gaining this independence was complicated by problems of working out what the most effective forms of government, under varying circumstances, might be. In most areas most people continue to subsist on the desert-oasis economic system, but this has been affected in many ways by the products and demands of the Machine Age. The discovery and exploitation of petroleum has so far benefited only some parts of the Middle East, and it perpetuates certain foreign imperial interests, notably those of the United States and the Soviet Union.

Early in this chapter I emphasized the precariousness of the farming-herding-commercial economy. By now the fact should be clear that the precarious element in Middle Eastern life is not limited to the problems of gaining a living from this economy. The precarious element has also been inherent in the experience of every Middle Eastern person who has had to cope with the effects of the invasions and dynastic successions and other self-serving acts of particular human groups, a few highlights of which have been sketched in this chapter. More than once I have reminded the reader that the basic elements of village-pastoral-commercial life continued in spite of military adventures or political upheavals. That is true, but long-term survival and cultural continuity have been accompanied by injustice, disaster, and extinction for some people all along the way, and these misfortunes are often remembered as specific grievances or generalized fears among the living.

The machine age has not brought an end to such events. Consider the massacres of Armenians in Turkey during World War I and the flight of the survivors; the flight from Palestine of Muslim and Christian Arabs, and some Armenians, who feared terrorism by the Zionists; and the horrors of the Algerian war of independence. These are only a few of the well-publicized episodes. To them could be added the many small-scale atrocities that have accompanied the campaigns of several central governments to "sedentarize" the pastoral nomads within their borders.

The natural environment of the Middle East is such that subsistence is continually precarious for most of its inhabitants most of the time. In some respects Middle Easterners seem to have learned long ago to adapt themselves to this precariousness—to have learned conventional ways of taking what comes. No simple environmental determinism is involved here, however. An important part of each person's taking what comes is coping, both as insider and outsider, with the covetous, embittered, recalcitrant, and striving reactions that are perpetually renewed in all those kinship, religious, linguistic, and national groups. Very gradually their identities change, but the pluralism in the precarious environment persists, and it seems as if the Middle Easterners may have evolved a cultural system that has considerable capacity for incorporating such changes without being easily altered. Perhaps it is persistent because it involves stress and resilience in continual tension with each other, and not because it is "stable." The net result, in any case, is a set of cultural patterns that are distinctive for this particular cultural region of the world.

REFERENCES

Aswad, Barbara C. "Social and Ecological Aspects in the Formation of Islam." In *Peoples and Cultures of the Middle East: An Anthropological Reader*, vol. 1, edited by Louise E. Sweet, pp. 53–73. Garden City, N.Y.: Natural History Press, 1970.

Flannery, Kent V. "The Ecology of Early Food Production in Mesopotamia." In *Peoples and Cultures of the Middle East: An Anthropological Reader*, vol. 1, edited by Louise E. Sweet, pp. 29–52. Garden City, N.Y.: Natural History Press, 1970.

ANNOTATED BIBLIOGRAPHY

The Desert-Oasis Ecology

Coon, Carleton S. *Caravan: The Story of the Middle East.* Rev. ed. New York: Holt, 1958.

The first chapter, "Land, Wind, and Water," provides a vivid overview of fundamentals.

Cressey, George B. *Crossroads: Land and Life in Southwest Asia.* Chicago, New York, Philadelphia: Lippincott, 1960.

Includes Egypt and the Sudan but not the other African parts of the Middle East. Except for this omission, the book is extremely valuable. It is richly illustrated with photographs and maps and discusses history and culture, although its primary orientation is geographical.

Maktari, A. M. A. *Water Rights and Irrigation Practices in Lahj.* Cambridge: At the University Press, 1971.

A study of the application of customary and Islamic law to the problems of water rights in an extremely arid desert-oasis location in South Yemen. Though very specialized, the book will reward selective reading by nonspecialists.

Planhol, Xavier de. *The World of Islam.* Ithaca, N.Y.: Cornell University Press, 1959.

The subtitle of the original French edition was "Essay in Religious Geography." The author is a cultural geographer with a keen sense of history.

Vidal, F. S. *The Oasis of Al-Hasa*. Arabian American Oil Company, 1955.

An ecological study, by an anthropologist, of the complexities of a large oasis in eastern Saudi Arabia. It contains photographs, maps, and other illustrations.

Map

"A Cultural Map of the Middle East." *National Geographic*, July 1972.

Printed on both sides of the sheet, this map shows the entire area, is particularly clear on land forms, and shows the names and locations of important ethnic groups, with color codes for the different linguistic families.

Prehistory

Adams, Robert McC. *The Evolution of Urban Society: Early Mesopotamia and Prehispanic Mexico*. Chicago: Aldine-Atherton, 1971.

Despite the publisher's blurb about "great transformations," the book is a highly sophisticated anthropological study of the ecological complexities of the development of the earliest cities in the southeastern Fertile Crescent (compared with Mexican Indian urban developments).

Adams, Robert McC., and Hans J. Nissen. *The Uruk Countryside: The Natural Setting of Urban Societies*. Chicago: University of Chicago Press, 1972.

Covering some of the same ground as Adams (1971), a very important feature of this book is its ecological history of the Uruk area from the first city there to the present, beautifully illustrating the desert-oasis fluctuations in settlement, water use, pastoralism, farming, and city life.

Braidwood, Robert J. *Prehistoric Men*, 8th ed. Glenview, Ill.: Scott, Foresman, 1975.

A renowned specialist in Middle Eastern archaeology, the author clearly and imaginatively places the preagricultural and early agricultural technologies of the Middle East in the context of Eurasia and Africa.

Hamblin, Dora Jane and the Editors of Time-Life Books. *The First Cities*. New York: Time-Life Books, 1973.

Has the virtues of popularized, commercial books—such as vivid illustrations and interesting maps—but also the faults: in particular, treating as confirmed fact, rather than as hypothesis, the idea that eighth millennium B.C. fortifications and trading settlements were full-fledged cities.

Leonard, Jonathan N., and the Editors of Time-Life Books. *The First Farmers*. New York: Time-Life Books, 1973.

Has the same virtues as Hamblin (same format in same series of books: "The Emergence of Man"). The book includes some material from the Americas, but much of the emphasis is on the Middle East.

History

Brockelmann, Carl. *History of the Islamic Peoples.* New York Putnam, 1947.

Out of date as far as recent history is concerned, this book serves as a concise reference for historic sequences in the entire Middle East, rather than only in certain regions of it or for certain periods. Middle Eastern historians with whom I have consulted do not recommend Brockelmann (saying it is out of date, too condensed, and not very readable, and that it contains errors). However, they agree that it is unusual in that it encompasses the entire Middle East. Most of the large number of Middle Eastern history books do not attempt to do this. Rather, they are usually specialized in regard either to time periods or subtopics, among which Arabs, Iran, Turkey, and the Maghrib (as set apart from the rest) are typical.

Esin, Emel. *Mecca the Blessed, Madinah the Radiant.* New York: Crown, 1963.

This is primarily a history of the origins of Islam, illustrated (with photographs by Haluk Doganbey) by present-day conditions in Mecca and Madina (to which the Turkish author and photographer had access). It presents a sensitive treatment of early Islam's roots in many ancient traditions.

Grabar, Oleg. *The Formation of Islamic Art.* New Haven, Conn.: Yale University Press, 1973.

Sophisticated, insightful, and stimulating for specialists, this book is written in a straightforward and readable style that recommends it to nonspecialists, also. Two major arguments of the book run closely parallel to, and are supportive of, points made in this chapter. First, early Muslim art forms—with considerable emphasis on architecture—were continuations of pre-Islamic forms, with new interpretations, combinations and functions. Second, the "first Muslim classical movement," with variations from region to region, took place in the ninth and early tenth centuries—in other words, at the end of the Florescent time frame. Also discussed at some length is the well-known and highly debatable issue of animal and human representational forms in Islamic art.

Grube, Ernst J. *The World of Islam.* London: Paul Hamlyn, 1966.

A richly illustrated survey of Islamic art, this book sets the subject in the context of the Conservative Islamic time frame. It contains maps and time charts.

Hodgson, Marshall G.S. *The Venture of Islam: Conscience and History in a World Civilization.* Three volumes. Chicago: University of Chicago Press, 1974.

A history of all the Middle East, focused on Islam from the seventh to the 20th centuries, A.D., with a brief consideration of pre-Islamic times. Very comprehensive, it may be too long and too detailed for some readers, especially nonspecialists.

Lewis, Bernard. *The Arabs in History.* New York: Harper and Brothers, 1960.

Recommended by other historians, it is succinct and readable. Its major limitation is that, except occasionally, it considers only the Arabs.

Smith, W. Robertson. *The Religion of the Semites.* New York: Meridian, 1956.

Originally published in 1889, this is a classic. An orientalist, Smith is also claimed by some as having been an early anthropologist. The book is a reconstruction of religious behavior in the Formative or early Florescent time frames.

Bibliography

Atiyeh, George N. *The Contemporary Middle East 1948–1973: A Selective and Annotated Bibliography.* Boston: G. K. Hall, 1975.

Arranged into major sections by geographical regions that closely correspond with those discussed in Chapter One of this book, plus major sections on the Middle East as a whole, the Arab-Israeli conflict, and the arts. Source materials on history, politics, economics, and sociocultural behavior are all well covered. There are author and topical indexes for the 6,491 items.

Hopwood, Derek, and Diana Grimwood-Jones, ed. *The Middle East and Islam: A Bibliographical Introduction.* Zug, Switzerland: Inter Documentation Co., 1972.

Basic references compiled for the establishment of a department of Islamic Studies, organized under reference, Islamic studies (including history), various disciplines besides history, subregions of the Middle East, and Arabic literature.

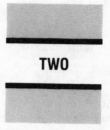

TWO

PERIL AND REFUGE

A PARADOXICAL CONSISTENCY

Two common generalizations about the Middle East are that its people are extremely group oriented and that they are extremely individualistic. Often cited as examples of group orientation are fanatic zealousness in sectarian and religious matters and intense loyalty to kin groups. Examples of extreme individualism include each Muslim's one-to-one relationship with God (no human or superhuman intermediaries) and Middle Easterners' great difficulty in achieving sustained, well-coordinated, or well-disciplined group endeavors, despite the great formal deference that is paid by those of inferior rank to their superiors.

The trouble with these generalizations is, first of all, the labels ("group oriented" and "individualistic"), and, second, the implication that each is all-inclusively true. How can the Middle Eastern person be both extremely group oriented and extremely individualistic? This seems like a contradiction in terms.

If the labels are put aside and the examples of actual behavior are considered in their own right, the problem of impossible contradictions disappears. What emerges instead is a paradoxical, but not impossible, situation. Individuals whose group identities and loyalties are clear-cut and well known, and who are sociable and ceremonious, are also wary, cantankerous, volatile, and seemingly withholding of themselves from others. It is almost as if the typical individual were both other-directed and inner-directed, to use David Riesman's terms. Accompanying these portrayals of personal modalities are portrayals of social groups that are also paradoxical. Certain group memberships are extremely important to individuals, and yet the same groups seem haphazardly organized and likely to be torn apart by dissension.

The data on all this are too numerous, too varied in detail, and observed by too many different people under too many different circumstances to be discounted, gainsaid, or explained away. In order to make some sense of them we need to put aside some of the more usual preconceptions about personality structure and group dynamics and look at the subject in a somewhat different way: social life as a continual interplay between sense of peril and sense of refuge from peril.

In Chapter One the perilous modes of Middle Eastern life were set in an ecological context and given time depth. In this chapter I shall outline how the paradox of peril and refuge is to be found at every level of Middle Eastern life. With this as a framework I believe that the details of the various behavioral observations and studies used as source material are made comprehensible because of the thread of consistency that is woven to link them. This thread is the supposition that within every phenomenon that is perceived to be a refuge against peril there are perilous elements. No refuge, in other words, is complete or absolute. This idea is easy to grasp in connection with the well-recognized inconstancy and unreliability of political alliances. It may not be so easily recognized in connection with such well-known refuges from sociocultural peril as the so-called "ingroup" and—the most private refuge of all—the ego-structure of the individual. Yet it is in precisely these phenomena in the Middle East that peril, as well as refuge, seems to be inherent—as well as in the other aspects of existence where both peril and refuge are more generally acknowledged. I think that it is the interplay of feelings of peril and refuge that underlies the impression conveyed in many publications on Middle Eastern life that even in what are expected to be secure relationships there is a quality or "feeling tone" of insecurity, unreliability, instability, or tension.

This peril-and-refuge idea is properly open to challenge, as are all of the other binary conceptualizations of human behavior. The question should always remain open: Is this a stereotype, an oversimplification that distorts reality more than it clarifies it? Or is it a heuristic concept, an oversimplification whose helpfulness in explaining reality outweighs the distortions inherent in the oversimplifications? The distinctions between the two can be difficult to draw, and they should be regarded as tentative and always subject to reevaluation in the light of new interpretations or new evidence.

The peril-and-refuge idea consists of several heuristic generalizations. While peril and refuge in themselves are certainly not peculiarly or exclusively Middle Eastern, they are expressed in terms of specifically Middle Eastern cultural details. Furthermore, I think that Middle Eastern people are, on the whole, less free from the sense of peril in life than are many other people in the world, including American middle-class professional people, for example. Middle Easterners are not only highly sensitive to peril, but it also permeates their perceptions of many aspects of their social world and of themselves as individuals. This highly intense and widely ramified sensitivity is distinctively Middle Eastern.

LAND OF GOVERNMENT, LAND OF DISSIDENCE

The French colonial regime in Morocco in the 1920s and 1930s conceived of the country as being divided into two geographical zones called bled al-makhzen ("land of government") and bled al-siba ("land of dissidence" or "insolence" or "disorder"). Many specialists on Morocco have emphasized this view of the country, for example Montagne (1931), Coon (1958), Hoffman (1967), and Hart (1973), but David Seddon, in a lengthy introduction to his English translation of Montagne's monograph, refers to it as a stereotype (Seddon 1973, p. xxiv). Whether or not it unduly distorts the fine details of Moroccan history and culture, I think that it can be extended and generalized to the Middle East as a whole, past and present.

Bled al-makhzen refers to the territory that is under the direct control of a recognized ruler. In Morocco the ruler is the sultan, and the territory has essentially been the Atlantic plains with their cities and villages. Bled al-siba has been, in contrast, the mountainous regions whose inhabitants have refused to submit to the sultan's authority, particularly in such matters as paying taxes. However, through time, bled al-makhzen and bled al-siba have expanded or contracted in relation to each other depending on the effectiveness of the sultan, and his officers and troops, in maintaining and enforcing his authority. From the sultan's point of view bled al-siba's inhabitants have been perpetually dissident. But this has not necessarily been their point of view of themselves. They have regarded their tribal leaders and councils as legitimate and their territory as a refuge against the peril posed by the sultan's armies and taxes. As for the inhabitants of bled al-makhzen, they at times may have regarded the sultan's troops as a protection against tribesmen, but at other times those troops have themselves been a threat. This is one of the reasons for the instability of bled al-makhzen. The leadership in both bled al-makhzen and bled al-siba claims legitimacy; each regards the other as perilous and itself as providing refuge from the peril; and the villagers, pastoralists, and townsmen have had reason to regard both as being sources of both peril and refuge.

Each of the empires discussed in Chapter One was a maximum expansion of the land of government, always challenged and repeatedly eroded away by lands of dissidence. For instance, the Abbasid caliphate at one point controlled the entire Middle East, except for Anatolia, plus the Iberian Peninsula. But it did not do so for long, and dissidence was in the minds of many of its subjects even at its zenith. The Neo-Umayyads in Spain and the Maghrib and the Fatimids in Egypt and the Levant were dissidents against the Abbasids, but they themselves claimed the legitimacy of the caliphate. When the last Abbasid caliph was killed by the Mongols in 1258, the Abbasid land of government had been reduced to his palace in Baghdad, but by that time there were other lands of government, each claiming legitimacy against what it regarded as dissidence.

From Morocco to Iran and Afghanistan, the most usual lands of government have been headed by kings or other potentates, with their power base in cities and city hinterlands, while at the same time the land of dissidence has generally consisted of more remote village and pastoral areas. This does not mean, however, that land of government is equivalent to urban areas and land of dissidence equivalent to pastoral nomadic areas. Plausible as this may seem, there is too much factual divergence from it to allow its acceptance as a valid generalization. A few examples will illustrate some of the permutations of these divergences. In Morocco and Jordan city-based kings have recruited pastoralists to serve as their troops against dissidents. In Iran high-ranking city-based Shia clerics long ago worked out a theory of legitimate government that defines all secular rulers since the disappearance of the Twelfth Imam as usurpers, a theory that has provided a rationale for much resistance to the power of the shahs. While the land of government's core may seem to be in the cities where the major political institutions are located, cities are by no means refuges from dissidence and rebellion. Many revolts have been spearheaded in them, as for example in the fourteenth and fifteenth century cities of Egypt and Syria (Lapidus 1967) and in eighteenth and nineteenth century Aleppo (Bodman 1963). At the present time the fear of rebellion and dissidence in cities is particularly focused both on the squatter settlements on the outskirts of many of the cities and on the old quarters in their centers where parties regarded by the government as rebels may take refuge—as indeed they did in 1958 in Beirut and Tripoli, Lebanon.

The point is this: The land of government/land of dissidence image is of limited usefulness if it is seen only in a geographical sense. While it certainly is acted out on a geographical stage, it is basically a state of mind that is expressed in the disdainful but fearful subjection of Middle Eastern people to their government of the moment, coupled with the necessity to be prepared actively or passively to accommodate themselves to some new government that may overthrow the present one. In this state of mind the sense of peril and the sense of refuge from peril are interrelated with each other like yin and yang.

As far as those who seek, hold, and exercise power are concerned, Shakespeare put it succinctly: "Uneasy lies the head that wears a crown." This can be readily inferred from Middle Eastern political history, and it is explicit in some major studies of the present-day situation. Two of these are Waterbury (1970) and Zonis (1971) on political behavior in Morocco and Iran, respectively.

They are quite different in style due to the different research methods that were used and to differences between the two countries. However, their findings are, in certain fundamental ways, very similar. In both cases the sovereigns are continually engaged in defensive tactics that will protect the power that they exercise. The sultan of Morocco has traditionally fought, bought off, resettled, or reconciled various tribal groups that challenge his power (Waterbury 1970, p. 17), and the makhzen, of which he is head, is a coalition of competing interests in which there is a "defensive preoccupation with survival" (Waterbury 1970, p. 31). The Shah of Iran buys off opposition by strategic appointments (Zonis 1971, p. 24) and by various means acts to prevent the formation of coalitions that might overthrow him (Zonis 1971, p. 82). Waterbury portrays the general situation among the ruling elite of Morocco as one in which today's ally can be tomorrow's enemy, where one must protect one's flanks against friends who may become enemies but at the same time maintain communications with enemies who may become friends—a situation, in short, of "moral relativism" and "pervasive tension" (Waterbury 1970, p. 66). Zonis (p. 11) characterizes the attitudinal dimensions of political behavior in Iran as "cynicism, personal mistrust, manifest insecurity, and interpersonal exploitation," and he devotes considerable space to examining and elaborating upon each of them. While Waterbury and Zonis emphasize the power elites of the two countries, they both seem to feel that political concerns are also important among the relatively powerless and that the political behavior of the latter has the same characteristics as that of the powerful. The complex system of protective behavior and attitudes of the essentially vulnerable Qashqai pastoralists of Iran would seem to be a case in point (Beck 1973).

Zonis analyzes the structure of a particular case of the land of government, while Waterbury and Beck analyze the interfaces between land of government and land of dissidence in other cases. Rounding out the picture is Fredrik Barth's study of the Pathans of Swat State in northern Pakistan, which is an analysis of the internal political structure of an example of the land of dissidence (Barth 1959, p. 133). The Pathans are a highly self-aware cultural aggregate of Sunni Muslims who inhabit extensive areas of Afghanistan and Pakistan. Spread over a diversified region, they are themselves diverse in many of their customs. For example, they include pastoralists, villagers, and townsmen. Yet they conceive of themselves as all being descended from the same common ancestor (who lived at the time of Muhammad), and they have a strong sense of cultural identity. This is epitomized by their speaking the Pashto language (a member of the eastern Indo-Iranian family) and by their "doing Pashto," which means living in accordance with certain very particular expectations of behavior. These include a sharp segregation of the sexes that involves strictly secluded females on the one hand and aggressive males competing for honor and power in the public sphere on the other hand (Barth 1969, pp. 119–120).

The Swat Pathans are villagers living in a mountainous river valley. Their domain is divided into thirteen subtribal territories, each of which is in turn subdivided according to the principles of segmentary patrilineal descent groups (Barth 1959, pp. 13–14). (These groups as they occur generally in the Middle East will be discussed later.) The main focus of the Swat Pathans' loyalties is in their villages, where local chiefs maintain guest houses for the men. Here the chiefs extend lavish hospitality in order to secure the loyal following of their guests or clients (Barth 1959, pp. 80–81). Ordinary men can, and frequently do, shift their allegiance from one chief to another, and the chiefs must therefore continually revalidate their leadership. The main concerns of everyone are the most advantageous control possible of land and the constant disputes and negotiations that are entailed. The men's high sensitivity to their honor (izzat) makes direct negotiation difficult, and the major mediators are men who are known as saints because of their descent from the Prophet or some famous saint in the past, plus their reputation for piety and the exercise of mystical powers in curing and other types of problem solving (Barth 1959, pp. 96–103). With the assistance of the saints the chiefs are continually in the process of forming, revalidating, and reforming alliances with other chiefs, and this process results in the Swat Pathans' being divided into two opposed power blocs. There are members of each bloc in almost every community.

In other words, the members of each bloc live in discontinuous parcels of land each adjacent to parcels belonging to members of the other bloc. This comes about because the main lines of cleavage between the two blocs are the tensions over the inheritance and control of land among the descendants of particular common ancestors—among "agnatic collaterals" as Barth puts it (1959, pp. 108–109). There is perennial internal divisiveness in the major kinship groups (within which land is inherited), and each contending kinsman seeks support and advantage through allegiance to a chief (who may or may not be a member of the same lineage). Each chief, in turn, seeks greater power through alliances with other chiefs. The overall situation seems to be one of perpetual contention and realignment.

CATEGORIES OF IDENTITY

In Middle Eastern culture there are five characteristics that are very commonly perceived as categories of identity. These are:

1. Same language
2. Same religion
3. Same ancestry

4. Same sex
5. Same territory

Each of these serves as the basis of cohesion among people who already know each other. Each can also be invoked for the purpose of making new alliances among people who are only newly acquainted. The existence of aggregates of people sharing these identities constitutes a resource for the formation of new, active groups and a justification for the maintenance of already existing groups. Whether it is an actual, or only a potential, criterion of group membership, each category of identity is at the very least a potential source of refuge and also of peril. This point will be developed in this chapter, while details of the group structures will be discussed in later ones.

Social class, occupation, and ethnicity are not, for various reasons, included on the list. Social class, status, and rank distinctions are very marked in the Middle East, but most of the literature makes it very difficult to differentiate them from kinship and/or sectarian groups. That is to say, kinship and sect (or religion) seem to be the primary criteria of identification. The same, in general, applies to occupations, although it could be argued that the traditional guilds (though not apparently as cohesive as the European ones were) and the new, embryonic unions and professional associations (modeled on Western prototypes) are identity groups in their own right. As for ethnicity, it is only a catchall term for various combinations of the categories of identity that are already on the list.

Same Language

Middle Eastern people are highly sensitive to the diversity of their languages and dialects, to the cultural identities associated with each language and dialect, and to the antagonisms that are likely to come to the surface when speakers of divergent languages and dialects come into contact with one another.

In most Middle Eastern countries one language is usually predominant because it has the largest number of speakers and is the official language of the government. At the same time, in many of these same countries, other languages are also spoken by substantial numbers of people. Language differences are significant in Afghanistan, Iran, Iraq, Turkey, Israel, and the countries of the Maghrib. In every case the speakers of the predominant language are felt to be a peril by the speakers of the "minority languages," but the latter, in conferring a definite identity on their speakers, provide a refuge for them at the same time that they make them a target. The Armenians in Turkey were a case of linguistic *and* religious distinctiveness, and they survived there for many centuries, though they were eventually driven out. But in many cases linguistic distinctiveness takes precedence over other criteria as the primary cultural marker. The Arabic and Berber speakers in the Maghrib are mostly all Sunni Muslims; the Kurdish speakers in Iraq are Sunni Muslims like many of the Arabic speakers there; and in Iran the many non-Persian speakers are mostly Shia Muslims, as are most of the Persian speakers. Conversely, most of the Christians and Jews in the predominantly Muslim countries speak the vernacular language of the majority in the area where they live, but they characteristically preserve a special, distinctive language in their religious rituals.

The linguistic diversity of the Middle East is far greater than it may seem from these examples. Each of the major languages —Arabic, Berber, Persian, and Turkish—is divided into a number of dialects, some of which are so different from each other as to be almost mutually unintelligible. On the whole, these dialects are markers of regional identities, and the distinctions become so fine as to set apart one city from another and even different sections of the same city from one another. To the communications problems that are involved in all this must be added the reputations borne by certain dialects. There is a tendency to regard one particular dialect of each major language as being the superior one, in terms of which all the others (and their speakers) are viewed with contempt. This is connected with the fact that many of the spoken dialects diverge considerably from the form of the language in which they are written, and it is of course only the literate people (still in an overall minority in most of the countries) who know the written language.

In the macrocosmic sense the Middle East is highly diverse in languages and dialects of languages. These divergences are also felt at microcosmic local levels, just as are the transitions between desert and oasis. This is most evident in the cities where different languages are commonly spoken and multilingual individuals are relatively frequent. The smaller the city or town, the less there usually is of such heterogeneity, but even in remote villages the inhabitants are often accustomed to coping with visiting outsiders who speak differently.

Same Religion

Mortal peril in connection with religious identities in the Middle East is too well known and well documented to need any summary here. To be a member of a particular sect (that is, a socially organized religious group) has normally meant to be in peril at the hands of some other sect, or, on the other hand, to feel justified in imperiling some other sect.

Consequently, the religious and sectarian diversity of Middle Eastern culture is remarkable, and it suggests that refuges are also felt to be inherent in the groups concerned. Each of the groups is a refuge but not an absolute or ultimate one. Religiously faithful Middle Easterners would argue that in God there is, in fact, an ultimate and absolute refuge. This is, however, a religious response that does not answer the crucial question: Why the great diversity of organized religious groups, all of which avow their faith in the same one God? Perhaps we should leave the question unanswered, as a spur to meditation, as did Ferdowsi (ca. 935–ca. 1020–1026), the famous Persian epic poet, who likened his own sect (Shia Islam) to one of seventy-seven ships, each representing one of the sects of mankind and all afloat on the sea of eternity. Whatever we may be inclined to do with this metaphysical issue, we remain confronted with the formidable reality of Middle Eastern sectarian diversity.

Muslims are an overwhelming majority in every Middle Eastern country except Israel and Lebanon, but where Christians (in a wide variety of sects) and Jews are present they are noticeable, and special accommodations (such as the Ottoman millet system) have been made for them. There are also other sects, such as the Yezidis in northern Syria, the Druze in Israel, Lebanon, and Syria, and a few Zoroastrians in Iran. Furthermore, Islam itself is internally divergent. The Shia-Sunni division is present and intensely felt in parts of Iran and Turkey and throughout the Fertile Crescent where the Shias are, in turn, subdivided into such sects as the Alawites, the Ismailis, and the Mitwalis. Even in Saudi Arabia, where there is minimal diversity, the intense fundamentalism of the ruling Wahhabi sectarians sets them apart as special Muslims and creates tensions in other parts of the peninsula where their influence is felt.

In Egypt, predominantly Sunni, there are about 3 million Coptic Christians (about 8 percent of the population) living both in villages and in cities. In the Maghrib Christians are negligible in number, but rural and urban Jewish groups have been important, and many of the Sunni Muslims belong to distinctive, sometimes competing, religious brotherhoods, each devoted to the cult of a particular saint. In addition there are groups like the Mzabites, descendants of what was originally a heretical Muslim sect, who have a distinctive subculture and reputation in the Maghrib. While there are ever-present reminders of Islam as a refuge (the enclosed, uncluttered, sheltered serenity of mosques and the sense of communicable blessedness in saints' shrines), there are also ever-present reminders of the sectarian divisions within it.

One of the most sensitive intersectarian issues in the twentieth-century Middle East involves the Jews and the establishment of Israel. The idea of Israel was largely that of European—not Middle Eastern—Jews. In 1947 there were apparently about 700,000 Jews living in the Middle East, not counting those in Palestine. By the early 1970s there were apparently about

200,000 of them still living in various parts of the Middle East outside of Israel. Possibly all of the latter may move to Israel, but it should be remembered that Jewish identity has for a long time been an integral part of Middle Eastern culture generally. This integration, as in all the other sectarian cases, has been characterized by an interplay of peril and refuge. The establishment of Israel has meant a regrouping of forces but a perpetuation of the same old interplay of peril and refuge.

Same Ancestry

The acknowledgment or recognition of a common ancestor by two or more individuals, or two or more groups of people, is an important means by which kinship is established and maintained between them. Kinship ties and alliances are important in all cultures for at least some of the regulating of sexual relationships and for the care of infants and small children. Beyond these considerations, however, the importance of kinship ties and obligations varies greatly from one culture to another.

Most observers of Middle Eastern culture have attributed much importance to its kinship aspects—so much so, in fact, that "the family" often emerges in the literature as a rock of absolute stability. Political alliances may be treacherous and uncertain, and one's religion may make one the target of persecution—not to mention the perils of drought, famine, and pestilence—but kinsmen can be relied on for absolute loyalty and unstinting assistance. In other words, kinsmen are the ultimate refuge. This is the image, and it can certainly be filled out with examples of actual behavior, proverbs, and statements of ideal norms.

But the image is only partly correct. It is true that kinsmen are often one's first line of defense—or one's last resort—and that there is ideological backing for the expectation that they can be relied upon to perform these roles. However, it is also true that bitter quarrels among close kinsmen are common, and this is evidence that they cannot be automatically relied upon to serve as an absolute or ultimate refuge against the perils of life. Ironically, it seems that the bitterness of the quarrels is accentuated by the very weight of the demands that are made upon relatives—demands that are based on high expectations of performance. Because the demands and the expectations are so high, they often cannot be met and may have to be ignored out of sheer necessity, if for no other reason. Overdependence breeds disappointment, which, in the absence of alternatives, perpetuates overdependence.

The larger aspects of this paradoxical situation have been recognized for some time, but scholars are only now beginning to try to put the parts of the paradox together. They must be put together because that is how they are experienced by Middle Eastern people. Feuds that keep kinsmen apart, or create new divisions among kinsmen who had previously been unified, are reported from all over the Middle East, but so also is the very strongly expressed ideology of the unity of brotherhood. The latter may be an expression of a sincere sentiment, but it can also be mainly an invocation against the realistic fear that the ideology of brotherhood itself is likely to be violated. Waterbury—writing of social groups generally—observes that in Morocco hostility is most intense *within* groups because it is there that the control and distribution of the group's patrimony is debated (Waterbury 1970, p. 78).

The larger dimensions of the instability of kin groups in the Middle East have been analyzed by several observers in terms of the balanced antagonisms and segmentation of lineages. These concepts were originally set forth by the British anthropologist E. E. Evans-Pritchard in 1940. They have subsequently been adapted by several anthropologists for the analysis of various Middle Eastern settlements and areas: Eastern Orthodox Christian Lebanese village (Gulick 1955), Druze Lebanese village (Ayoub 1955), Iranian village (Alberts 1963), and Moroccan tribes (Hart 1973). The segmentation of lineages in itself has been reported from every location in the Middle East where long genealogies are recorded. Segmentation means the division of a kin group acknowledging the same common ancestor into two or more different groups acknowledging different common ancestors. A simple case would be a group descended from A segmenting into two groups whose ancestors were two sons of A, namely B1 and B2. In the course of time groups composed of B1's and B2's descendants will themselves segment into various sets of groups (C1 and C2, C3 and C4) whose ancestors were sons of B1 and B2, respectively. If all the people concerned retain a memory of A as a common ancestor and of all the subsequent ancestors of subgroups, there is then a tribal group (A) subdivided into two major lineages (B1 and B2) each of which, in turn, is divided into two minor lineages, C1 and C2, and C3 and C4. The four minor lineages may all be quarreling with each other at a given time, but circumstances may change, and C1 and C2 may unite (as group B1) in opposition to members of B2. Under still other circumstances, all may unite as group A against a group with an entirely different common ancestor, say X. When that issue is resolved, the A people may revert again to the antagonisms of the various C groups. As I have suggested elsewhere (Gulick 1955, p. 162), what all this means for each individual actor is that he must be able to respond to different, situationally varied cues in his relationships with kinsmen. Alliance may be replaced by antagonism, while erstwhile enemies may become allies.

The conception of common and segmented ancestries provides a model in terms of which these shifting alliances and antagonisms can be expressed. It is a flexible model, adapted to perilous ecological and political realities, providing a modicum of stability while

allowing room for maneuver. Relatives may or may not be agents
of refuge, depending on the circumstances, and the model allows
people to rationalize these uncertainties while at the same time
holding on to the ideal of continuous stability that is implied by
the concept of common ancestry. The notion that Middle Eastern genealogies can be accepted at face value, as being literally true,
is no longer entertained by specialists. Too many instances of manipulation, of adjusting the model of descent lines to fit present-day
changes in segmentation and alliance, have been discovered. Consequently, the genealogical model is now generally seen by Middle
Eastern anthropologists as being a metaphor of social relations
expressed in the idioms of kinship, rather than an exact replica of
the structure of kinship groups.

Waterbury's study of Morocco (1970) is an excellent recent
example of this metaphorical perception, but two of the earliest
studies that alerted Middle Eastern anthropologists, and other area
specialists, to it are Barth's monograph on the Swat Pathans (1959)
and Peters' paper on the pastoralists of Cyrenaica (1960). Barth says
that while the typical Pathan genealogy defines a segmentary
hierarchy of groups and subgroups, it "has no finality; it simply
offers an idiom for the expression of changing social alignments,
and the only criterion of 'correctness' is its fit with [present-day,
actual] social organization" (1959, p. 29).

Cyrenaica is the northeastern part of Libya. Its pastoral
nomadic population is divided into eastern and western aggregations, and the eastern one is subdivided into plains and foothills
dwellers. Each of these aggregations is believed to descend from a
common ancestor, these ancestors in turn being descendants of the
common ancestor of all, a woman. Peters explains how the
Cyrenaican pastoralists keep this early part of their genealogy constant, thus reflecting their large present-day ecological divisions.
Each of the latter is divided into smaller territories occupied by
tribal groups descended from the earlier ancestors. The whole system is a "hierarchy of ordered territorial groups" (Peters 1960, p.
31). The tribal groups are divided into primary, secondary, and
tertiary levels. The tertiary units are the actual residential groups
that live and move together for eight months of the year. Each
consists of from 150 to 200 people who constitute a lineage segment that is descended from a common ancestor. Generally speaking, these tertiary common ancestors lived about five generations
(supposedly) in the past.

In order to survive, each tertiary group must make the most of,
but also avoid overtaxing, the carrying capacity (especially the
water resources) of its territory, and in order to do this it must be
able to diminish, hold constant, or enlarge its numbers to fit the
erratic conditions of the environment. This is where the various
manipulations of the genealogies play their part. The genealogies

may be "telescoped" by eliminating names that intervene between the common ancestor and the living—identical names of different ancestors may be fused into one, and present-day descent lines that seem to be dying out may be grafted onto others, thus losing their genealogical identity (Peters 1960, pp. 32–36). These manipulations counteract the tendency for genealogies to enlarge and broaden through time, and they are necessary so that the genealogical conception of social groupings can be adapted to fit the actual ecological distribution of the people. Coping with peril is an underlying theme of this behavior, and peril is highlighted when tertiary groups actually segment or break apart. This is signalled in various ways: refusal to continue to be responsible for paying blood money on behalf of erstwhile fellow members of the lineage; demanding blood money payments, as compensation for homicide, from the same; failing to attend obligatory mourning observances for relatives; and ceasing to worship at the same saint's tomb (Peters 1960, pp. 47–48).

This genealogical conception of social unity and divisiveness is characteristically Middle Eastern, and it is not limited to tribal minorities like the Pathans and the Cyrenaican pastoralists. Variations on the same basic theme are manipulated by politically ambitious people among tradesmen in suburban Beirut, for example.

The smallest kinship group is the nuclear family, consisting of husband and wife and their dependent, unmarried children. In the Middle East the nuclear family is normally assumed to be strongly affiliated with the husband's brothers, their parents (while they remain alive), and the brothers' children (this larger group constituting what is generally called the patrilineal extended family). Within the extended family the ideology of brotherhood is invoked to the maximum, including the idealized preference for marriage between the son and daughter of brothers. Farsoun has discussed the importance of this group as it functions among modern business-oriented people in Beirut, Lebanon. He puts it in the context of "amoral familism," that is, distrust of all nonkin persons (Farsoun 1970, p. 265). Yet it is precisely *within* this group that Waterbury's observations about the intensity of hostility also apply. Coupled with the ideology of brotherhood are many accounts of bitter and irrevocable quarrels between brothers.

Same Sex

This review of the peril and refuge idea now comes to the level of the individual person, female or male. In every culture there are definitions of female and male gender: behavior, attitudes, and expectations considered appropriate or inappropriate for persons of each sex. Gender definitions are the result of long cultural experience and are not necessarily linked directly to the biological components of sex. But many people are unaware of this, and the result is the stereotyping of genders—the insistence that female and male gender patterns be mutually exclusive, polar opposites. "Feminine mystique" and "machismo" are examples. Insistence on such stereotypes imposes behavior on people of one sex or the other and forces on each person the idea that only certain types of behavior are appropriate for her or him. Cultures differ in the intensity with which they exhibit these differentiations.

Middle Eastern culture is one of those in which there are major differences in the definitions of female and male gender. "Man's world" contrasted with "woman's world," each being very much separate from the other, is the way the situation is often phrased. Details will be discussed later. Here I will consider the traditionally sharply differentiated female and male gender definitions only in terms of peril and refuge.

It is to a large extent true that Middle Eastern women are, by various means, secluded from exposure to strangers, their lives confined to domestic affairs. This is certainly the generally recognized norm or expectation, and although there are many instances of activities that do not neatly fit it, they are usually treated as exceptions rather than as normal variations.

One aspect of the male gender image is doing battle with the perils of public experience (that is, experience that takes place outside one's own home and family affairs), while the female gender is sheltered in, and a part of, that home, which is clearly perceived as a refuge. Are the two genders themselves emotional refuges in the sense that each defines in clearcut terms what is and is not expected of females or males? Possibly they are to some extent, for certain people, at certain times, and under certain circumstances, but that is as far as we can safely generalize.

Most of the many descriptions and discussions of the seclusion of women in the Middle East convey the feeling that it is a defense against peril rather than a secure haven. One reason is that women cannot be sheltered completely from the "outside world." In one way or another it cannot be prevented from obtruding into their lives. Another, perhaps more important, reason is that the main source of outside peril is perceived to be men—all men who are not within the woman's circle of mahram relationships. Mahram, in this instance, designates people with whom sexual activities would be considered incestuous, such as father, uncles, brothers, and some others. All other men are potential sexual threats. Hilal observes that men are felt simultaneously to be protectors of some women (such as their sisters, wives, and daughters) and exploiters of other women (Hilal 1970, p. 82). There is also an apparently widespread feeling that women (in complete contrast to the stereotype of Western Victorian women) are insatiably lustful. Put the "naturally" exploitive man and the insatiably lustful woman into contact, and the results will be inevitable. In order to minimize the likelihood of this result, women are secluded. Yet the seclusion does not forestall continual anxiety about the virginity of unmarried women or the faithfulness of married ones. The security system does not really protect against the perils to which it is explicitly addressed. Why doesn't it?

A woman's sexual transgressions are felt to bring dishonor not only to her but also to the men with whom she is closely connected. There are innumerable instances in the literature of a man's honor (and that of his kin group) being besmirched by his sister's premarital loss of virginity. This is different from the cuckolded husband's sexual jealousy and grievance, and I do not think that we fully understand the motivations involved. For the time being, however, one thing seems clear: Female and male genders are felt to be mutually threatening *and* vulnerable to each other. The seclusion of women seems to be a set of reactions to these feelings and not a prevention of them. Barth, in his discussion of the seclusion of women among the Pathans, suggests that it is an important support for the men because it allows them an opportunity for a private life that will not affect their all-important public image. It keeps their sexuality completely separate from public scrutiny, possibly resulting in trusting relationships between the men and their secluded women. However, he admits that this is difficult to document, and he says, "a male is dependent on, and vulnerable through, his women" (Barth 1969, p. 122).

Hanna Papanek, in her study of female seclusion in Pakistan (Papanek 1973), has made what may be an important breakthrough observation on the subject. Consider the man who kills his unmarried sister because she has—or is rumored to have—lost her virginity. Accounts from all over the Middle East emphasize that a man is honor bound to severely punish, if not kill, his sister under these circumstances. If sexual jealousy is not the motive, how is the man's "pathological rage," as Papanek (p. 308) calls it, generated? Papanek's hypothesis is that most Middle Eastern men feel, with good reason, that on the whole the social world they live in is dangerous, unpredictable, and uncontrollable. In defense against these feelings, a set of cultural patterns has evolved wherein men seclude women for whom they are responsible, thus gaining a sense of safety, predictability, and control over at least one important segment of life (pp. 317–318). In the terms of this chapter, in other words, the seclusion of women is a psychological refuge for the men. The sexual transgressions of a secluded woman are evidence that this refuge has been violated, and Papanek's idea is that men who are particularly dependent on the refuge react particularly violently to the threatened or actual loss of it. The dangerous and uncontrollable social world goes right on, however, and so the elaborate defensive mechanism is perpetuated.

Another warning about stereotypes is necessary. The subject under discussion lends itself to the picture of the "typical" Middle Eastern man's being a sexual fanatic and the Middle Eastern woman's being totally subdued by his fanaticism. Such an extreme view taken literally is inaccurate and unfair. There *are* dramatic incidents that have been reported and a whole complex of distinctive cultural patterns that I have summed up with one word: seclusion. These must be accounted for, and I have put them into the context of peril and refuge. But we do not know how many Middle Eastern men are *not* exploiters of women, how many brothers have *not* beaten up (let alone killed) their errant sisters, how many women are *not* insatiably lustful, and so on. Indeed, we must recognize that there may be very large numbers of such people. Nevertheless, the reports and descriptions are there, and another point also seems to be clear: Whatever their internal emotional sets may be, Middle Eastern females and males generally are careful to observe the proprieties of gender definition, for to do otherwise would be to run the highly feared risk of being damaged by gossip.

Same Territory

The various categories of identity that have been discussed have clearly recognized territorial expressions. This territorial clarity is probably facilitated by the desert-oasis environment, which involves sharp demarcations between well-watered (densely inhabited) and less well watered areas. There is a general tendency for sects, languages, and dialects to be distributed on a regional geographical basis. Furthermore, within any given region, villages usually consist of tightly concentrated clusters of houses surrounded by land that has definite (though often disputed) boundaries. Neighboring villages may, because they are so clearly demarcated, accommodate differing sects or dialects. Internal division of single villages into quarters can accommodate such distinctions on an even more minute scale, though village quarters most often express kin group differentiations. Similar considerations apply, on the whole, to larger towns and, to some extent, even to very large cities. And everywhere the individual dwelling, be it a tent or a house, demarcates a protective territory with special concern for gender identities.

Territorial identity per se is perceived in some groups, such as clusters or associations of migrants living in large cities. In general Middle Eastern territoriality is, certainly, the stage on which identity-oriented behavior is acted out, and it is a dimension of aggregate identity of which Middle Eastern people are very much aware. Canfield has shown how, in Afghanistan, the territorial distributions of three Islamic sects result from the many interactions of central government-people relations, geographical conditions, ecological adaptations, and kinship alliances and realignments. These territorial, ethnic and sectarian groups are not only different subcultures but also "political units existing in tension within their socio-political contexts" (Canfield 1973, p. 117). He sees the interplay of peril and refuge quite clearly, and indeed his study encapsulates a number of the points made in this chapter.

The Self

Finally, we must consider the individual alone, apart from alliances, kinsmen, and even gender. The literature emphasizes the great sociability of Middle Eastern people and their styles of interaction. Nevertheless, there is also a "loner" theme in many observations. The great sociability—including highly elaborated verbal courtesies and highly valued patterns of hospitality—may, it seems, be presentations of reassurance among individuals who must, ultimately, be wary of everyone else. Ultimate reliance on oneself only has been suggested in various ways by Waterbury (1970, p. 77), H. Williams (1958), and J. Williams (1968, p. 92), among others.

There is one particular manifestation of the perception of self in relation to others that, in conclusion, I will mention. This is the widespread belief in the Evil Eye. The belief is not confined to the Middle East; it is found all around the Mediterranean and elsewhere. Often presented as some other culture's irrational mumbo jumbo, it has not been given enough serious attention. Years ago Westermarck (1933) published an extensive discussion of it in the Middle East, emphasizing its wide occurrence and its pre-Islamic origins. The essence of belief in the Evil Eye is that things or persons one holds dear are continually vulnerable to damage or destruction caused by other people's envy projected through their eyes. Unexplainable misfortune, of which there is much in life, can also be attributed to the Evil Eye. Possession of the power to cause Evil Eye damage is believed to be involuntary, and particularly people who on occasion may be thought to have unusual Evil Eye powers are not treated as scapegoats. The belief system is significantly different in this respect from witchcraft beliefs. Everyone and anyone can be an agent of the Evil Eye, and it is reasonable to suppose that basically it is a projection of the destructively envious feelings that large numbers of people harbor. The projection is onto the "generalized other," onto other people in general rather than onto specific individuals, perhaps because of subliminal awareness that everyone is envious. The belief system itself includes no cures for the Evil Eye, only a large variety of defensive, protective rituals and devices. Other people's malevolence, in other words, is felt to be a normal condition of social life, triggered by envy. Envy is very understandable as a commonly felt emotion where subsistence is precarious, where there are not enough of the good things of life to be shared equitably, and where personal lives are subject to abrupt changes of fortune.

Rather than being thought of as a bizarre, irrational superstition, belief in the Evil Eye can perhaps more constructively be regarded as a mental set that has evolved in realistic reaction to styles of life in which individuals are both agents of peril to others and also imperiled themselves by others.

PERIL, REFUGE, AND MODERNIZATION

My hypothesis is that there is a peril-refuge mentality that has been present in the Middle East for a long time. It is anchored in certain objective realities (external to any individual's subjective state of mind), but it also is reinforced by many kinds of behavior and attitude. Collectively, these many kinds of behavior include various recurrent types of groups, alliances, and institutions. In other words, there are strong tendencies for the peril-refuge mentality to be self-perpetuating. Consequently, Middle Eastern people are likely to try to adapt their behavior patterns to modern innovations in their culture without changing the mentality.

Which changes that have taken place in the Middle East during the Machine-Age Islamic time frame have been sufficiently radical to result in the emergence of any alternative mental sets among substantial numbers of people? Automobiles? Airplanes? Electricity? Increased literacy rates? Movies? Radio and television? Modern medical techniques? Democracy? Socialism? Petroleum revenues? This question must be asked whenever one encounters evidence of "modernization" (most of which is visual and material) and wonders to what extent these changes are only superficial. It is certain, in any case, that many aspects of Middle Eastern culture that existed long before these changes were introduced continue in the lifeways of large proportions of Middle Eastern people. Perhaps in a less than ideal world the peril-refuge mentality is a still-viable system of trade-offs between stresses and satisfactions. If some aspects of it seem highly undesirable, what alternatives could be substituted, by whom, and how?

Several Middle Eastern governments now recognize that the very rapidly increasing populations of their countries may result in disaster of unprecedented proportions. Involved are high birth rates (anchored in long-established patterns of behavior governed by familial values and gender definitions) and recently reduced death rates owing to modern preventive medicine. Are the perils of disastrous overpopulation great enough to induce people to change behavioral patterns that have been part of the traditional peril-and-refuge mentality? Must that traditional mentality itself be altered if this new peril is to be averted?

In presenting an anthropological perspective of the modern Middle East, I invite the reader to bear these important questions in mind as we proceed from one major aspect of Middle Eastern culture to another.

REFERENCES

Alberts, Robert C. *Social Structure and Culture Change in an Iranian Village.* Ph.D. dissertation, University of Wisconsin, 1963.

Ayoub, Victor F. *Political Structure of a Middle East Community: A Druze Village in Mount Lebanon.* Ph.D. dissertation, Harvard University, 1955.

Barth, Fredrik. *Political Leadership Among Swat Pathans.* London School of Economics, Monographs on Social Anthropology, no. 19. New York: Humanities Press, 1959.

Barth, Fredrik. "Pathan Identity and its Maintenance." In *Ethnic Groups and Boundaries,* edited by Fredrik Barth, pp. 117–134. Boston: Little, Brown, 1969.

Beck, Lois Grant. "Masks and Mirages: Social Distance among Pastoral Nomads." Paper presented at annual meeting of Middle East Studies Association, November 7–11, 1973.

Bodman, Herbert L., Jr. *Political Factions in Aleppo, 1760–1826.* Chapel Hill: University of North Carolina Press, 1963.

Canfield, Robert L. *Faction and Conversion in a Plural Society: Religious Alignments in the Hindu Kush.* Anthropological Papers, no. 50, Ann Arbor: University of Michigan, 1973.

Coon, Carleton S. *Caravan: the Story of the Middle East.* Rev. ed. New York: Holt, 1958.

Farsoun, Samih K. "Family Structure and Society in Modern Lebanon." In *Peoples and Cultures of the Middle East: An Anthropological Reader,* vol. 2, edited by Louise L. Sweet, pp. 257–307. Garden City: Natural History Press, 1970.

Gulick, John. *Social Structure and Culture Change in a Lebanese Village.* New York: Viking Fund Publications in Anthropology, no. 21, 1955.

Hart, David M. "The Tribe in Modern Morocco: Two Case Studies." In *Arabs and Berbers: From Tribe to Nation in North Africa,* edited by Ernest Gellner and Charles Micaud, pp. 25–58. London: Gerald Duckworth & Co., 1973.

Hilal, Jamil M. "Father's Brother's Daughter Marriage in Arab Communities: A Problem for Sociological Explanation." *Middle East Forum* 46, no. 4 (1970): 73–84.

Hoffman, Bernard G. *The Structure of Traditional Moroccan Rural Society.* The Hague: Mouton & Co., 1967.

Lapidus, Ira M. *Muslim Cities in the Later Middle Ages.* Cambridge, Mass.: Harvard University Press, 1967.

Montagne, Robert. *The Berbers: Their Social and Political Organization.* London: Frank Cass, 1973 (First published in 1931).

Papanek, Hanna. "Purdah: Separate Worlds and Symbolic Shelter." **49**
Comparative Studies in Society and History 15, no. 3 (1973): 289–325.

Peters, Emrys. "The Proliferation of Segments in the Lineage of the Bedouin in Cyrenaica." Journal of the Royal Anthropological Institute
90 (1960): 29–53.

Seddon, David. Introduction to Robert Montagne's The Berbers: Their
Social and Political Organization. London: Frank Cass, 1973, pp. xiii-xl.

Waterbury, John. The Commander of the Faithful: The Moroccan Political
Elite—A Study in Segmented Politics. New York: Columbia University Press, 1970.

Westermarck, Edward. Pagan Survivals in Mohammedan Civilisation.
Amsterdam, Netherlands Philo Press, 1973 (First published in 1933).

Williams, Herbert H. Some Aspects of Culture and Personality in a
Lebanese Maronite Village. Ph.D. dissertation, University of Pennsylvania, 1958.

Williams, Judith R. The Youth of Haouch el Harimi, a Lebanese Village.
Cambridge, Mass.: Harvard Middle Eastern Monographs, no. 20, 1968.

Zonis, Marvin. The Political Elite of Iran. Princeton, N.J.: Princeton University Press, 1971.

ANNOTATED BIBLIOGRAPHY

The idea of peril-and-refuge, as set forth in this chapter, is an
interpretative synthesis of many studies that have varied contents
and viewpoints. Consequently, there are very few works that concentrate on the subject itself, and most of the works that I have
found particularly useful—such as those cited in the text of this
chapter—belong under other topics as much as, if not more than,
they do under this one. Furthermore, this chapter has touched on
several topics that will be dealt with in more detail in later chapters, and the bibliographies pertaining to those subjects will be
annotated at the ends of those chapters. In this bibliography some
of the publications already cited will be grouped and briefly discussed, and a few more publications will be annotated in order to
highlight certain aspects of the subject.

Peril and Refuge: Two Views

Gulick, John. "The Ethos of Insecurity." In Responses to Change, edited
by George DeVos. New York: D. Van Nostrand, 1976, pp. 137–156.

Concentrates on the peril aspects of the subject with main emphasis
on kin groups and gender. First written in 1968 and presented at the
Eighth International Congress of Anthropological and Ethnological
Sciences in Kyoto, Japan, it was subsequently greatly revised and
presented at the Conference on Psychology and Near Eastern Studies,
Princeton University, May 7–9, 1973. It includes a fifty-five-item
bibliography.

50   Ardalan, Nader, and Laleh Bakhtiar. *The Sense of Unity: The Sufi Tradition in Persian Architecture.* Chicago: University of Chicago Press, 1973.

> Ultimate refuge in the Sufi's mystical union with God is seen in the context of architectural adaptations to the perils of the desert-oasis environment. This book is beautifully illustrated with line drawings, diagrams, maps, and photographs.

Bled al-makhzen/Bled al-siba

As already indicated in the text, Waterbury (1970) and Zonis (1971) are two very important works on this subject. Though emphasizing the political, both authors define "political behavior" broadly, and they take into account many other dimensions of culture than political institutions, such as kin groups and personality characteristics. Canfield (1973), dealing with yet another country, is an excellent presentation of the interrelatedness of various dimensions of culture. Canfield tends to approach the phenomena of power from the bottom up rather than from the top down as do Waterbury and Zonis.

Jacobs, Norman. *The Sociology of Development: Iran as an Asian Case Study.* New York: Praeger, 1966.

> Overlaps to some extent with Zonis but concentrates on details of interpersonal relations, the presentation of self, and the nature of the self. This work is particularly relevant to the last section of the chapter, where questions are raised about cultural change and the peril-and-refuge mentality.

Kin-Group Segmentation and Antagonisms

Canfield (1973) can appropriately be cross-referenced here with Gulick (1955), Ayoub (1955), Alberts (1963), and Hart (1973). Gulick borrowed the basic concepts from Evans-Pritchard, who had developed them in connection only with kin groups (among the Nuer of the southern Sudan). Gulick adapted them to a greater variety of groups and aggregates (similar to the categories of identity in this chapter). Alberts adapted Gulick's formulation to fit his Iranian material and added another point of considerable importance. Traditional patterns of culture that continue to function in the midst of change were interpreted by Gulick (1955) as being "resistant" to change. Alberts suggests that a more accurate and useful interpretation may be that they continue to function because they are successfully adapted to change. Hart (1973) derives the concepts directly from Evans-Pritchard, which suggests a kind of independent confirmation of the applicability of the concepts to the Middle East. Peters (1960) also uses Evans-Pritchard's concepts but shows how the Cyrenaican pastoralists' manipulations of their segmentary system differ from those of the Nuer.

Gender

Hilal (1970) is a thorough and critical review of professional interpretations of the rather technical issue of father's brother's daughter marriage. It is also insightful on female-male relations in general. Judith Williams (1968) is a rare study of modern Middle Eastern teenagers in a Sunni Muslim village in Lebanon. She deals with the differentiations of female and male genders in specific detail. Papanek (1973) is a major review article on the seclusion of women, with an extensive bibliography, comparing the Muslim details from Pakistan (which seem largely applicable among Muslims farther west) with Hindu seclusion of women in India.

In addition to these works, which are cited in the text, two others are mentioned below. They are very different from each other in a number of respects, but both document the differentiation of female and male genders in specific terms.

Fuller, Anne H. *Buarij: Portrait of a Lebanese Muslim Village*. Cambridge, Mass.: Harvard Middle Eastern Monographs, no. 6, 1961.

Field work done in 1937–1938. The study concentrates on adults.

Kendall, Katherine W. *Personality Development in an Iranian Village: An Analysis of Socialization Practices and the Development of the Woman's Role*. Ph.D. dissertation, University of Washington, 1968.

Field work done in 1965–1966. This dissertation concentrates on infants and small children.

Population and the Population Problem

Baer, Gabriel. *Population and Society in the Arab East*. New York: Praeger, 1964.

Limited to coverage only of the Arab nations and dated (both in its statistics and its sources on qualitative matters), it is nevertheless comprehensive and relates demographic data to cultural patterns, ranging from the family to aggregates of identity.

Clark, J. I., and W. B. Fisher, ed. *Population of the Middle East and North Africa: A Geographical Approach*. New York: Africana Publishing Corporation, 1972.

Covers the entire area and is excellent as a comprehensive source book on such matters as population aggregates and densities.

Wade, Nicholas. "Sahelian Drought: No Victory for Western Aid." *Science* 185, no. 4147 (July 19, 1974): 234–237.

A specific instance of regional disaster: the drought and famine since 1968 in the southern border zone of the Sahara. Overpopulation and its various consequences are co-causes, with short-term drought, of the disastrous conditions that have ruined the previously viable but precarious ecological systems of the Sahel.

Tension and Stress

Miner, Horace M., and George DeVos. *Oasis and Casbah: Algerian Culture and Personality in Change.* Ann Arbor: Museum of Anthropology, University of Michigan, Anthropological Papers, 15, 1960.

Based on Rorschach tests and ethnographic observations, this study's emphasis is on the intrapsychic effects of an external world generally perceived as perilous.

THREE

FOOD PRODUCTION COMMUNITIES

In this chapter I shall review the literature on Middle Eastern villages, pastoral-nomadic groups, and small towns, in that order. The farmers and animal husbandmen who live in these communities are the people who raise food and produce raw materials for all the inhabitants of the Middle East. The towns serve as regional or district marketing and processing centers. Locally produced goods are exported from them, while imported goods from other districts, regions, and nations are redistributed in their shops and markets. In addition, towns are almost invariably administrative centers where the power of national governments (concentrated in the national and provincial capital cities) is felt at the local level and manifested in such institutions as health centers, high schools, gendarmerie stations, jails, and courts.

The literature will be reviewed in terms of the cultural-ecological regions discussed in Chapter One in order to give some indication of those cultural patterns that appear to be widely recurrent and those that appear to be more narrowly confined.

DESERT-OASIS SUBSISTENCE

Agriculture, animal husbandry, and commerce have been the means of subsistence of Middle Eastern people since the Formative period of cultural development. Commerce includes both the processing and distribution of vegetable and animal products and the creation and distribution of artifacts.

Most villagers are agriculturists of some sort, but many are also craftsmen, shopkeepers, or shepherds. Most nomads are animal husbandmen, but some also raise crops. Some town and city dwellers are farmers and animal husbandmen, but most earn their living by a wide variety of means only hinted at by such terms as wage labor, commerce, crafts and manufacturing, professions, and government administration. Considering all this variety, there are many different life styles, some of which may seem quite distinctive.

Three fundamental points must be kept in mind: (1) A system in which agriculture, animal husbandry, and commerce are interrelated has evolved over a long time, providing maximum exploitation of the desert-oasis environment. (2) The countless geographical interpenetrations of desert and oasis mean that people exploiting these different environments are in continual contact with each other. (3) Many individuals have, during their lifetimes, changed from one major type of subsistence activity to another, or have friends or relatives who have done so, or have observed other individuals or groups doing so. This is a highly complex subsistence system, offering many alternative opportunities and risks.

PROBLEMS OF GENERALIZATION

While no systematic sampling of the various Middle Eastern ecological communities has been done, there are various generalizations about them that must, at the outset, be considered.

First of all, there are vivid, highly judgmental stereotypes of "the nomad," "the peasant," and "the city dweller" in Middle Eastern culture itself. Many Middle Easterners apparently assume these stereotypes to be objective facts, just as many Americans and Europeans regard the stereotypes of various ethnic groups in their midst. To confuse matters further, many observers of the Middle East have accepted Middle Easterners' stereotypes of themselves as if they were confirmed facts and have presented them as such in their publications.

Briefly, the stereotypes of nomad, peasant, and city dweller, when taken literally, give the impression that they are completely different kinds of people, and that there is only one kind of nomad, one kind of village dweller, and one kind of city dweller. These oversimplified impressions are so inaccurate that they should be considered false. There *are* distinctive features of pastoralism, of villages, and of cities, but they are only *some* of the features of pastoralism, villages, and cities, respectively. The nonheuristic quality of these stereotypes is now generally recognized by area specialists, and much of the recent literature that I draw upon is written with a view to disposing of them.

The stereotypes consist of oversimplified classifications of people, and they are also expressions of judgment as to the "quality" of people. These characterizations are vivid and also ambivalent, so that they can be fitted to one's frame of reference to suit one's convenience. Thus: Nomads are the epitome of bravery, nobility, hospitality, manliness, and poetic imagination; they are also warlike, treacherous, and ignorant. Peasants are clods, for they work with their hands in earth and manure; but compared to city dwellers, they are honest and straightforward, albeit capable of shrewdness. City dwellers are clever, "cultured," literate, and "live the good life"; they are also dishonest, devious, and physically and morally corrupt.

These multipurpose, protean caricatures are quite understandable as accompaniments—rationalizations, justifications, and explanations—of the various experiences encountered in the interplay of peril and refuge. In fact they are a part of the peril-and-refuge mentality or ethos itself. They involve the denigration of manual labor, some form of which (including farming) is the means of livelihood of more Middle Easterners than any other large category of work. That the essential work of a culture's basic food production should be conventionally disdained is a striking fact. Thaiss, in his study of the bazaari subculture of Tehran, suggests, drawing on the ideas of Max Weber, that each group of people feels a need for distance and opposition between occupational categories in order to enhance its style of life (Thaiss 1973, p. 18). I am not certain how far this can be pressed, but it does certainly seem to apply at this general level. A very unromantic reason why farming (and, by extension, manual labor in general) is denigrated may be that for many centuries farming, never easy under the best of circumstances in the desert-oasis environment, has been burdened by exploitation—sharecropping, indebtedness, and heavy taxation—and therefore kept at a level of drudgery from which many persons born to it would be only too glad to escape. These negative feelings have even been expressed in specific terms in the central valley of Lebanon, where natural conditions are relatively good and about half of the farmers own their own land (Fetter 1961). Perhaps it is a comforting rationalization, under such circumstances, to think and to claim that one disdains being a farmer because of one's noble nomadic heritage or ancestry. It is very risky, however, to mistake this rationalization for a historical explanation, for in its latter guise it would presuppose such unsubstantiated assumptions as that all settled people have nomadic ancestors, that present-day nomads are prototypical of all the other inhabitants, and that ancestral behavioral characteristics can be inherited.

The village-urban stereotypes are very ancient in the Middle East and the Mediterranean area generally (Baroja 1963), and some social scientists continue to be fascinated by the romantic image of the pastoral nomads—even while they recognize the stereotypic and exaggerated elements in the romanticism. For example, Patai, in a major recent work on the Arabs (all Arabic-speaking people) entitles two chapters "The Bedouin Substratum of the Arab Personality" and "The Bedouin Ethos and Modern Arab Society" (Patai 1973). And Polk, in his introduction to a very handsome illustrated edition of "The Golden Ode," a pre-Islamic Arabic poem by Labid Ibn Rabiah, emphasizes the remote, pure nobility theme of then and now, despite disclaimers that, after all, present-day nomads have modern materialistic desires (Polk 1974).

As for the peasants—who are the largest single occupational category in the Middle East and constitute a very large proportion of the people who migrate to cities and become new city dwellers—there is beginning to become available to general western readers through translation a variety of modern fiction by Middle Easterners that reflects the ambivalent stereotypes but leavens them with the complex subtleties of reality. For instance Rathbun (1972) discusses how, from about 1920 to 1955, Turkish writers who were largely urban people wrote stereotypic accounts of Turkish village life. Makal (1954) was, however, a controversial counteraction—expressing the author's own biases but from the vantage point of personal experience in villages. Taieb Salih's amusing and evocative short story, "The Doum Tree of Wad Hamid," is set in a village on the Nile and vividly conveys the sense of the villagers' acceptance of a tough life and their very realistic appraisals of the fallibility of outside agencies that insist on interfering with them, supposedly for their own good (Salih 1967). The opening of Yahia Haqqi's "The Saint's Lamp" catches, in one paragraph, some city dwellers' contempt for villagers' expressive piety at a saint's tomb in Cairo, other city dwellers' empathy for them, and the fact that some of the peasants themselves became city dwellers (Haqqi 1973).

Recognition of these stereotypes is a necessary first step in coming to terms with problems of generalization about Middle Eastern communities. A very important point that emerges from this process is that villagers, pastoralists, and city dwellers are highly aware of each other because they are so interdependent. Their interdependence, in turn, makes it very difficult to neatly characterize the "typical" traits of pastoral groups, villages, towns, and cities, except in very general ways. These entities are varied, and often the distinctions between them are unclear. Indeed, there is merit in the increasingly popular idea that Middle Eastern cultural patterns should be studied, and portrayed, in regional terms wherein village, pastoral, and urban cultural ecologies are treated as parts of a single cultural system rather than as separate entities, as emphasized by the stereotypes. Unfortunately, very few such regional analyses have yet been made, and almost all of the data we have were gathered under the traditional assumption of there being a tripartite division of Middle Eastern culture. It is impossible to revise these data to fit the new concept. However, the growing awareness of towns as being intermediate in various ways between villages and cities is a step in the direction of regional analysis, and fortunately several good studies of towns are available.

Beginning, then, with the villages, what generalizations can meaningfully be made about them? There are several hundred thousand of them in the Middle East, and 70 percent of the Middle Eastern people supposedly are villagers, while 5 percent and 25 percent supposedly are pastoralists and city dwellers respectively. These are, incidentally, very rough, approximate figures that are composites of figures derived from such sources as national censuses. The proportions differ in different countries, but in many countries they are not really known, owing to the absence or inaccuracy of data sources. Also troublesome is the fact that "urban" and "rural" populations are defined arbitrarily, as well as differently, in different countries. Frequently, "urban" is defined as any place with a population of 5,000 or more. Is one to assume that everyone in a smaller place is a peasant but that no one in a place of 5,000 or more is a peasant? This is only one of many such questions that must be asked concerning demographic cutoffs between "rural" and "urban." Unfortunately, demographic sources rarely provide any answers to questions such as these that are concerned with cultural patterns, life styles, and values.

Attempts to generalize about the number and size of Middle Eastern villages are similarly frustrating. For instance, the number of villages in Iran is estimated at between 50,000 and 60,000, and the rural population of the country was about 17 million in 1966. From such figures one can calculate an approximate average village size of 280 to 340 people for the country. Could one then project this average size to the rest of the Middle East? Definitely not. The average size of villages in Iraq for example is 265 people, as opposed to 600 to 700 people in western Lebanon. Villages with less than 100 people have been described, as have villages with several thousand. Perhaps the best that can be said is that a sample of villages picked at random in the Middle East would probably have populations somewhere between 100 and 1,000 people.

As to the number and total population of nomadic groups, estimates are even more difficult, one reason being that many Middle Eastern governments wish to deemphasize the number of nomads within their borders. In Jordan a probably rather accurate count indicates about 6 percent of the population as living in tents, while estimates for Saudi Arabia range between 17 percent and 21 percent. The official number in Iran is somewhat under 1 percent, but some observers think it is really more. All indications are that in the past few decades the number of nomads has been decreasing, and it is certain that there have been massive movements of rural people to the cities, especially the larger ones where job opportunities are thought to be the most numerous.

There is no doubt that the great majority of Middle Easterners live in villages and that those villages are varied in size, in their relationships to larger regional systems, and in other respects. No one has yet published a typology that satisfactorily accounts for all the major permutations in the entire Middle East, but I will summarize two studies, each of which makes a beginning: Kolars (1967) and Fernea (1972). Neither pretends to be a definitive typology for the entire Middle East. Fernea's later work appears to have been developed independently of Kolars', and there are interesting similarities and differences between them. The important point is that both identify certain variables that are undoubtedly important everywhere in the Middle East. Both are based on research already done.

Kolars' typology (p. 69) is based on Turkish materials only and is as follows:

Urban-directed villages
 1. Shadow
 2. Annexed
 3. Satellite
 4. Summer dormitory
Rural-directed villages
 5. Market-seeking
 6. Market-recognizing
 7. Market-ignoring

Shadow villages are enclaves of people from particular villages living in large cities. They are migrants' neighborhoods or quarters. They have been reported from cities all over the Middle East. Important questions concerning them include the extent to which these people maintain contact with the home village and what effects the maintenance of these contacts have on their adaptation to living in the city. Kolars hypothesizes that they serve as channels to occupational specialties, city-dwelling migrants from certain villages or rural regions often becoming known as specialists of one sort or another.

Annexed villages are former farming villages that have been engulfed by growth of a particular city. The village name may be retained as the name of a city quarter, complete with the suffix "köy," which means village. I know of specific and exact parallels in Baghdad, and Isfahan, and annexed villages are presumably common wherever large Middle Eastern cities have been growing rapidly. Kolars says that in Turkey farming has become rare and anomalous in annexed villages. An example is Balgat, which is featured in a well-known publication by Daniel Lerner (1958), and which has now been annexed to the city of Ankara (Kolars 1967, p. 70).

Satellite villages are within commuting distance of a large city. Kolars defines this as one to two hours on foot or bicycle or the equivalent by bus or train. The economy of such villages may include traditional farming by some of the inhabitants. There are many satellite villages outside of cities in other parts of the Middle East.

Kolars says that although summer dormitory villages certainly exist in Turkey, no research has been done on any yet (p. 71). It is a long-time custom in Turkey for many city dwellers to go to mountain or seaside villages in the summer, and presumably one of the effects on these villages is greater income and greater influence of urban life styles. What is meant here is not newly created resort settlements but old villages that to some extent become summer resorts. There are definitely such villages in the mountains adjacent to Beirut and Tripoli, Lebanon, and presumably elsewhere. One of the important variables that needs exploration is the extent to which the summer visitors are total strangers to the village, as opposed to being people who, at an earlier point, migrated from the village to the city and by spending the summer in the village are simply maintaining their ties with it.

Kolars' categorizations of rural-directed villages are based on the degree to which the village is tied to an external market system, and this depends on the village's resources and various historical factors (Kolars 1967, p. 72).

In market-seeking villages there is, in addition to subsistence production, enough production of surplus so that there can be continuing expansion toward cash crops, local craft specialties, or local industry. Such villages become "incipient towns" when people from elsewhere begin to come to them for special services that have been developed in them (Kolars 1967, pp. 76–77).

Market-recognizing villages have limited cash crops and occasional marketing of subsistence crop surpluses—with some inhabitants, but not others, benefiting from saleable surpluses (Kolars 1967, pp. 73–74).

Market-ignoring villages have no crop surpluses, and some inhabitants may have to do seasonal work elsewhere in order to survive. In Turkey Kolars sees them as belonging to two types: plateau grain producing villages that may be able to switch to good cash crops, and many mountain and forest villages that have little potential for change. This type of village—its economy often dominated by sharecropping, in which a substantial ill-afforded "surplus" is given to absentee owners—is very common, if not the most common of all, in the Middle East generally.

Kolars' concern is with economic change and development. He points out that fifty years ago in Turkey more villages than now were market-ignoring, and he discusses other patterns or paths of change from one situation to another. His concluding point is that the great variety of village situations suggests that there should be a variety of development plans and procedures, not just one (Kolars

1967, p. 83). These considerations should be applicable in other countries.

Fernea's typology emphasizes political, more than economic, variables. There are two dimensions of these variables: the degree to which influences from cities are imposed on villages and the extent to which individual villages are linked to others by means of tribal organizations.

The classification (Fernea 1972, p. 77), with identifying numbers changed from those in the original in order to make each type stand out more distinctively, is as follows:

I.   Villages that are tribally organized
- A. High degree of urban influence
  1. Economic dependence
  2. Political dominance
- B. High degree of independence from urban centers
  3. Corporate economic interests
  4. Private ownership of resources and of means of production

II. Villages lacking tribal organization
- A. High degree of urban influence
  5. Politically administered
  6. Economically dominated
- B. High degree of independence from urban centers
  7. Corporate economic interests
  8. Private ownership of resources and means of production

III. Villages containing tribal and nontribal elements
  9. High degree of urban influence
  10. High degree of independence from urban centers

Fernea bases his ten types on twenty-eight sources, mostly from the Fertile Crescent, the Nile area, Anatolia, and Iran. Tribal organization means social organization based on the concept of descent from a common ancestor, where individual villages are linked to other villages, and sometimes to nomadic groups, resulting in villages and other settlements that are segments or sections of kinship-defined regional political structures. Villages defined as lacking tribal organization are usually internally organized in terms of such kin groups but not externally tied to other villages by them. Political urban influence may be minimal (limited to tax collection, conscription, and some law enforcement), or it may be much more intensive. Economic urban influence ranges from ownership of the entire village by urban landlords to local corporate or private ownership patterns on which there is no urban influence at all. Corporate economic interests consist of common property held and administered by the villagers, of which there may be very little or much, as opposed to privately owned property and means of production.

Fernea's typology is valuable in that it shows the many permutations of these variables. Most of the cases he uses would fall into Kolars' rural-directed category, although two or three might qualify as satellite, and even perhaps summer dormitory, villages. Among these urban-directed villages is one that is tribally organized and, by reason of being so, integrated with the national city-dominated political system. While many other urban-dominated villages (as in the Nile Delta and the immediate hinterlands of other cities) lack tribal organization, there are still other villages lacking tribal organization that are not urban dominated. In other words, there is no necessary affinity between urban and nontribal or between nonurban and tribal.

Once again, the existence of many types of villages, involving a variety of urban-village relationships, should warn us against assuming that there are always sharp, contrasting differences between "the village" and "the city." Food production is primarily a village and a pastoral concern, while life styles associated with elite social classes and the most important Muslim institutions are almost exclusively urban. These are indeed contrasts. But segmentary kinship structure, factionalism, major gender distinctions, various details of domestic family organization, awareness of identity differences, and commercial awareness are basically common experiences and themes to villagers, pastoralists, and city dwellers (Gulick 1969).

VILLAGE STUDIES

Much of the anthropological field research that has been done in the Middle East has been done in villages. Anthropologists have traditionally preferred to do their research in locations where they can live for a relatively long time, become well acquainted with a variety of the inhabitants, and be able to observe the full cycle of life at close hand. Villages are ideal "natural" locations for these purposes. Since most Middle Easterners are villagers, anthropologists' village studies have therefore sampled variants of one of the mainstreams of Middle Eastern life.

In this section I will highlight certain subjects that illustrate what I think are probably important and very widespread features of village institutions and structure. Some are emphasized more in some cases than in others. Does this mean that certain features are not as widespread as others, or, to put it another way, some features are typical of certain regions but not of others? In the present state of our knowledge one often cannot answer this with confidence, but I will at least raise the question when appropriate. This is a composite view of "the Middle Eastern village," formed from diverse parts. Certain themes will recur, as follows:

1. Segmentary kinship structure, whether "tribal" or limited to the particular village; whether strictly genealogical or also politically metaphorical
2. Degree of autonomy from larger economic and political systems, as signaled by Fernea's and Kolars' typologies
3. Social inequality, with emphasis on sectarian and ethnic considerations

The point is that the issues involved in each of these themes are reported with sufficient frequency for us to postulate that in one form or another they may be universal characteristics of Middle Eastern villages. However, this postulate must remain tentative; the questions must remain open.

The Fertile Crescent

Beginning in the southeastern extremity of the Fertile Crescent, I shall proceed northwestward and then southward, ending in Israel.

Ech-Chibayish is a large village (population nearly 10,000 in 1947) on the Euphrates River in the extensive marsh area north of the seaport city of Basra. The marshy environment itself is certainly unusual for the Middle East, but it is, nevertheless, a form of oasis surrounded by desert. The source of information is the monograph (1962) by Shakir Mustafa Salim, a British-trained Iraqi anthropologist.

The village is built on about 1,600 very small islands that extend along the river for 3 miles, but it is only 50 to 150 yards in width. Fernea includes it in his type 1 (tribally organized, dependent on urban economy), and Kolars might well consider it to be an incipient town, for it is a minor administrative center and a market center to which people from the surrounding area come for various commercial services. Wet rice is grown, but the main crop is a commercial one: harvesting reeds, which are used for a variety of purposes, including mats for the roofing of houses.

The inhabitants consider themselves to be members of one tribe of Arabian desert-pastoralist origins. Until 1924 the tribe was led by a hereditary shaykh. The sense of tribal unity is now dissipated (Salim 1962, p. 44), but the subdivisions of it (clans and lineages) continue to be important. Also, there are five social classes: (1) "holy men" (belonging to eight families) who claim descent from one or another of the Shia Imams; (2) members of the ex-ruling clan; (3) members of other clans ("commoners"); (4) descendants of former slaves of the former ruling clan; and (5) thirteen Mandaeans—remnants of an, until recently, larger group of Christians (special devotees of John the Baptist)—who have been specialists in boat building (Salim 1962, pp. 62). Social inequality associated with sharply differing levels of prestige attached to certain occupations is an element that is given considerable emphasis.

Daghara is another settlement on the Euphrates, about 100 miles northwest of ech-Chibayish. (Between the two of them, incidentally, is the site of Uruk, one of the earliest cities, referred to in Chapter One). The major sources on Daghara are a technical monograph by Robert Fernea (1970) and a very readable and informative autobiographical book by his wife, Elizabeth Fernea (1969).

Robert Fernea includes Daghara in type 3 of his village typology (tribally organized, high degree of independence from urban centers), but he himself recognizes that there are, in its culture, elements of something more than simply an agricultural village: Namely, it is a minor administrative center, and it is a marketing center for surrounding hamlets. Irrigation agriculture, nevertheless, is the subsistence base. The El Shabana, the people of Daghara, are one of twelve tribal segments of a larger intertribal confederation, and they are subdivided into several levels of segments. The El Shabana have a hereditary shaykh, and they claim ultimate ancestry among Arabian "Bedouin," but Fernea notes that settled and nomadic people in this area have many cultural traits in common (1970, p. 77). There is a particularly lucid discussion of the tribal system as a metaphor of social relations, as opposed to the many socioeconomic realities that do not neatly fit the metaphor (1970, pp. 80–83). Further, despite his placing Daghara where he does in his typology, the settlement *is* influenced by city-based government agencies and personnel, and, in fact, the theme of the book is the adaptations of the tribal system to changing government structures and influences. In other words, a "high degree of independence from urban centers" does not mean *complete* independence, a condition that would be very difficult to find anywhere in the Middle East.

The people of ech-Chibayish and Daghara are Arabic-speaking Shia Muslims, both tribally organized, both claiming remote Arabian-desert ancestry but both thoroughly involved in sedentary ecologies. The source materials on them focus on the two individual villages and therefore place less emphasis on wider tribal connections. The next two studies, in contrast, focus on small districts in which there are numerous villages and pastoral nomads. One of these is Barth's study of Kurdish-speaking Sunni Muslims east of Kirkuk, Iraq (Barth 1953), and the other is Aswad's study of Turkish- and Arabic-speaking, recently sedentarized, villagers in the Hatay Province of Turkey (Aswad 1971). Study of a map will show that these districts are, respectively, in the northeastern and the northwestern extremities of the Fertile Crescent.

Barth's study delineates three aggregations of Kurds living in the same region: Jaf nomads, Hamawand tribal villages, and nontribal ("feudal") villages. The Jaf are organized according to the segmentary idiom discussed earlier, and so are the Hamawand village residents. All of the latter recognize a common ancestor

(Hamma) who lived nine generations earlier than the living adult group. There are four subgroups of villages, each claiming descent from one of the four sons of Hamma (according to one version but not others). There are four subgroups, in any case, each with its hereditary agha, or chief, and a council of the aghas of component villages (Barth 1953, pp. 45–47). Whereas the tribal farmers largely own their own land, the nontribal villagers are largely tenants of absentee owners, and there is no wider kinship system that links the nontribal villages together. For the Hamawand villages there is an intermediary tribal structure between themselves and the governmental authorities; for the nontribal villages there is not. In both types of village there are definite social class differences; for example, kinsmen of aghas, commoner farmers, tenant farmers, laborers, and serfs. Barth also sees certain cultural differences between the tribal and nontribal villages in such matters as frequency of marriage between kinsmen and relative importance of feuds (pp. 68–72).

Of particular importance is the complexity of differences within just one ethnic aggregate (Kurdish) that Barth's study presents. Presumably the same is true of the other cultural groups in the immediate vicinity, which includes towns, village areas, and pastoral nomadic dry areas that Barth only touches upon.

Similarly complex is the situation studied by Aswad. Her central interest is in the processes by which a Turkish-speaking and an Arabic-speaking group have, over the past century, become settled as villagers. The Turkmen, who had been long-range herders, experienced forced settlement by the government, resulting in their notables' acquiring large estates on which lower-ranked tribesmen are now sharecroppers. There is considerable commercialization on the estates, and the large kin groups (lineages) do not hold property corporately. The general situation seems somewhat reminiscent of the nontribal village situation among the Kurds.

The Arabic-speaking Al Shiukh were short-range herders, they were not forced to settle, and they established villages on a kin-group basis, forming alliances with wealthier settled patrons, both rural and urban. There now are, among them, what Aswad calls "core villages," each dominated by a patrilineal kin group holding its property corporately and competing with other such groups, and "fringe villages," with mixed dominant and dominated kin-group memberships (Aswad 1971, pp. 111–112).

East of Hatay, and south of the Syrian city of Aleppo, is the village of Tell Toqaan, studied by Sweet (1960). Tell Toqaan is a newly settled village and has a heterogeneous population of tribal and nontribal Arabs, plus Circassians, Turks, and Kurds. The first mentioned of these include people who were formerly pastoral nomads. Others moved to Tell Toqaan from other villages. The village has a mixed agricultural and herding economy, and Sweet emphasizes that it also has close ties with urban-based commercial systems, a situation that is of long standing in the area (p. 229).

So far the cases have repeatedly involved recent sedentarization of nomads or traditions of nomadic origin, and one could easily be tempted to generalize from these cases and conclude that Fertile Crescent villagers as a whole are "sedentarized nomads," or that nomadism in general is ancestral to village life. However, it would be incorrect to do this. It happens that since about 1800 there has been considerable sedentarization in the desert fringe areas of the Fertile Crescent. This has been documented and directly observed. However, in previous times, the areas that have been recently sedentarized had villages and towns, as the numerous tells (habitation site mounds) prove. Over the centuries there have been waxings and wanings, alternately, of the farming and the nomadic pastoral ecologies. We in the present era happen to have observed a waxing period of the farming ecology in this desert-fringe area.

Farther west, in the better-watered hills and mountains of Syria and Lebanon, there are both tribally and non-tribally organized villages whose inhabitants either have no traditions of pastoral-nomadic ancestry at all or have such traditions that are dubious and vague. Among these people are the Alawites of the Syrian coastal mountains south of Hatay and north of Lebanon. They are a Shia-derivative sect who numbered about 200,000 in the 1930s, when they were studied by Weulersse (1940). He describes them as farmers living mostly in small hamlets and trading towns and divided into four tribal confederations, which are subdivided into twenty-five tribes, each confederation occupying discontinuous parcels of territory. Weulersse is very doubtful about their supposed "glorious" Arabian desert ancestry (p. 328). He was also, earlier perhaps than many other observers, aware of an idea that is now more widely accepted and has already been introduced, namely that the genealogical ("tribal") model of social relations is a metaphor, an abstract expression, rather than necessarily an exact plan whose details can automatically be accepted as literally true. Weulersse wonders, for example, at the dispersal of the Alawite tribes and suggests that it may well be the result of different groups at different times attaching themselves to a particular notable for protection and better advantage (p. 333). Such political alliances were then presumably formalized by various genealogical fictions. This is the genealogical metaphor at work, and it has been observed elsewhere in the Middle East.

Farther south, in Lebanon and Jordan, there are several villages that have been studied by anthropologists that are not tribally organized and where possible pastoral nomadic ancestry is either not part of local folklore, is not mentioned by the author in question, or is mentioned only as a vague possibility. Those in Lebanon include the Maronite Christian villages of Hadchite (H. Williams 1958) and Hadeth el-Jobbeh (Touma 1958), the Eastern Orthodox Christian villages of al-Munsif (Gulick 1955) and Bishmezziin (Tannous 1942), the Sunni Muslim villages of Buarij (Fuller 1961) and Haouch el-Harimi (J. Williams 1968), and a Shia Muslim village (Peters 1963). The two Sunni Muslim villages in Jordan are Baytin (Lutfiyya 1966) and Kufr al-Ma (Antoun 1972). Some of these villages have close economic and communications ties with cities, but others do not—or did not when they were studied—and so it cannot be said that their nontribal, nonpastoral-nomadic characteristics are simply due to some sort of urban influence.

Following Fernea and Barth, I have been referring to "tribal" and "nontribal" villages as if they were clearly distinct types. They are not, for the same principles of structure apply to both. All persons concerned understand the metaphor of patrilineal descent from a supposed common ancestor and the basic system of segmentary lineages derived therefrom. In some instances the inhabitants of a district that is comprised of a number of villages will acknowledge a common ancestor and be organized politically on this basis. Such villages are called "tribal." In other instances there is no intervillage or district kinship structure, and such villages are called "nontribal." However, the internal structure of these villages is based on the same segmentary kinship metaphor as the "tribal" villages are and as the larger regional tribal structure itself is. Furthermore, particular villages may change through time from "tribal" to "nontribal," or the reverse, depending on the presence or absence of forceful leadership, government interference, and changing economic conditions.

All of the villages listed have internal kinship structures that are basically the same, though none is exactly the same as any other. There are several lineages that may or may not collectively acknowledge a single common ancestor. Lineages that do not acknowledge any common ancestor with other lineages in the village often have a tradition of having migrated to the village from somewhere else. Even in cases where there is a single common ancestral tradition for an entire village, original settlement of the site, under difficult conditions (such as being forced to move from some other location), is a common theme of local folk histories. Being a member of a larger ("tribal") kinship system is not, as already explained, a common theme in these particular villages, but there are suggestions of it in a few cases. In Tell Toqaan *some* of the inhabitants, but not all of them, are affiliated with larger, external kin groups (Sweet 1960). Kufr al-Ma is in a district where descendants of the same common ancestor are found in several different villages, including Kufr al-Ma itself (Antoun 1972, p. 37). But these descendants do not act as members of a unified tribe (perhaps they would if the requisite leadership were present), and not all of the lineages in Kufr al-Ma acknowledge descent from this ancestor anyway. In the Shia village studied by Peters some of the inhabitants claim descent from Ali as-Saghir, who was son of the martyred Husayn and was also the Fourth Imam, and thus have special prestige inhering in their particular lineage that would be recognized by Shias generally. However, it does not apparently link them (let alone the village as a whole) into a larger specific tribal structure. An additional point is that in most villages there are residents who are not members of *any* of the major lineages. Often recent settlers, they are typically regarded as "outsiders" for a long time and have no land-use rights in the village or any rights to common property (musha) that the village may hold. These people are frequently farm laborers who must be prepared to move from one village to another in order to find work.

While these particular Lebanese and Jordanian villages are not, in general, linked into wider political systems on the basis of kinship, they very frequently are subject to the influence of a regional political boss (zaim) who is himself a manipulator of the formal administrative framework in which all of these villages are set. And there is one anthropologically documented village that *is* part of a tribal structure. This is the Lebanese village called "Kallarwan" in the publications of Victor Ayoub (1955; 1965). The inhabitants of Kallarwan are divided into three lineage groups: two large Druze lineages (segmented into smaller units) and one small Christian one. The Druze in Lebanon conceive of themselves as divided into two hereditary groups (tribes), and both of these are represented in Kallarwan. They are highly competitive with each other—the rivalry involves national as well as local politics—and thus Kallarwan is linked to a modern national political system through a tribal organization.

If the two factional Druze tribes of Lebanon are generally distributed as they are in Kallarwan, it follows that the membership of each is geographically dispersed in a discontinuous fashion. Such discontinuous tribal distribution was, it will be remembered, found among the Alawites of Syria, and something similar is suggested, at least, in the "checkerboard" distribution of the soffs and leffs of the Maghrib (see Hoffman 1967, pp. 104–109). When it is remembered that the affiliation of a group with a particular tribe is subject as much to that group's momentary allegiance to a particular leader as it is to rigid adherence to genealogy (often the genealogy is adjusted to the political realities), these intricate and changeable arrangements should be more comprehensible than they might be otherwise (see the analysis of leadership and the territorial distribution of the power blocs among the Swat Pathans in Barch, 1959).

Coming now to Israel, we are confronted by some special situations. Three types of village in Israel have been studied by anthropologists: (1) the kibbutzim, special communal settlements conceived and first established by the early European Zionists before the establishment of the state of Israel; (2) Arab villages that remain from what was Palestine before 1948; and (3) the moshavim, settlements established by the state of Israel for new immigrants, these very often being Jews from other Middle Eastern countries. The kibbutz has received an enormous amount of attention because of the many social innovations, including the collective socialization of the children, that are involved. Conceived and established largely by European Jews, the kibbutzim and the moshavim are unique in the Middle East, and at the present time there is little about them that can be informatively generalized to non-Israeli Middle Eastern villages, or vice versa. A brief discussion of them, with further references, will be found in Weingrod (1971). There is, however, one important direct tie between these innovative communities and non-Israeli Middle Eastern culture, and this is the settlement of Jews from other Middle Eastern countries in moshavim (Goldberg 1972; Shokeid 1971; Weingrod 1966).

In different ways Rosenfeld and Cohen both emphasize the continued importance of kinship groups in Arab villages in Israel, but their interpretations differ. Rosenfeld sees these villagers as a "residual peasantry," heavily dependent on wage labor in the cities yet motivated, and limited, by the lineage system that previously controlled landholding (Rosenfeld 1964, pp. 228–229). Cohen's major theme, on the other hand, is that the kinship-based political system of the Arab villagers, having previously been weakened, has been reasserted under the new political conditions (Cohen 1965). This interpretation is consistent with the general view that the segmentary lineage system is flexible and adaptable to various conditions—as is amply exemplified by the different forms of it in the Fertile Crescent village studies that have been considered.

Weingrod (1966) and Shokeid (1971) have studied Arabic-speaking Moroccan Jews who were settled in moshavim in the Negev. Drastic cultural change and relearning of life styles were involved and necessary. Both authors convey the feeling that the adaptations—including learning mechanized farming techniques instead of being craftsmen and shopkeepers as they had been in Morocco—were successful. Weingrod interprets this in terms of the idea that total rapid change may be easier than more gradual change, aided by the help that the immigrants received from longer-established Israelis (p. 196). Shokeid notes the inability of the immigrants he studied to assume formal leadership roles because their division into kinship groups (very like those one would expect among other Middle Eastern people) was a divisive influence (1971, Chapter 7 in particular).

The immigrants studied by Goldberg were from Libya and settled in a moshav in central Israel (better watered than the Negev) near other moshavim and former Arab villages, and in fact the moshav had a citrus grove owned by an Arab who had fled in 1948–1949 (Goldberg 1972, p. 56). One of Goldberg's major conclusions is that despite the drastic changes involved in the move from Libya to Israel, considerable cultural continuity was maintained, and the general adaptation was successful, particularly because of excellent leadership (p. 6). This leadership, in some contrast to the situation studied by Shokeid, was able to counteract the divisive effects that the various kin groups might otherwise have had. In their original homes these three immigrant groups were by no means the same, and the details of their adaptations in their new homes are also quite different.

This review of community studies in the Fertile Crescent has focused on villages and perhaps resulted in neglect of the pastoral nomadic elements in the ecology. We need to be reminded that, despite the general historical trend toward sedentarization, there still are pastoral nomadic groups interacting with the sedentary people all along the desert fringes of the Crescent, but I will review the pastoral nomadic studies separately.

The Nile

One of the major concentrations of villages and peasant life in the Middle East is in the Nile Delta, but very little anthropological research has been done there. Saunders (1968) reports on the continued importance of extended kinship ties in one Delta village where migration to cities, and travel back and forth between the village and cities, is an important aspect of village life—as is generally the case. However, Berque's (1957) is the major single study of a village in this area, and the village (Sirs al-Layyan) is probably unusual at least in one respect: it is extremely large. Its population is 22,000, divided into twenty-nine quarters, and there is sociocultural differentiation among the inhabitants on the basis of property and degree of adoption of new life-style items from the cities. Nevertheless, the social organization is of the usual segmentary kin-group type, without a wider tribal organization but, until recently, with frequent feuds between kin groups. In these and other respects Sirs al-Layyan sounds representative of what is generally considered typical of Lower Egypt. Saints' festivals are given considerable attention by Berque, as they are by other observers of Nile village life, but festivals of this sort are not unique to the Nile area. The Nile area is, however, special in regard to another matter that is mentioned by Berque and others. This is clitoridectomy, the excision of the clitoris of young girls, an operation that is, or has been until very recently, practiced more commonly in the Nile area than anywhere else in the Middle East, apparently. There will be more discussion of it in Chapter Six.

Kaum al-Arab (Barclay 1966) and Kafr el-Elow (Fakhouri 1972) are both near Cairo. The former is, in fact, a satellite village, in Kolars' terms, while the latter is eighteen miles upstream, with a large proportion of its labor force working in industrial mills nearby. Both studies illustrate the continuation of extensive kinship functions, and intensive concern for saints and other religious matters, at the same time that wage labor outside the village has become a major means of livelihood and an alternative to farming. The people of Kaum al-Arab, along with the people of several other villages in the vicinity (near the Pyramids), claim membership in a section of a pastoral-nomadic tribe of the western desert of Egypt. Although their forebears began gradually becoming sedentarized 150 years ago and are now indistinguishable from other peasants in the area, they still refer contemptuously to the latter as peasants, or "fellahin," as opposed to desert dwellers, or "bedu" (Barclay 1966, p. 143). This general tribal association illustrates the broadest application of the common ancestor metaphor in the sense that this has been referred to in the Fertile Crescent. Otherwise, intervillage tribal organization does not seem to be strong in Lower Egypt generally. Direct government controls and massive absentee landlordism (only recently affected by government-supervised land reform measures) may be part of the reason.

Blackman (1927) and Ayrout (1938) are two of the oldest village studies in Upper Egypt and, as a matter of fact, the Middle East generally. Both present composite materials and do not focus on any particular village. The major study of a single village in Upper Egypt is Ammar (1954), a study concerned chiefly with the psychological aspects of child rearing. Ammar also describes the village as divided into nine clans (lineages) that, in turn, belong to a regional tribal aggregation, the G'afra, who are opposed by another such aggregation, the Ababda. The G'afra claim descent from Ja'far al-Sadiq, great-great-great-grandson of the Prophet, while the Ababda claim descent from a collateral relative of the Prophet (Ammar 1954, pp. 45–46). Ammar does not mention it, but one wonders whether, among these Sunni villagers, it matters that Ja'far al-Sadiq was the Sixth Shia Imam. Although the two regional descent aggregations do not have hereditary shaykhs, membership in one or the other does affect contemporary political behavior (Ammar 1954, pp. 47–48). This somewhat attenuated expression of tribal structure is reminiscent of the Qays-Yaman factions of the southwestern Fertile Crescent, mentioned by many observers, in which descent from extremely ancient, perhaps mythical, characters is used as the metaphor for present-day factional identification.

Farther upstream, among the Nubian villagers, Fernea has drawn attention to two different social structures, one being the segmentary tribal structure. The other, which may be unique, places greater emphasis on each individual's mother's close kinsmen and father's close kinsmen. Among the Fedija Nubians who have these bilateral groups (called nogs), feuding behavior, which is virtually an integral part of the segmentary lineage system, is absent (Fernea and Gerster 1973, pp. 19–21).

Buurri al Lamaab is a village on the outskirts of the city of Khartoum, Sudan, and because of its closeness to the city, it is becoming a satellite, or, as Barclay calls it, a suburban village (Barclay 1964). The village has a rather heterogeneous population and a new saint's shrine, and most of its inhabitants participate in a lineage system—but one in which the units are not as clear-cut as they are in Egypt. By this Barclay means that, unlike Egyptian lineages, those in Buurri al Lamaab do not have guesthouses or lineage heads that are as influential (Barclay 1964, pp. 82–83). Once again we encounter variations on a theme, for lineage or "tribal" chiefs (shaykh or agha) are intermittently present elsewhere, along with their guesthouses (mudifs, madafas, or in Egypt, diwans).

The Maghrib

Tribal territories are characteristic of the mountains and desert fringes of the Maghrib. Within these territories villages are clustered—as in oases in the plains or along mountain streams—and by reason of being clustered are separated from other villages, as, for example, among the Seksawa of the High Atlas Mountains (Berque 1955). In addition to the village ecology there is the pastoral ecology, and the two, as usual, interpenetrate each other. Incursions of one on the other have been continual, as illustrated in the recent study of the Ait Atta of Morocco (Dunn 1973). This is a notable instance of the perilous social environment, and one of the conspicuous features of the Saharan fringe of Morocco is the fortified settlement (kasbah or qsar), of which there are many, each usually identified with a tribal group.

Pastoral-agricultural conflicts of interest and disputes over water rights among villagers are among the basic sources of difficulty, plus the exertions of city-based power structures and the alliances with them, or resistances to them, on the part of village and pastoral people. These differences and conflicts, acted out in a broken and difficult terrain, express themselves in the usual genealogical concept of tribal membership. However, common tribal membership is not sufficient to allay intratribal conflicts here, any more than elsewhere, in the Middle East. In the Maghrib, however, a special terminology has developed that sometimes makes this region seem unique in the Middle East, this special quality being accentuated by the Berber names and Berber or Berberized-Arabic vocabularies that are peculiar to the Maghrib.

The notable case in point, already referred to, consists of the cross-tribal alliance units known as leffs in Morocco and soffs in Algeria (Montagne 1931, p. 36; Hoffman 1967, p. 104; Bourdieu 1962, pp. 12–16; Hart 1970, pp. 40–45). *Tada* is another term for "alliance" that is also encountered frequently. The literature is often detailed, but it fails to yield a clear perception of the structure of these units. A possible key to the lack of clarity may be that, where and when observed, they have been momentary responses to situational cues (see Vinogradov 1973, p. 80) and thus, over the long term, are changeable and ephemeral. This important item in Middle Eastern anthropology is not well understood and needs more field study, if that is possible.

In the Maghrib, as elsewhere in the Middle East, lineal descent is also a metaphor for alliance and is thus subject to the manipulations of conflicting interests. A relatively constant phenomenon is the rather strict adherence to a particular line of descent when the descent line is reinforced by religious prestige. For example, Gellner (1969) has analyzed the descent lines of marabouts (holy men in their lifetimes, becoming saints with hereditary blessedness, or baraka, after death). Such lineages become the upper-class cores of villages as well as the leadership cores of religious brotherhoods with very far-flung memberships. However, while particular details of the saint complex may be peculiar to the Maghrib, the basic phenomenon is pan-Middle Eastern, as we shall see later.

A large number of mountain villages in the Maghrib are small hamlets whose inhabitants must rely on regional exchange systems for various goods and services. Market towns frequently serve this function, but in the Maghrib it is also served by regular open-country markets (without towns). Activities in these markets are not only commercial, but the markets also provide an arena where tribal conflicts can be adjudicated and mitigated (Benet 1970). However, Benet emphasizes the fragility of these functions of the market and the ever-present danger of the outbreak of sudden violence, or nefra'a (p. 191).

There have been very few intensive studies of individual villages in the Maghrib, but there are four of them that I will comment upon. The first is of Mediouna, a coastal village in Morocco near Tangier, studied by William Schorger. The economy (as observed in 1948–1949) is a combination of wheat and millet agriculture, animal husbandry, and the cutting of millstones for cash (Service 1963, pp. 417–419). Recent changes in this economy have included the sale of considerable amounts of farming land to outsiders and considerable confusion in village leadership in the course of making adjustments to changes in the economics and politics of Tangier and Morocco (Schorger 1969).

The other three villages are in Tunisia. One of them is Souailha, a small hamlet of about fifty people in the well-watered plains west of Tunis. As might be expected with such a small settlement, its members belong to a larger kinship group encompassing other hamlets, and it maintains a saint's shrine and an adjoining cemetery where the villagers bury their dead (Bardin 1965, p. 111). Bardin seems to have mixed reactions to the present state of the village, faced as it is by increasing large-scale mechanization of agriculture all around it. On the one hand, he points to unemployed males loitering in the nearby market town (p. 115), and, on the other hand, he concludes his study by refusing to predict that the traditional agriculture and animal husbandry of the village will necessarily soon disappear (p. 136). A very different study, by Nadia Abu-Zahra, is of a much larger village she calls Sidi Mateur. As this pseudonym implies, the village was founded, more than 300 years ago, by a man regarded as a saint (sidi). He was not only the patron saint of the village itself but also of a regionally popular brotherhood. The population of Sidi Mateur is divided into two factions, each living in its own quarter. The Zawya (250 in number) are the descendants of the saint, and they, as in many other similar circumstances in the Middle East, are believed to inherit his blessedness (baraka), enabling them to effect cures and ward off various ills. The other faction consists of the Ramada, 2,000 people of diverse origins divided into four lineages plus some unaffiliated families. Until the independence of Tunisia was achieved, the Zawya controlled the political leadership of the village and the endowed sectarian properties known as habous (more generally known in the Middle East as waqf). Because of this the Zawya did not have to engage in manual agricultural labor (as did the Ramada) and could afford more education for their children. With independence came the government's liquidation of habous properties in 1957 and its campaign against the saint cult (Abu-Zahra 1972, p. 274). One of the Zawyas' adjustments to their loss of privileges is permitting their previously veiled and secluded women to take white collar and other jobs in the city of Sousse, whereas among the Ramada, whose women used to participate perforce in their men's manual labor, the better-off women, at least, are now more veiled and secluded than they used to be (Abu-Zahra 1972, p. 275).

Souailha and Sidi Mateur are in relatively well watered parts of Tunisia, but Shebika, the fourth village under consideration, is a small oasis in the stark desert west of Gafsa, very near the Algerian border. Duvignaud's book (1970) begins with a long description of the individuals living in the village (as he subsequently came to know them) and the arrival of his team of researchers—mostly young urban Tunisians wholly inexperienced in this village aspect of their own national society. The concerns of the book are to describe the extreme poverty of the village and nearby pastoral nomads, the dilemmas caused by alienation of land to outsiders, the desire of many villagers to escape, and (perhaps above all) the failures of communication between the village and various government agencies with their promises of help. The climax is the villagers' defiance of the government: refusing to quarry any more stones for the construction of an unwanted public building. Instead, they wanted help for badly needed reconstruction of their houses. The style is impassioned, vividly anecdotal, and based on five years of experience in the village.

Anatolia

Stirling's *Turkish Village* (1966) is actually a study of two nearby villages near the city of Kayseri. In both villages (despite various differences) Stirling was impressed by various similarities, including de-emphasis on social rank, emphasis on the individual household (mostly nuclear family households) as the major organized group, and a strong sense of village identity (p. 236). Both villages are divided into quarters, and these are to some extent identified with lineages, but these particular Turkish lineages apparently become evident in village life only when people are called upon to take sides in feuds. Of some interest are the guest rooms that some villagers maintain, which are the nuclei of gossip groups (pp. 240–241). Hospitality and visiting, with strategic motives very much in mind, are involved here, and this is an aspect of Middle Eastern life that is commonly commented on but that has not been given much systematic attention until very recently (see *Anthropological Quarterly* 1974).

Social, cultural, and psychological differentiation is the theme of the first chapter of Lerner's *The Passing of Traditional Society* (1958), most of which consists of analyses of questionnaire surveys on exposure to the mass media that were done in several Middle Eastern countries. The first chapter, however, is a "parable" based on Lerner's own direct experience in Balgat, a village that was rather rapidly annexed and absorbed into Ankara in the 1950s. The differing personalities of the grocer and the mayor of the village, and their differing adaptations to change, are the foci of the "parable." "Transformation" is the lasting image in any case. Being so close to a city, and in a country where modernization has been pursued as a policy longer than in most Middle Eastern countries, Balgat and its transformation should not be considered typical of Middle Eastern villages generally.

Alborz-Zagros Mountains

Three studies that have been done in Iran bring into high relief the subject of social inequality in villages, together with the related subject of land ownership and land tenure. Yossouf-Abad is an Azeri-speaking village of about 800 people located north of the city of Tabriz, not far from the border of the Soviet Union. When visited and briefly studied by Hanessian (1963), it was owned by an absentee landlord whose manager (mubashir) was resident in the village and was a member of its upper class. Also prominent were the mayor and a council of elders. Village mayor ("mukhtar" in

Arabic and Turkish, "kadkhuda" in Persian, and usually called "omda" in the Nile area) is a position found everywhere. The incumbent is not necessarily a strong figure in his own right, but the position usually constitutes the formal link between the village and the governmental administrative hierarchy. Where the village is owned by an absentee landlord, the mayor must of course accommodate himself to his interests.

Hanessian provides a list of five categories of land ownership in Iran that will serve to illustrate conditions that are fairly general throughout the Middle East. The list is Hanessian's, but the further comments are mine:

1. *Vaqf* lands (from Arabic waqf, commonly called habous in the Maghrib). Lands that have been made over to Islamic sectarian administrators, the making over being an act of piety. In theory the income from the land, or its usufruct, is used for such sectarian purposes as clerics' salaries and upkeep of mosques. From the point of view of the peasant it may make no difference whether his village is owned by the waqf administration or a secular absentee landlord.
2. *Khaliseh* lands. Owned by the state. Miri is another term used with similar meanings elsewhere. The state may grant (or rescind) usufruct rights to such lands to persons who, in turn, will assume the role of absentee landlords as far as the villagers are concerned.
3. *Amlak* lands. Personal crown lands of the Shah.
4. *Khurdeh malikin.* Peasant-proprietors who live and work on their own lands.
5. *Milk* lands. Privately owned, usually by absentee landlords.

In one way or another, all of these arrangements, except the fourth, involve absentee landlordism, the target of the various land reform programs that have recently been promulgated in various Middle Eastern countries, including Iran. Peasant proprietors do occur here and there, but most Middle Eastern peasants have been until recently—and many still are—tenants. However, the conception of being a member of the village by reason of being a member of one of the component lineages established in it, conveys to many peasants at least the security of use rights to land that they do not themselves own.

Not all peasants, however, have such use rights, let alone private-property rights. Consequently, in addition to individual status distinctions (such as mayor, owner's agent, and others) there are group distinctions. I have already made references to cases of special group status based on descent from some sacred figure or membership in a lineage in which the status of tribal chief is hereditary. Property rights, or use rights, among nonelite people tend to be hereditary also. Ajami's study (1969, p. 65) of three villages near the city of Shiraz differentiates among three social classes:

1. Farm operators: large holdings; market oriented; cash crops. 12 percent of sample.
2. Peasants: former sharecroppers who, with land reform, received ownership rights because they previously had had use rights in the villages. 35 percent of sample.
3. Khwushnishin: landless farm laborers. 53 percent of sample.

The large number of Khwushnishin is apparently representative of the general situation in the country (see Hoogland 1973), and it is quite possible that massive differentiations of this kind —in villages—are more important than most existing village studies would lead one to believe. Anthropologists' attention to social inequality in Middle Eastern villages perhaps has been drawn overmuch to "sacred" lineages on the one hand or to low-status ethnic groups like the Haratin of the Sahara (Briggs 1960, pp. 67–68) on the other.

Robert Alberts' study of Davarabad, a village about eighty miles southeast of Tehran, is the most detailed and thorough study of an Iranian village now available. I will mention only two of the topics that he discusses. One is the close interrelation of the farmers of Davarabad with pastoral nomadic groups in the environs of the village. Members of the latter regularly take care of herds of sheep and goats owned by the villagers, this care including seasonal migrations (Alberts 1963, pp. 420–422). The other is the matter of social inequality to which Alberts devotes an entire chapter. The basic villagers' conception in this is the distinction between "big" people and "little" people (in local terminology), with the arbobs (landlords) at one end of the scale and the Khwushnishin at the other (p. 745).

The khwushnishin, and the many people living under similarly disadvantaged circumstances in other Middle Eastern countries, must be distinguished from the small groups of outcastes who are encountered almost everywhere. Generally referred to loosely as Gypsies, they are itinerant and invariably despised. They earn their living as musicians and dancers and as tinkers or the like. They are socially shunned, often on the grounds that contact with them is polluting, and are often regarded as being a subhuman race. Little social-science attention has been paid to them, but there is an article on the cultural patterns of one group of them, the Luti of western Iran (Amanolahi and Norbeck 1975).

Arabian Peninsula

The last village to be considered is in the Shaykhdom of Bahrain in the Gulf area, where almost no other anthropological field work has been done. The study (Hansen 1967) is of the Shia village of

Sar, and considerable emphasis is put on the material culture of the village and on details of religious belief and practice. The context of social differentiation is in evidence here, too, for the villagers of Bahrain are generally Shia, while the ruling elite and the town dwellers are Sunni (Hansen 1967, p. 25). Evidently the low status of the village Shias in the eyes of the town-dwelling Sunnis is not affected by the claims of the Shias that they are direct descendants of Imam Husayn (p. 34). Elsewhere we have seen that such a claim can, under different circumstances, be the rationale for high status. Here it cannot.

PASTORAL NOMADS

Fernea's village typology provides something of a bridge between villagers and pastoralists by recognizing cases where tribal political structures encompass both villagers and pastoralists. In some of those cases, as we have seen, the villages are the result of relatively recent sedentarization of some of the pastoralists, but this is not always the case. The stereotypes to the contrary not withstanding, villagers and pastoralists have common concerns in regard to animal husbandry, and, to put it over simply, there are village-dwelling shepherds and there are nomadic herdsmen who are part-time farmers. Village farmers may hire pastoralists to take care of their herds, and pastoral groups may own villages where others do the farming for them. Farmers and pastoralists are reciprocally dependent on each other for their various products.

Spooner, in a major article on pastoral nomads in the Middle East and adjacent areas, concludes with a set of six generative rules of nomadic adaptation (1973, p. 41). In abbreviated and paraphrased form they are:

1. Nomadic pastoralism developed from animal husbandry among farmers due to population pressure on agricultural resources.
2. Herds and groups of pastoralists must be maintained at optimum sizes.
3. Local groups of pastoralists are unstable because individuals and their individually owned animals must frequently transfer to other groups and herds in order to maintain optimum sizes.
4. Local instability is counteracted by the conceptual stability of larger scale aggregations (for example, tribe).
5. Leadership roles are based on personality except where sedentary populations influence the matter otherwise.
6. Religious expression reflects "a stoical, unritualized relationship between man and an intractable supernatural."

The migratory patterns of pastoralists, necessitated by the search for optimum water supplies and fodder in maximally fragile environments, are not random. Use rights and territorial rights are highly elaborated, and conflicts of interest must be continually negotiated with other nomads, villagers, and city-based governments.

Seemingly remote from city life, nomadic groups have in fact, on occasion, seized and held control of city-based governments (becoming sedentarized in the process); the heads of large pastoral groups are often city-dwelling notables who exercise political influence; and pastoral groups have (in the past anyway) interfered directly in city matters by raiding commercial caravans or exacting tribute for their safe passage. Sometimes rebels and sometimes co-opted as government troops, pastoralists have sometimes epitomized the land of dissidence but at other times have served the land of government.

Recent anthropological studies of Middle Eastern pastoral nomads for the most part show conscious awareness of the traditional stereotypes and seek to counteract them. In the process the complexities of the ecologies of pastoral groups (including symbiosis with sedentary groups) are given emphasis, as are internal social differentiations involving considerations of power, authority, and rank.

Anthropologists tend to concentrate their work on particular groups largely because their studies are mostly done while in residence with particular groups. Therefore their studies tend to be either of a single village (with subsidiary references to urban and pastoral-nomadic contacts) or of a single pastoral group (with subsidiary references to village and urban contacts). The overall result is insufficient emphasis on the interrelationships, despite the often better intentions of many of the authors.

Barth has recently recommended, as a remedy, field research focus on *regions* where activity systems—including the symbiotic production systems of villagers and nomads—can be studied as systems rather than in terms of separate parts (Barth 1973, p. 12). Some examples have already been adduced, but his recommendation pinpoints a definite need. Meanwhile, most of the available studies of villagers and of pastoral nomads emphasize one or the other. This is a major reason why I am considering the pastoral-nomadic studies in this separate section.

General opinion now is that characterizations like "pure" nomad as opposed to "seminomad" should not be used. These seem to have been based on misperceptions, such as the erroneous idea that some nomads subsist entirely on the camel ("pure" nomadism), coupled with the snobbish romanticism that led many European observers to portray all camel herders as a noble and pure aristocracy (a native Middle Eastern stereotype that I have previously tried to put into perspective). Spooner, in any case, goes so far as to suggest that "nomadism" itself is a word whose usefulness is now dubious, a word that should perhaps be used only in reference to a particular trait of cultural ecology (Spooner 1972, p. 130) rather than to a whole subculture. In reviewing some of the recent studies of "nomads" I shall not attempt to classify them into types but rather let the varieties and the symbiosis speak for themselves.

Swidler's description of the seasonal subsistence cycle of the Brahui of West Pakistan illustrates what is sometimes called transhumance. Like many pastoralists, the Brahui make use of highlands and lowlands, the former being relatively cooler and better watered in the summer, when the particular lowlands are too dry and hot for subsistence activities (except, of course, where there *is* enough water for sedentary farmers to maintain themselves). The Brahui live in highland hamlets from March to November, where they both care for their animals and also raise crops. In November they migrate to the lowlands for better grazing, returning to the highlands in February (Swidler 1972, p. 70).

Farther west, in the Iranian-Pakistani border country of Baluchistan, live two Baluch tribes that have been studied by Salzman, who explicitly attacks the older ideal-type conceptualizations of nomadism that I have already mentioned (Salzman 1972, p. 67). These people have what Salzman calls a tripartite multiple-resource ecology of animal husbandry, date cultivation while living in hamlets, and wage labor in towns (at the same season in which they used to raid settled communities).

Cole, in his study of the Al Murrah of Saudi Arabia (1973), emphasizes that this case illustrates the high degree of pastoral-sedentary interaction *without* its being confused by interethnic issues such as those found elsewhere, as in Iran (Vreeland 1969). Saudi Arabia is the homeland of the Bedouin stereotype, and Cole's study is especially valuable in its counterbalance of it. The main grazing territory of the Al Murrah for winter pasturage is in the Rub al-Khali (the so-called "Empty Quarter" featured on most maps). They are among the most highly mobile camel herders in Saudi Arabia, Cole says. Nevertheless, in the summer they live in date-grove oasis villages (they do not have access to cool highlands as do the pastoralists of Iran and the Maghrib). Their kinship ties link them with village dwellers, in addition, and their notables have contacts with important city dwellers. Access to religious instruction and sectarian affiliations are among their village and town interests. Recently, they have contributed manpower to the modern Saudi Arabian army. Cole's main point is that however isolated some segments of the Al Murrah may seem at certain times of the year, it is impossible to conceive of them as being anything but completely integrated in the same ecological and national system with villagers and city dwellers (Cole 1973, p. 114). This is wholly at variance with the popular image of the Bedouin Arab.

The Yörük are a pastoral-nomadic group who seasonally migrate between the Hatay province, where Aswad, as we have seen, studied recently sedentarized nomads (Aswad 1971), and a region to the north not very far from the villages studied by Stirling (1966). Bates' meticulously detailed study (1973) makes it very clear how the Yörük maintain their pastoral subsistence while at the same time interacting with villagers all along their migration route. Careful seasonal timing, and the use of fallow lands so as not to conflict with farmers' interests, are among the many strategies involved. The Yörük have managed to remain pastoralists because they are a small, unthreatening group, unlike some others, who have worked out delicate modes of interaction with settled peoples.

Sometimes such interactions occur *within* a single sociopolitical identity. One such group is the Abu Gwe'id, who are one of the four Arabic-speaking tribes in the Sullam tribal group of the northern Negev of Israel (Marx 1967). The Abu Gwe'id are divided into four named groups, in the largest of which the position of shaykh is hereditary. Each of the groups has a core lineage of pastoralists plus related and unrelated pastoralists, farmers, and former slaves (Marx 1967, pp. 68–69).

Barth's widely quoted study of the Basseri (1961) is outstanding for its careful attention to social, political, and economic aspects of life, from the level of the household and camp to the national position that the tribe has occupied in Iran. In it can be found details, pertaining to *one* social system, on many important topics that have already been mentioned. Among these are: the lineal descent and segmentary system that can, through fictions, accommodate nonrelatives; pastoralists who also raise crops; different segments of the same lineage, some of whom are pastoralists but others of whom have become villagers; and the hereditary role of chief (khan), which is crucial in the external relations of the tribesmen. It is on the last that I will concentrate my comments on the Basseri.

The Basseri are one of the five tribes of the Khamseh ("five") Confederation. They are Persian speaking, whereas the other four include one Arabic-speaking and three Turkish-speaking tribes. No common ancestor is acknowledged by this motley aggregation, though the principle is applied, as usual, within each of the five groups. Rather, the confederacy was put together in the nineteenth century by the Ghavam merchant family of the city of Shiraz. The Ghavams sought a counterweight to the threat of the Qashqai confederacy, being particularly concerned about protection of their caravans (Barth 1961, p. 88). In return for Khamseh assistance, the Ghavams served as intermediaries for, and protectors of, the Khamseh tribesmen's interests vis-à-vis the Shah. Though the details are unique to the case, the role of a powerful urban intermediary between pastoral and sedentary tribesmen on the one hand, and the Bled el-Makhzen on the other hand, is by no means unique. The chief of the Basseri, who is the head of one of the major lineages of the tribe, must maintain a house in the city of Shiraz and make frequent visits to Tehran (Barth 1961, p. 97). This is true of the leaders of other tribal groups in Iran, and the net result is that "tribal nobility" is one of the elements of the recognized nationwide upper class of Iran (Bill 1972, p. 8).

Two other examples from Iran will illustrate other economic and political permutations. Among the Baluch of southeastern Iran there are four social status categories: hakomzat (chiefs), baluch (pastoralists), shahri (peasants), and gholam (former slaves, now generally propertyless laborers) (Spooner 1969, p. 140). A detail worth noting—because it is probably connected to the "noble nomad" stereotype—is that "baluch" means tent dweller (Spooner 1969, p. 149). This is a close parallel to the generic meaning of "arab," with noble connotations, that has been expanded to mean anyone who speaks Arabic but with the lingering notion in some minds that the only "true" Arabs are nomads.

The Yomut Turkmen of northeastern Iran are divided into the charwa, who are predominantly pastoral, and the chomur, who are predominantly agricultural but live in tents and are not, Irons emphasizes (1971, p. 145), to be thought of in the same terms as the exploited village-dwelling peasants characteristic of the Middle East generally. Irons discusses how, during the past fifty years, the Yomut have been forced to stop raiding sedentary people and how, at the same time, the charwa and the chomur have developed different intensities of relationships with villagers and with the government.

The last three pastoral cultures I shall mention are the Kababish and the Baggara of Sudan, and the Touareg of the Sahara.

Cunnison's study of the Baggara (1966) and Asad's of the Kababish (1970) are both very detailed analyses of Arabic-speaking, predominantly pastoral, tribes. Both emphasize the patrilineal, segmentary concept of social organization, and both illustrate how this is used as a model for social relations, a model that is, in fact, manipulated. The closing point in Cunnison's book is that alliances among the Baggara are continually changing. In particular, the cohorts of any given leader are constantly realigning themselves and cannot be simply predicted on the basis of patrilineal descent (Cunnison 1966, p. 192). This point has been mentioned repeatedly, and Cunnison's book provides ample illustrations of it.

Asad, near the end of his book, reaches a conclusion about the Kababish that I see as an instance of support for my hypothesis that the "land of dissidence" is a state of mind. After a long analysis of the structure and functions of the ruling lineage of the Kababish, Asad says that the ordinary Kabbáshi considers his relationship to his superiors as being one of compulsion, not of duty, and that ordinary Kababish individuals conceive of each other (but not themselves) as "liars, thieves, and deceivers" in relation to their superiors. The only resistance they can make to the power of their rulers is some sort of evasion (Asad 1970, p. 242). Though very different in local details, this is not fundamentally different from what has been mentioned earlier in connection with the behavior of the urban political elite of Iran, for example.

The Touareg are an aggregation composed of seven main groups living primarily in the Sahara, where they dominate the oasis settlements. They range all the way from the mountain fringe regions of Algeria in the north to the transition zones in the south, in Mali and Niger. They speak one of the Berber languages and have an alphabet in which some of them can write it. They are famous because (1) their men wear veils; (2) their women appear to be less secluded than Middle Eastern women generally; (3) they owned black slaves (the Haratin), who did agricultural labor for them, well into the twentieth century; and (4) they were very warlike, making a specialty of raiding caravans. Like other pastoral nomads, they have (or have had) regular, seasonal migration routes (Lhote 1955, pp. 360–361) that are part of a larger ecological system, including the agricultural labor and produce of the Haratin.

Keenan notes that the Algerian government now considers the old political structure of the Touareg to have been destroyed —meaning the end of raiding, slavery, and exploitation by the nobles of vassals (Keenan 1973, p. 360). Thus much of what has been described by Lhote (1955) and Coon (1958, pp. 204–210) in regard to them may be out of date. This would include the power of the noble lineages, traced matrilineally from a common female ancestor, in contrast to the prevailing patriliny of the Middle East.

Nevertheless, when studied by Murphy in 1959–1960, Touareg men still wore the veil, and Murphy's analysis of this behavior can be related to wider situations in Middle Eastern culture. Indeed, he relates it to humanity generally: "Alienation is the natural condition of social man" (Murphy 1970, p. 314). His specific observations are that by veiling, most (but not all) Touareg men hide the expressive mouth region of the face from others, thus creating social distance, and that by creating some measure of social distance, they allow for flexibility in social conditions that are not clearly defined by the kinship system (which appears to be highly varied now among the Touareg). This permits some autonomy in the threatening quality of such interactions (p. 312). Murphy draws a thought-provoking parallel between Touareg men's veiling and the commonly observed practice of wearing dark glasses for other reasons than protection against the glare of the sun. It has been suggested that ta'rof, the elaborate verbal formalities for which the Iranians are famous, and mujamalat, which serve the same function generally among Arabic speakers, also provide social distance and maneuverability. They, too, are forms of concealment for purposes of gaining social advantage, and in this light Touareg men's veiling, though unique, appears to be an expression of a very generally felt need. No one knows why the Touareg adopted this particular expression. Possibly it is some form of reaction to the unusually unsecluded status of Touareg women, which is presumably connected with matrilineal descent, at least among the nobles. However, the relative freedom of women among the Touareg may not be unique to them. There are suggestions of it—expressed in different ways—among the Ouled Nail and the Mzabites, north of the Touareg in Algeria, and among the Hausa, south of the Touareg in Nigeria. If there are systemic relationships among these otherwise quite different, yet contiguous, ethnic groups in regard to the status of women, this may be a significant and substantial variant of Middle Eastern culture.

All the pastoral-nomadic peoples of the Middle East have, in recent decades, been under pressure from various central governments either to become sedentary or to change certain of their cultural patterns. Decline of pastoralism is one result. It is more than ever necessary for the remaining pastoral-nomadic people to try to exercise as much control as they can over the relationships that they have with sedentary people in general and governmental agencies in particular. The shaykhs, aghas, and khans of various tribal groups have always served this function, but in many cases they have lost their power. Now, it seems, there may be a need for a more flexible role, less bound by the traditional kinship system. At any rate, one such instance of a "cultural broker," a man influential on the pastoral scene and in the sedentary power structure, has been described by an anthropologist, Gerald Obermeyer (1973, p. 160). The people are the pastoral nomads of western Egypt, and the brokerage functions are between them and the provincial government offices in the coastal town of Marsa Matruh.

TOWNS

First we shall consider Timbuktu (Mali) and the towns of the Mzab (Algeria). Then we shall move eastward—to Turkey, Jordan, and South Yemen—concluding with two towns in Afghanistan.

There is no clear-cut category of settlement different from both village and city in Middle Eastern parlance or thinking, as far as I know. There is a felt difference between village and city, but the criteria are many and occur in many different combinations, with sometimes illuminating results. For example, Fernea found that natives sometimes called Daghara a "village" and sometimes a "city" (Fernea 1970, p. 198). When calling it a city, they had in mind the presence of government agencies and city-bred government personnel, these criteria momentarily outweighing, in their minds, its agricultural, "village" character. In another example Iranians from other cities than Isfahan have been heard to refer, snidely, to Isfahan (a former imperial capital with a present population of about 500,000) as "the biggest village in Iran" because they feel its inhabitants behave in village ways with respect to family life and religion (Gulick and Gulick 1974, p. 442). Again, we encounter the matter of stereotypes with which this chapter began.

In this chapter, we have been concerned with food-producing villages and pastoralists, the two together producing cereals, vegetables, fruits, meat, and milk. Hides, animal hair for weaving cloth, timber, stone, and nonedible cash crops like cotton are also important products of these people. I have referred to the growing opinion that these activities can best be understood in regional terms. Regions involve nodes of communication, exchange, processing, transportation, and governmental supervision and administration. For our purposes "town" denotes a relatively small node of this sort, usually serving a relatively small region and often being the locus of food production as well as a node.

Some economic geographers have specialized in quantified formulations of regional settlement hierarchies. Such analyses have been done in Turkey, and there is a very detailed one of the hinterland of the city of Yazd in Iran (Bonine 1973). Someday there may be sufficient coverage of the Middle East by means of such studies to provide a more rigorous framework in which to place the great variety of settlements that have now been sampled, but for now I will not attempt to put the few studies included in this section into such a framework.

Timbuktu is a trading town at the southern end of trans-Saharan trade routes. Miner, who studied it in 1940, says that it then had a population of about 7,000. It now apparently has many more. One of Miner's main objectives was to demonstrate that the widely accepted "urban-rural" polarity is stereotypic as a characterization of any actual place, for Timbuktu's culture has both "rural" and "urban" characteristics. Miner's study was an important early effort in the struggle for freedom from this influential ideal type (Gulick 1973, p. 988), but I will not discuss this matter further here. It will suffice to mention that Timbuktu is divided into residential quarters. They are ethnically distinctive, including Arab and Touareg ones (Miner 1965, p. 43).

It was in the close community life of the quarters that Miner saw some of the "rural" characteristics of Timbuktu. Villages themselves are also typically divided into quarters (usually identified with particular kin groups living in them), and most of the village studies I have cited discuss the pertinent details. A particularly striking additional instance is represented by the case of Sukhnah, a small town in the Syrian Desert. Subsisting on transportation services and the production of potash, it is reported by Boucheman (1937) to have been divided into tribal quarters. They are shown with overlays on aerial photographs. The theme of quarters will become more prominent as we further consider towns and, in Chapter Four, cities.

Northeast of Timbuktu, 1,250 miles across the Sahara, are the five towns of the Mzab in Algeria. Remote from the more densely settled coastal and mountain areas of northern Algeria, these towns were founded by the Ibadites, an early dissident Islamic sect. Linked by an underground hydraulic system that is fed by very sparse rainfall, each town is an oasis in a small oasis system, the valley of the Mzab. Its population is about 38,000, of whom half live in Ghardaia, the chief town (Etherton 1971, pp. 139–140). Each town has a fort and a mosque in the center, concentric rings of houses around the center, and groves of date palms on the narrow outskirts. The people are famous for their fierce factional disputes, their austere brand of Islam, and the men's specialization as merchants elsewhere. Like the Swasa, who are migrants from the Sous valley in southwestern Morocco (Waterbury 1972), the Mzabite men are shopkeepers and merchants all over Algeria and have a reputation for cleverness and success. It is for this reason that the Mzabite women, though restricted to the oasis, have important and public responsibilities within it. As Alport says, they are "guardians of the hearth . . . of the whole city" (Alport 1973, p. 150).

Disturbed now by the effects of transportation to and from the Algerian oil fields, the Mzabites are also faced with a master plan that would preserve certain old parts of the oasis but would also accommodate new forms of settlement (Etherton 1971, p. 147).

Hureidah is a town with a population of slightly more than 2,000 people. It is located in the Hadramaut valley of South Yemen, approximately 100 miles inland from the coast of the Indian Ocean. The location is an oasis—relying on the careful regulation of occasional flood waters—in an extremely harsh desert. Like other towns in the area, Hureidah was an independent city state until World War II. Isolated in some ways, its people, like the Mzabites, have many wider contacts. Indeed, the area has been so little studied by outsiders that its actual isolation has perhaps been exaggerated.

The theme of Bujra's study is that the highly stratified social structure of this town has (as of the early 1960s) survived recent political changes in the area. The privileged upper class has managed to adjust itself to changes so that it continues to hold its privileges. The social hierarchy of Hureidah (Bujra 1971, p. 14) is as follows:

1. Sadah: 30.2 percent of population
2. Mashaikh and Gabail: 32.4 percent of population
3. Masakin: 37.4 percent of population

The Sadah control much of the property in the town, and its leadership is hereditary within their ranks. They also maintain the saints' shrines, and some of the rituals at these draw large regional crowds. The leadership of the Sadah is, in part, legitimized by their claim of descent from Husayn, grandson of the Prophet. However, they are Sunnis and are very conscious of their difference from the Shia Zaydis in Yemen to the west. The Sadah not only own more property than the other groups, but they (and some of the Mashaikh)) also control the town's waqf properties. In general, their situation seems quite comparable to that of the Zawya in Sidi Mateur before Tunisian independence. Just outside of Hureidah live some pastoral-nomadic people who are in various ways interconnected with the townspeople.

Al-Karak is a town of about 7,400 people (1961) in Jordan, south of Amman and on the north-south trade route linking the Fertile Crescent and western Arabia. Gubser's study of it, like Bujra's of Hureidah, pays considerable attention to its historical background and its diverse inhabitants. Gubser is also very conscious of al-Karak's being part of a region including townspeople, villagers, and pastoralists, and in large measure his study is an exposition of the kinship-political structure of the region (see, especially, Gubser 1973, pp. 41–59). Emphasized in the study is the recent rise of a particular lineage to political prominence.

From a consideration of desert-oasis towns we next turn to two that are in the mountainous *maritime* province of Mughla in southwestern Turkey. They are Ula (Benedict 1974), slightly inland, and Bodrum (Mansur 1972), which is a small seaport.

Like Gubser, Benedict devotes great attention to the history and the regional context of the town he is studying. In negative reaction to some of the urban stereotypes I have mentioned, Benedict's approach to Ula is that it is a "mediating center" for a hinterland that includes plains and mountain villagers, each with somewhat different ecologies and self-conscious attitudes toward one another (Benedict 1974, pp. 72–73). The inhabitants of Ula (population about 4,600) recognize four social levels among themselves: landlords (the hinterland is agricultural), merchants, civil servants, and craftsmen (p. 75). This is a division that must surely be basically similar to that of the hundreds of Middle Eastern towns in general. Recent trends in Ula include the diminution of the influence and power of the landlords, to the benefit of some of the merchants, and Ula's becoming less important regionally than it used to be. This trend is due to the fact that Ula's civil servants and their agencies are now merely links in a bureaucratic chain with the national government. Formerly, final decisions on various administrative and religious matters were made in Ula (Benedict 1974, Chapter 7). This is a specific instance of the effects of changes that have been generally observed in the Middle East at national levels: centralization of governmental functions and what is felt by many to be excessive growth of, and concentration of activities in, the largest cities—to the detriment of smaller cities and towns.

Bodrum has a population of 6,500 people living in eight quarters. It has a double economy: one part concentrated on fishing and sponge collection (with the consequent importance of boatbuilding and boat repair) and the other on the agricultural hinterland. There is a large number of shops, mostly operated part time (Mansur 1972, p. 52). Tourism has recently become important, and Mansur feels that for this and other reasons a distinct concept of leisure, as opposed to work, has entered Bodrum's ethos. Nevertheless, she concludes with the thought that the inhabitants are still "provincial and peasant" (Mansur 1972, p. 257).

Mansur does not say very much about the maritime aspects of life in Bodrum, but at least she mentions them. This is important, for, apart from some observations on the dhows that ply their trade in the Red Sea and the Indian Ocean (see Villiers 1970), there is very little material on the maritime aspects of Middle Eastern culture. However, one anthropologist has made a recent study of the schooners that ply their trade from just east of Bodrum around the coast to Alexandria (Prins 1969). Prins feels that despite great competition from motorized craft, the schooner masters may be able to make adaptations of rig that would enable them to stay in business.

In the northwest corner of Anatolia, a few miles from the coast, is the town of Susurluk (Magnarella 1974). Until the first half of the twentieth century it was essentially a large village whose farming inhabitants were in close interaction with remnant pastoral nomads, chiefly the Yörük and the Turkmen. In addition to the long-time Turkish residents, there were various immigrant ethnic groups such as Georgians, Circassians, and Turks from the Balkans. Though these people have now become strongly identified with a common Turkish national culture, they are still conscious of their diverse origins.

Typical of towns generally, Susurluk is a marketing center for an agricultural hinterland and an administrative center for a subprovince. The establishment of a sugar beet factory in the 1950s radically changed the standard of living and expectations of its people, and it provided impetus for the various modernization policies of the Turkish government.

With a population in 1970 of about 12,000 (increased from 5,000 in 1940) Susurluk is divided into six residential quarters. These are governmental administrative units, their elected officers often helping their constituents cope with the larger bureaucracy. Sense of quarter identity is particularly strong in those cases where ethnic homogeneity is considerable and turnover of resident population is moderate. One way in which this identity is expressed is the people's felt responsibility for the care of the mosque in the

quarter. This is notable in view of the widespread idea that modernizing Turkey is highly secularized.

Within each quarter are "defended neighborhoods," as Magnarella calls them (1974, p. 43). He sees them as extensions of the
private households, where the women maintain networks of trust
and cooperation primarily in "response to perceived fears of invasion from the outside"(p. 44). Magnarella's portrayal of these defended neighborhoods epitomizes the peril-and-refuge mentality,
and he documents a phenomenon that must be universal in the
Middle East. However, it has not been generally documented. One
reason probably is that the very nature of these female-dominated
neighborhoods precludes the systematic study of them, at least by
men.

Aq Kupruk and Tashqurghan are in northern Afghanistan not
far from the city of Mazar-i Sharif. The region is ethnically diverse
and includes Sunnis and Shias, Pashtuns (the predominant Afghan
aggregate), and several other ethnic groups otherwise associated
with Soviet Central Asia (Uzbeks, Tajiks, and others). This diversity is emphasized in Dupree's study of Aq Kupruk (1970) and in
both of the studies that have recently been done in Tashqurghan
(Centlivres 1972; Charpentier 1972).

Dupree says that Aq Kupruk is "a town of about 1,500 men"
(1970, p. 368), leaving the total population indefinite. It is a regional market center with a bazaar of over 100 shops. Seventy
percent of the men own land, while the others are tenant farmers
(p. 353). From May to September nomads pass through Aq Kupruk,
and many of them have traditional economic understandings with
the farmers (for letting their herds graze on certain lands) and with
the bazaar merchants (pp. 365–367). In regard to this and to the
socially ranked ethnic diversity of the town, Dupree's exposition
provides an excellent example of the nomadic-agricultural-
commercial symbiosis. Like Ula, Aq Kupruk has recently become a
less important locus of administrative influence than it used to be,
owing to reorganization at the national level.

Tashqurghan (this name was officially changed to Khulm in
1963) has a population of about 30,000 people, much larger than
any of the other towns that I have considered. The two studies of it
that have recently been done (independently of each other) both
concentrate on the bazaar. Bazaars ("souqs" in Arabic) are those
complex networks of roofed-over streets on which the shops and
workshops of the old parts of Middle Eastern large towns and cities
are located. Can the bazaar continue much longer to function in
the face of the many socioeconomic changes that are occurring in
the Middle East? In order to answer this one must learn how
still-functioning bazaars work, and this was clearly the purpose of
both Centlivres and Charpentier. In Chapter Four I will again
mention this matter, drawing on other recent studies in cities.

Charpentier, whose study was done 2 to 3 years later than Cent-livres', leaves the big question of ultimate survival open. However, he notes that some of the older crafts are dying out, partly because "westernized" materials have been introduced, and that the distribution area, on the whole, has been narrowed. Nevertheless, new trades are becoming established in the bazaar (Charpentier 1972, p. 186), a possible indication that it is adapting to change. It is in the bazaars that the raw materials produced by farmers and animal husbandmen have been converted into various products and where the farmers and animal husbandmen (as well as the town and city dwellers) have bought local and imported products. Whatever may happen to the covered streets and the small shops clustered together by specialty, these functions in the general symbiotic system must be maintained. These functions are at the core of much of the life of Middle Eastern towns and cities.

This discussion may give the impression that interrelations among animal husbandmen, villagers, and town and city dwellers are entirely commercial in nature. This is not true. While the commercial elements are very important, there are other aspects of, and motives for, these interrelations. For instance, Magnarella (1974, p. 52) points out how many people in Susurluk are linked to relatives and friends in surrounding villages and are constantly providing each other with help, news, and ideas, as well as exchanging goods. A useful way in which to view these links is in terms of channels of communication, some of which have been discussed by Laura Nader (1965). These channels involve constant movement of people, long and short visits, and long- and short-distance travel, as well as the disembodied communications of the mass media. This constant movement—some of it resulting in permanent or long-term resettlement—is the immediate reality of the people who earn their living by means of the pastoral-agricultural-commercial system.

CONCLUSION

The outstanding characteristics of most of the communities and groups that have been reviewed in this chapter evolved in adaptation to certain general conditions. Among these conditions were (1) adversary relationships between communities and governments, (2) social and economic exploitation of the food-producing population in general, and (3) competition for access to the "limited good" among the various food-producing groups.

It is little wonder that what evolved under these conditions was a system of defensive structures, tactics, and values. These are emphasized in most of the Middle Eastern anthropological studies that have been done. Influenced strongly by the structural-functional approach, these studies explain continuities and fixities of cultural patterns and social behavior such as defensive structures, but they do not help us to understand how individuals and communities respond positively to changes, let alone how they may themselves become innovators. While there is a strong bent for conservatism and fixity in human communities (Nisbet 1969, p. 271), and structural-functional studies show how this bent actually operates, it is also obvious that communities can and do change. Among the changes that have been referred to in this chapter (and that are being given greater attention in the more recent studies) is the decrease in the relative isolation of villages and pastoral groups from the centers of power and innovation in the cities. One effect of this that has already been felt is the transformation of some villages into towns. More widespread, however, and not sufficiently emphasized in many of the source materials, or in my review of them, is the greatly increased awareness of, and participation in, national political and economic policies on the part of village people. Land reform, the cooperative movement, education, and military service as ways out of the older exploitive system are all innovative activities and options that engage increasing numbers of the people with whom this chapter has been concerned.

To the extent that these innovations reduce the adversary relationships and the preoccupation with defensive tactics that have been traditional, cultural patterns like the tribal metaphor of social solidarity and conflict may be radically changed. Some observers think they are already changing, but they have by no means disappeared. But will an agro-business technology and social structure largely replace the older symbiotic system we have described, and to the extent that it does, will it reduce the exploitation and social inequalities produced by the older system? Perhaps. Yet if greatly increased wealth—such as that derived by some countries from petroleum—is largely monopolized by a few individuals and groups, "limited good" will continue to be the perception by most Middle Eastern people of their resources. The sense of relative deprivation that is already acute among many modernizing Middle Easterners may evolve into a prolonged "culture of discontent" (see Magnarella 1974, p. 183). If this happens, and it seems inevitable that it will unless population increase rates are greatly lowered in the very near future, then the system of defensive structures and values may be perpetuated as an adaptive process, unless, of course, it is displaced by truly revolutionary movements. Further considerations of these prospects will be found in subsequent chapters.

REFERENCES

Abu-Zahra, Nadia M. "Inequality of Descent and Egalitarianism of the New National Organizations in a Tunisian Village." In *Rural Politics*

and Social Change in the Middle East, edited by R. Antoun and Iliya
Harik, pp. 267–286. Bloomington: Indiana University Press, 1972.

Ajami, Ismail. "Social Classes, Family Demographic Characteristics and Mobility in Three Iranian Villages." *Sociologia Ruralis* 9, no. 1 (1969): 62–72.

Alberts, Robert C. *Social Structure and Cultural Change in an Iranian Village.* Ph.D. dissertation, University of Wisconsin, 1963.

Alport, E. A. "The Mzab." In *Arabs and Berbers: From Tribe to Nation in North Africa,* edited by Ernest Gellner and Charles Micaud, pp. 141–152. London: Gerald Duckworth and Co., 1973.

Amanolahi, Sekandar, and Edward Norbeck. "The Luti, an Outcaste Group of Iran." *Rice University Studies,* vol. 61, no. 2, "Studies in Cultural Anthropology," 1975.

Ammar, Hamed. *Growing Up in an Egyptian Village.* London: Routledge & Kegan Paul, Ltd., 1954.

Antoun, Richard T. *Arab Village: A Social Structural Study of a Transjordanian Peasant Community.* Bloomington: Indiana University Press, 1972.

Asad, Talal. *The Kababish Arabs: Power, Authority and Consent in a Nomadic Tribe.* New York: Praeger, 1970.

Aswad, Barbara C. *Property Control and Social Strategies: Settlers on a Middle Eastern Plain.* Ann Arbor: University of Michigan, Museum of Anthropology, Anthropological Papers no. 44, 1971.

Ayoub, Victor F. *Political Structure of a Middle East Community: A Druze Village in Mount Lebanon.* Ph.D. dissertation, Harvard University, 1955.

Ayoub, Victor F. *Political Structure of a Middle East Community: A Lebanese Village."* *Human Organization* 24(1965): 11–17.

Ayrout, Henry Habib. *The Egyptian Peasant.* Boston: Beacon Press, 1968 (First published in 1938).

Barclay, Harold B. *Buurri al Lamaab: A Suburban Village in the Sudan.* Ithaca, N.Y.: Cornell University Press, 1964.

Barclay, Harold B. "Study of an Egyptian Village Community." *Studies in Islam* (New Delhi, India). July 1966, pp. 143–166; October 1966, pp. 201–226.

Bardin, Pierre. *La vie d'un douar.* The Hague: Mouton & Co., 1965.

Baroja, Julio Caro. "The City and the Country: Reflexions on Some Ancient Commonplaces." In *Mediterranean Countrymen,* edited by Julian Pitt-Rivers. The Hague: Mouton & Co., 1963.

Barth, Fredrik. *Principles of Social Organization in Southern Kurdistan.* Oslo, Norway: Universitetets Etnografiske Museum Bulletin No. 7, 1953.

Barth, Fredrik. *Political Leadership Among Swat Pathans*. London School of Economics, Monographs on Social Anthropology, no. 19. New York: Humanities Press, 1959.

Barth, Fredrik. *Nomads of South Persia: The Basseri Tribe of the Khamseh Confederacy*. Boston: Little, Brown, 1961.

Barth, Fredrik. "A General Perspective on Nomad-Sedentary Relations in the Middle East." In *The Desert and the Sown: Nomads in the Wider Society*, edited by Cynthia Nelson, pp. 11–21. Berkeley: University of California, Institute of International Studies, Research Series no. 21, 1973.

Bates, Daniel G. *Nomads and Farmers: A Study of the Yörük of Southeastern Turkey*. Ann Arbor: University of Michigan, Museum of Anthropology, Anthropological Papers, no. 52, 1973.

Benedict, Peter. *Ula: An Anatolian Town*. Leiden, Netherlands: E. J. Brill, 1974.

Benet, Francisco. "Explosive Markets: The Berber Highlands." In *Peoples and Cultures of the Middle East*, vol. 1, edited by Louise E. Sweet, pp. 173–203. Garden City, N.Y.: Natural History Press, 1970.

Berque, Jacques. *Structures sociales du Haut-Atlas*. Paris: Presses Universitaires de France, 1955.

Berque, Jacques. *Histoire sociale d'un village Egyptien au xxeme siècle*. The Hague: Mouton & Co., 1957.

Bill, James A. *The Politics of Iran: Groups, Classes and Modernization*. Columbus, Ohio: Merrill, 1972.

Blackman, Winifred S. *The Fellahin of Upper Egypt*. New York: Barnes & Noble, 1968 (First published in 1927).

Bonine, Michael E. "A Settlement Hierarchy in Central Iran: The Functional Hinterland of Yazd, Iran." Paper delivered at annual meeting of Middle East Studies Association, Milwaukee, Wisc., November 8–10, 1973.

Boucheman, Albert de. *Une petite cité caravanière: Suhne*. Documents d'études orientales, vol. 6, Institut Français de Damas, 1937.

Bourdieu, Pierre. *The Algerians*. Boston: Beacon Press, 1962.

Briggs, Lloyd Cabot. *Tribes of the Sahara*. Cambridge, Mass.: Harvard University Press, 1960.

Bujra, Abdalla S. *The Politics of Stratification: A Study of Political Change in a South Arabian Town*. Oxford: At the Clarendon Press, 1971.

Centlivres, Pierre. *Un bazar d'Asie Centrale: Forme et organisation du bazar de Tashqurghan (Afghanistan)*. Wiesbaden, West Germany: Dr. Ludwig Reichert Verlag, 1972.

Charpentier, C. *Bazaar-e Tashqurghan: Ethnographical Studies in an Afghan Traditional Bazaar*. Uppsala, Sweden: Studia Ethnographica Upsaliensia 36, 1972.

Cohen, Abner. *Arab Border-Villages In Israel.* Manchester: Manchester University Press, 1965.

Cole, Donald P. "The Enmeshment of Nomads in Sa'udi Arabian Society: The Case of Al Murrah." In *The Desert and the Sown: Nomads in the Wider Society,* edited by Cynthia Nelson, pp. 113–128. Berkeley: University of California, Institute of International Studies, Research Series, no. 21, 1973.

Coon, Carleton S. *Caravan: The Story of the Middle East.* Rev. ed. New York: Holt, 1958.

Cunnison, Ian. *Baggara Arabs: Power and the Lineage in a Sudanese Nomad Tribe.* Oxford, England: Clarendon Press, 1966.

Dunn, Ross E. "Berber Imperialism: the Ait Atta Expansion in Southeast Morocco." In *Arabs and Berbers: From Tribe to Nation in North Africa,* edited by Ernest Gellner and Charles Micaud, pp. 85–108. London: Gerald Duckworth and Co., 1973.

Dupree, Louis. "Aq Kupruk: A Town in North Afghanistan." In *People and Cultures of the Middle East,* vol. 2, edited by Louise E. Sweet, pp. 344–387. Garden City, N.Y.: Natural History Press, 1970.

Duvignaud, Jean. *Change at Shebika: Report from a North African Village.* New York: Pantheon, 1970.

Etherton, David. "Concentric Towns—the Valley of the Mzab." In *The Growth of Cities,* edited by David Lewis, pp. 138–148. New York: Wiley, 1971.

Fakhouri, Hani. *Kafr el-Elow: An Egyptian Village in Transition.* New York: Holt, Rinehart and Winston, 1972.

Fernea, Elizabeth W. *Guests of the Sheik: An Ethnography of an Iraqi Village.* Garden City, N.Y.: Doubleday-Anchor, 1969.

Fernea, Robert A. *Shaykh and Effendi: Changing Patterns of Authority Among the El Shabana of Southern Iraq.* Cambridge, Mass.: Harvard University Press, 1970.

Fernea, Robert A. "Gaps in the Ethnographic Literature on the Middle Eastern Village: A Classificatory Exploration." In *Rural Politics and Social Change in the Middle East,* edited by R. Antoun and Iliya Harik, pp. 75–102. Bloomington: Indiana University Press, 1972.

Fernea, Robert A., and Georg Gerster. *Nubians in Egypt: Peaceful People.* Austin: University of Texas Press, 1973.

Fetter, George C. "Attitudes toward Selected Aspects of Rural Life and Technological Changes among Central Beka'a Farmers." Beirut, Lebanon: American University of Beirut, Faculty of Agricultural Sciences, Publication No. 13, 1961.

Fuller, Anne H. *Buarij: Portrait of a Lebanese Muslim Village.* Cambridge, Mass.: Harvard Middle Eastern Monographs, no. 6, 1961.

Gellner, Ernest. *Saints of the Atlas.* Chicago: University of Chicago Press, 1969.

94

Goldberg, Harvey E. *Cave Dwellers and Citrus Growers: A Jewish Community in Libya and Israel.* Cambridge: at the University Press, 1972.

Gubser, Peter. *Politics and Change in al-Karak, Jordan: A Study of a Small Arab Town and its District.* London: Oxford University Press, 1973.

Gulick, John. *Social Structure and Culture Change in a Lebanese Village.* New York: Viking Fund Publications in Anthropology, no. 21, 1955.

Gulick, John. "Village and City: Cultural Continuities in Twentieth Century Middle Eastern Cultures." In *Middle Eastern Cities,* edited by Ira M. Lapidus, pp. 122–158. Berkeley: University of California Press, 1969.

Gulick, John. "Urban Anthropology." In *Handbook of Social and Cultural Anthropology,* edited by John J. Honigmann, pp. 979–1029. Chicago: Rand McNally, 1973.

Gulick, John, and Margaret E. Gulick. "Varieties of Domestic Social Organization in the Iranian City of Isfahan." In *City and Peasant: A Study in Sociocultural Dynamics,* edited by Anthony LaRuffa, Ruth S. Freed, Lucie Wood Saunders, Edward C. Hansen, and Sula Benet, pp. 441–469. New York: Annals of the New York Academy of Sciences, vol. 220, article 6, 1974.

Hanessian, John, Jr. *Yosouf-Abad, an Iranian Village.* American Universities Field Staff: Southwest Asia Series, vol. 12, nos. 1–6, 1963.

Hansen, Henny Harald. *Investigations in a Shi'a Village in Bahrain.* Copenhagen: Publications of the National Museum, Ethnographical Series, Vol. 12, 1967.

Haqqi, Yahia. *The Saint's Lamp and other Stories.* Leiden, Netherlands: E. J. Brill, 1973.

Hart, David M. "Clan, Lineage, Local Community and the Feud in a Rifian Tribe." In *Peoples and Cultures of the Middle East,* vol. 2, edited by Louise E. Sweet, pp. 3–75. Garden City, N.Y.: Natural History Press, 1970.

Hoffman, Bernard G. *The Structure of Traditional Moroccan Rural Society.* The Hague: Mouton & Co., 1967.

Hoogland, Eric J. "The Khwushnishin Population of Iran." *Iranian Studies,* 6(1973): 229–245.

Irons, William. "Variation in Political Stratification among the Yomut Turkmen." *Anthropological Quarterly* 44, no. 3(1971): 143–156.

Keenan, Jeremy H. "Social Change Among the Touareg." In *Arabs and Berbers: From Tribe to Nation in North Africa,* edited by Ernest Gellner and Charles Micaud, pp. 345–360. London: Gerald Duckworth and Co., 1973.

Kolars, John F. "Types of Rural Development." In *Four Studies on the Economic Development of Turkey,* edited by Frederic C. Shorter, pp. 63–87. London: Frank Cass & Co., Ltd., 1967.

Lerner, Daniel. *The Passing of Traditional Society: Modernizing the Middle East.* Glencoe, Ill.: Free Press, 1958.

Lhote, Henri. *Les Touaregs du Hoggar.* 2nd ed. Paris: Payot, 1955.

Lutfiyya, Abdulla M. *Baytin: a Jordanian Village.* The Hague: Mouton & Co., 1966.

Magnarella, Paul J. *Tradition and Change in a Turkish Town.* New York: Wiley, 1974.

Makal, Mahmut. *A Village in Anatolia.* London: Vallentine, Mitchell & Co., 1954.

Mansur, Fatma. *Bodrum: a Town in the Aegean.* Leiden, Netherlands: E. J. Brill, 1972.

Marx, Emanuel. *Bedouin of the Negev.* New York: Praeger, 1967.

Miner, Horace. *The Primitive City of Timbuctoo.* Rev. ed. Garden City N.Y.: Doubleday-Anchor, 1965.

Montagne, Robert. *The Berbers: Their Social and Political Organization.* London: Frank Cass, 1973 (First published in 1931).

Murphy, Robert F. "Social Distance and the Veil." In *Peoples and Cultures of the Middle East,* vol. 1, edited by Louise E. Sweet, pp. 290–314. Garden City, N.Y.: Natural History Press, 1970.

Nader, Laura. "Communication between Village and City in the Modern Middle East." In *Human Organization* 24, no. 1(1965): 18–24.

Nisbet, Robert A. *Social Change and History.* New York: Oxford University Press, 1969.

Obermeyer, Gerald J. "Leadership and Transition in Beduin Society: A Case Study." In *The Desert and the Sown: Nomads in the Wider Society,* edited by Cynthia Nelson, pp. 159–173. Berkeley: University of California, Institute of International Studies, Research Series, no. 21, 1973.

Patai, Raphael. *The Arab Mind.* New York: Scribner's, 1973.

Peters, Emrys L. "Aspects of Rank and Status among Muslims in a Lebanese Village." In *Mediterranean Countrymen,* edited by Julian Pitt-Rivers, pp. 159–202. The Hague: Mouton & Co., 1963.

Polk, William R., trans. *The Golden Ode* by Labid Ibn Rabiah. Chicago: University of Chicago Press, 1974.

Prins, A. H. J. "The Syrian Schooner: Problem Formulation in Maritime Culture Change." In *Peoples and Cultures of the Middle East,* edited by Ailon Shiloh, pp. 403–423. New York: Random House, 1969.

Rathbun, Carole. *The Village in the Turkish Novel and Short Story, 1920 to 1955.* The Hague: Mouton & Co., 1972.

Rosenfeld, Henry. "Processes of Structural Change within the Arab Extended Family." *American Anthropologist* 60(1958): 1127–1139.

Rosenfeld, Henry. "From Peasantry to Wage Labor and Residual Peasantry: The Transformation of an Arab Village." In *Process and Pattern in Culture,* edited by Robert A. Manners, pp. 211–234. Chicago: Aldine, 1964.

Salih, Taieb. "The Doum Tree of Wad Hamid." In *Modern Arabic Short Stories,* edited and translated by Denys Johnson-Davies, pp. 84–96. London: Oxford University Press, 1967.

Salim, S. M. *Marsh Dwellers of the Euphrates Delta.* University of London: The Athlone Press, 1962.

Salzman, Philip C. "Multi-Resource Nomadism in Iranian Baluchistan." In *Perspectives on Nomadism,* edited by William Irons and Neville Dyson-Hudson, pp. 60–68. Leiden, Netherlands: E. J. Brill, 1972.

Saunders, Lucie Wood. "Aspects of Family Organization in an Egyptian Village." *Transactions of the New York Academy of Sciences,* ser. 2, vol. 30, no. 5(1968): 714–721.

Schorger, William D. "Evolution of Political Forms in a North Moroccan Village." *Anthropological Quarterly,* 42(1969): 263–286.

Service, Elman R. *Profiles in Ethnology.* New York: Harper & Row, 1963.

Shokeid, Moshe. *The Dual Heritage: Immigrants from the Atlas Mountains in an Israeli Village.* Manchester: Manchester University Press, 1971.

Spooner, Brian. "Politics, Kinship, and Ecology in Southeast Persia." *Ethnology,* 8(1969): 139–152.

Spooner, Brian. "The Status of Nomadism as a Cultural Phenomenon in the Middle East." In *Perspectives on Nomadism,* edited by William Irons and Neville Dyson-Hudson, pp. 122–131. Leiden, Netherlands: E. J. Brill, 1972.

Spooner, Brian. *The Cultural Ecology of Pastoral Nomads.* Reading, Mass.: Addison-Wesley Module in Anthropology, no. 45, 1973.

Stirling, Paul. *Turkish Village.* New York: Wiley, 1966.

Sweet, Louise E. *Tell Toqaan: A Syrian Village.* Ann Arbor: University of Michigan, Museum of Anthropology, Anthropological Papers, no. 14, 1960.

Swidler, W. W. "Some Demographic Factors Regulating the Formation of Flocks and Camps among the Brahui of Baluchistan." In *Perspectives on Nomadism,* edited by William Irons and Neville Dyson-Hudson, pp. 69–75. Leiden, Netherlands: E. J. Brill, 1972.

Tannous, Afif I. "Group Behavior in the Village Community of Lebanon." *American Journal of Sociology* 48(1942): 231–239.

Thaiss, Gustav E. *Religious Symbolism and Social Change: The Drama of Husain.* Ph.D. dissertation, Washington University, 1973.

Touma, Toufic. *Un village du Montagne au Liban.* The Hague: Mouton & Co., 1958.

Villiers, Alan. "Some Aspects of the Arab Dhow Trade." In *Peoples and Cultures of the Middle East*, vol. 1, edited by Louise E. Sweet, pp. 155–172. Garden City, N.Y.: Natural History Press, 1970.

Vinogradov, Amal R. "The Socio-Political Organization of a Berber Taraf Tribe: Pre-Protectorate Morocco." In *Arabs and Berbers: From Tribe to Nation in North Africa*, edited by Ernest Gellner and Charles Micaud, pp. 67–84. London: Gerald Duckworth and Co., 1973.

Vreeland, Herbert H. "Ethnic Groups and Languages of Iran." In *Peoples and Cultures of the Middle East*, edited by Ailon Shiloh, pp. 51–67. New York: Random House, 1969.

Waterbury, John. *North for the Trade: The Life and Times of a Berber Merchant*. Berkeley: University of California Press, 1972.

Weingrod, Alex. *Reluctant Pioneers: Village Development in Israel*. Ithaca, N.Y.: Cornell University Press, 1966.

Weingrod, Alex. "Israel." In *The Central Middle East*, edited by Louise E. Sweet. New Haven, Conn.: HRAF Press, 1971.

Weulersse, Jacques. *Le pays des Alaouites*, vol. 1. Tours, France: Arrault & Cie, 1940.

Williams, Herbert H. *Some Aspects of Culture and Personality in a Lebanese Maronite Village*. Ph.D. dissertation, University of Pennsylvania, 1958.

Williams, Judith R. *The Youth of Haouch el Harimi, a Lebanese Village*. Cambridge, Mass.: Harvard Middle Eastern Monographs, no. 20, 1968.

ANNOTATED BIBLIOGRAPHY

Bibliographies

Center for the Study of the Modern Arab World. *Arab Culture and Society in Change: A Bibliography*. Beirut: St. Joseph's University, Dar el-Mashreq Publishers, 1973.

Covers the nomadic, village, and city literature on the Arabs, and much more. Partially annotated, this bibliography includes English, French, German and Italian sources.

Coult, Lyman H., Jr. *An Annotated Bibliography of the Egyptian Fellah, 1798–1955*. Coral Gables, Florida: University of Miami Press, 1958.

Includes studies in Arabic, English and French.

Handelman, Don, and Shlomo Deshen. *The Social Anthropology of Israel: A Bibliographical Essay with Primary Reference to Loci of Social Stress*. Tel Aviv University: Institute for Social Research: Department of Social Anthropology. Mimeographed, 1975.

Strictly speaking, this is not so much a bibliography as it is an extended review article on the research literature. It covers studies of kibbutzim, moshavim, Arab villages, and city dwellers. The authors conclude that although there are many loci of social stress in Israel, anthropological research there, so far, has not contributed as much evidence as it could on them, owing to its theoretical preoccupations.

Sweet, Louise E., and Timothy J. O'Leary, eds. *Circum-Mediterranean Peasantry: Introductory Bibliographies.* New Haven, Conn.: Human Relations Area Files, 1969.

Contains a section on each European and Middle Eastern country, including two sections on the islands such as Cyprus. Each section consists of an introductory essay followed by a list of authors and titles.

Special Issues of the Anthropological Quarterly

Social and Political Processes in the Western Mediterranean. Preface by William D. Schorger and Eric R. Wolf. Vol. 42, no. 3, 1969

Five of the nine articles are on Italian communities, but two are on Morocco and one is a discussion of Europe and the Middle East.

Comparative Studies of Nomadism and Pastoralism. Introduction by Philip C. Salzman. Vol. 44, no. 3, 1971.

Five of the seven articles deal with the Middle East.

Visiting Patterns and Social Dynamics in Eastern Mediterranean Communities. Preface by Louise E. Sweet; Introduction by Amal Vinogradov. Vol. 47, no. 1, 1974.

One of the articles is on Greece. The others are on various Middle Eastern countries.

Anthologies

All but two of the following books have already been referred to at least once as the sources of articles cited in the text. Comments on each of the source books is necessary because they are in themselves important contributions to the anthropological literature of the Middle East.

Antoun, Richard, and Iliya Harik, eds. *Rural Politics and Social Change in the Middle East.* Bloomington: Indiana University Press, 1972.

Contains sixteen original papers and five general commentaries. Critiques by anthropologists of anthropological studies are combined with papers informed by history, economics, geography, sociology, and political science. This is a good source on the value and the limitations of village studies, particularly in regard to larger economic and political systems.

Churchill, Charles W., and Abdulla M. Lutfiyya, eds. *Readings in Arab Middle Eastern Societies and Cultures.* The Hague: Mouton & Co., 1970.

Contains fifty-three articles, most of which were originally published elsewhere. They are organized under seven headings: social organization, culture, social institutions and cultural change, social stratification, the family, urban life, and the role of communication. The editors are a sociologist and an anthropologist.

Fisher, W. B., ed. *The Cambridge History of Iran.* Volume I: The Land of Iran. Cambridge: at the University Press, 1968.

Most of the second half of this book is basic cultural geography of present-day Iran, including pastoral, village, and urban settlement patterns, and a concluding chapter ("The Personality of Iran") goes beyond geography and places Iran in the Middle Eastern cultural scene.

Gellner, Ernest, and Charles Micaud, eds. *Arabs and Berbers: From Tribe to Nation in North Africa.* London: Gerald Duckworth and Co., 1973.

Consists of twenty-three articles—mostly anthropologically oriented or concerned with political behavior. The four parts are: the traditional base, ethnicity and nation, ethnicity and social change, and the coup of 10 July 1971.

Gulick, John, ed. *Dimensions of Cultural Change in the Middle East.* Special issue of *Human Organization.* Vol. 24, no. 1, 1965.

Consists of fifteen original articles by a variety of behavioral scientists, with an introduction by the editor intended to integrate the papers.

Irons, William, and Neville Dyson-Hudson, eds., *Perspectives on Nomadism.* Leiden, Netherlands: E. J. Brill, 1972.

A critical review of concepts concerning pastoral nomadism. The book contains ten articles, mostly on the Middle East. Several of the same authors appear who contributed to the *Anthropological Quarterly's* special issue on nomadism.

Nelson, Cynthia, ed. *The Desert and the Sown: Nomads in the Wider Society.* Berkeley: University of California, Institute of International Studies, Research Series, no. 21, 1973.

Eleven articles by anthropologists on Middle Eastern nomadism. The title well indicates the predominant theme. This volume, together with *Anthropological Quarterly* 1971 and Irons and Dyson-Hudson, represents the most incisive recent anthropological thinking on the subject of nomads in the Middle East.

Pitt-Rivers, Julian, ed. *Mediterranean Countrymen.* The Hague: Mouton & Co., 1963.

Eleven articles, five of which are on the Middle East.

Shiloh, Ailon, ed. *Peoples and Cultures of the Middle East.* New York: Random House, 1969.

Twenty-five articles, all previously published either as journal articles or chapters in books. The editor, an anthropologist, begins the book with a culture history of the Middle East, and these five parts follow: the distribution of peoples, cultures and subcultures, population dynamics, culture change and conservatism, and the schoolteacher as anthropologist.

Sweet, Louise E., ed. *Peoples and Cultures of the Middle East,* 2 vol. Garden City, N.Y.: Natural History Press, 1970.

Despite its identical title, the contents of this two-volume anthology *never* duplicate Shiloh's selections. Volume 1 contains eighteen articles arranged into three parts: cultural depth and diversity, examples of Middle Eastern institutions and rural peoples of the Middle East: nomadic pastoralists. Volume 2 contains twelve articles arranged into two parts: rural peoples in the Middle East: agricultural enclaves and villages, and life in Middle Eastern towns and cities.

Sweet, Louise E., ed. *The Central Middle East. A Handbook of Anthropology and Published Research on the Nile Valley, the Arab Levant, Southern Mesopotamia, the Arabian Peninsula, and Israel.* New Haven, Conn.: HRAF Press, 1971.

Five anthropologists (all referred to in this chapter in connection with other publications) contribute review articles on the anthropology of each of the areas indicated in the subtitle. Most of the papers were written about 1960, but there was some effort to update them as of 1967. Each article has an annotated bibliography of the literature on each area. Sweet's bibliography on the Arabian Peninsula takes into account—among other things—the many "classics" that contributed so much to the romanticization of the Bedouin. (The word "Bedouin" itself is a pseudo-Arabic form of what is properly *bedawi* in the singular and *bedu* in the plural.)

FOUR

CITIES: ESTABLISHMENTS, INNOVATIONS, AND CONTINUITIES

THE PROBLEM: IDENTIFYING THE DISTINCTIVENESS OF CITIES

In Chapter Three cities were mentioned as being parts of the desert-oasis-commercial system of the Middle East, and towns like Aq Kupruk, Ula, and Susurluk were discussed as being nodes of commercial transaction and political administration at the level of relatively minor regions. The implication was that cities are nodes of commercial transaction and political administration at the level of major, rather than minor, regional systems. Such major systems would include substantial portions, if not the whole, of each of the cultural ecological regions that were outlined in Chapter One, the major provinces of national states, and, of course, national states themselves. The point of this implication would seem to be that towns are simply small cities and cities are simply big towns, that there are no important or sharp distinctions between them, and that the obvious differences in size and importance among the places in question are differences in gradation only.

This point of view is valid, but only up to a point. Its validity is based on the fact that many of the broad areas of most peoples' concerns—commerce, family life, protective alliances, and religious involvement—are expressed in patterns of behavior that are basically similar, when they are not identical, among city-dwellers, townsmen, villagers, and even pastoralists. These broad similarities are an essential component of the ecological system in which people from different segments must interact with each other effectively and must also be able to transfer themselves from one segment to another (for example, migrate from village or town to city) without too much culture shock.

However, it is also true that cities are special in the eyes of Middle Easterners and foreign observers. As illustrated by the stereotypes discussed in Chapter Three, this point of view has been carried to extremes, and one of the purposes of this book is to modify such extreme and unrealistic views. Nevertheless, while the extremes should be rejected, the sense of special qualities is real, and it must be recognized.

Actually, the sense of special qualities seems to apply not to "the city" in general but to certain cities in particular. These are places that, in addition to being large in ecological and political scale (as mentioned above), have prestige, attractiveness or glamor, and the excitement of variety or new opportunities. Though daily life for most people in these cities probably lacks these qualities, the applicability of the qualities to the cities in the abstract is real in many people's minds.

These qualities appear to be the result of several circumstances in the particular city's history, or in its present condition, or both. These are: (1) The city is now, or was at one time, the capital of a major ruler, dynasty, or power group, attracting wealth; (2) the city is, and has been for a long time, the location of important religious shrines that attract pilgrims, concentrate wealth, and convey a sacred aura to the locality; and (3) the city was founded, or occupied and transformed in many ways, by foreigners bringing different life styles, imposing new patterns of behavior, and stimulating change. The modernization—largely on Western models—of cities in the nineteenth and twentieth centuries is of course an example of this, but there have been many others in the past.

The most important cities are often those where all of these qualities apply. Cairo and Istanbul are cases in point, although, as has so often happened in other cases, Istanbul's prestige is less now than it was. In contrast, relatively new cities like Casablanca and Tehran have grown to spectacular prominence and size only very recently and mostly on the basis of foreign influences and the concentration of new nationalistic power.

Presumably, a scale or gradation of Middle Eastern cities, on the basis of these qualities and their permutations and varied intensities, could be constructed, but there is none, as far as I know, in the literature. Yet we come again to the reality of gradation in this connection as well as in the ecological one. Consider Fez, Damascus, and Isfahan, for example. They do not now have the prestige of Cairo and Istanbul, or the importance of Casablanca and Tehran, yet they are very special cities for the reasons already given. A case could even be made for the "cityness" of Hureidah, which was discussed in Chapter Three. With a population of only 2,000 it is nevertheless a center (in a very sparsely settled and isolated region). As such, it is a place where commercial, political, and supernatural forms of power are concentrated, where those phenomena involve social distance and differentiation among the inhabitants, and that has special prestige and attraction in the eyes of residents of the region. The same generalizations can be made of the much larger settlements I have mentioned, but they cannot be made of the vast number of peasant villages that are only a little smaller than Hureidah. Here are qualitative differences and distinctions, but there are no clear cutoff points that signal their presence or absence.

Hureidah lacks, of course, one of the qualities that is commonly associated with cityness: the presence of alternative life styles of foreign origin and the sense that the city is the place whence these foreign characteristics emanate to the rest of the society. It is very likely this element that is in the minds of those who have noted that the Middle East is becoming increasingly urbanized, meaning that increasingly large proportions of its people are living in places larger (normally) than villages—larger than 5,000, for example.

Actually, however, not enough studies have been done to show what specific effects this demographic trend may have on the cultural patterns of everyday living. It is known that the cultural continuities of everyday life between village and city are, for many people, very great. For them, differences in size of settlement have relatively little effect, although pressures for change may be stronger in the cities. Yet it is also true that there is a greater variety of subcultures, of cultural adaptations to living, in the larger cities. There is not just one city or urban pattern of life, but there are several, some of which are similar to rural patterns of life. This has always been true, as far as we know, in Middle Eastern cities. It remains to be seen whether one of the consequences of modernization—the growth of a few Middle Eastern cities to megalopolitan proportions—will have significant effects on those city cultural patterns that until now have seemed to be similar to noncity ones. Meanwhile, the heterogeneity of cities, whether traditional or modern in style, makes generalizations about "the city," "urbanism," "city people," and "urban culture" likely to be inaccurate and oversimplified.

Bearing in mind both the rural-urban cultural continuities and the special qualities that may inhere in Middle Eastern cities, we will now consider these cities in more detail. The subjects that will be discussed are: (1) change as always having been in process in Middle Eastern cities; (2) characteristics of what has most recently been the traditional form of Middle Eastern city; (3) profiles of four cities on which the literature is fairly abundant; and (4) aspects of Middle Eastern culture (religion, kinship, social inequality, and migration) in cities.

THE CHANGING CITY

While the desert-oasis ecology has been in operation for a very long time, and can therefore be regarded as a "constant," the specific locations of agricultural, pastoral, and commercial activities have been subject to shifts and changes. The long-term alternate displacement of pastoralists by villagers and of villagers by pastoralists in the desert fringe areas of the Fertile Crescent is one example of this that has been discussed.

Another example is the perilous careers of most Middle Eastern cities as revealed by their histories. Cities in general go back to the Formative period, but none of the important present-day ones is that old, and many once-important cities are now completely in ruins. A few important cities—such as Damascus and Jerusalem—have been more or less continuously inhabited since early Florescent times, but their present-day old parts have undergone drastic changes during the intervening period (for Damascus see Thubron 1967; for Jerusalem see Sharon 1973). Other important cities were founded later on in the Florescent: Alexandria and Istanbul, for example. In these, and in other pre-Islamic cities, there are traces of features that were long ago important but are no longer very apparent. Among them are traces of the rectilinear grid street plan that was favored by the Romans, as in Aleppo and many other towns and cities. Other examples are former churches converted into mosques, the churches themselves having sometimes been built on the sites of "pagan" temples.

The vicissitudes that many, if not all, of the existing pre-Islamic cities have undergone can be illustrated by the histories of Beirut and Tripoli in Lebanon. Both originated in the first millennium B.C. as Phoenician seaports, but hardly anything remains of the Phoenician or the subsequent Greco-Roman settlements. Tripoli was twice destroyed, first by the Crusaders and then by the reconquering Muslims who, at the end of the thirteenth century, moved the site of the town slightly inland from the shore. Beirut was destroyed by earthquakes in the latter part of the Florescent period. By the beginning of the Machine-Age Islamic period, both were small towns of a few thousand people apiece, Beirut protected on its inland sides by a wall. The morphology of these towns conformed to the general patterns of the traditional Islamic "old city" that will be described shortly. Subsequently, however, the "old city" of Beirut was completely obliterated; what are now the old parts of Beirut are the Europeanized business and residential districts that were built in the late nineteenth and early twentieth centuries replacing the "old city" (Khalaf and Kongstad 1973b, p. 117). On the other hand, in Tripoli, a city that has not grown nearly as rapidly or extensively as Beirut, considerable portions of the "old city" remained in the 1960s (Gulick 1967b). These two cities have changed radically and repeatedly over their long histories. In many instances, these changes have been caused by deliberate, wholesale destruction often followed, to be sure, by reconstruction along either similar or different lines.

Still other Middle Eastern cities were founded at the end of the Florescent by various Muslim potentates. There may have been older settlements nearby, but the establishment of each of the present cities appears to have been perceived as a major new beginning. Prominent among these are Fez, Morocco (Le Tourneau 1949), Cairo (Abu-Lughod 1971), and Baghdad (Lassner 1970; Hitti 1973). These cities, too, have changed radically through time. In each one the present-day "old city" is not at all what it was like originally. For instance, the present-day old parts of Cairo are not even in the same location as the original city, while the center of the original city of Baghdad was a unique circular palace precinct on the west bank of the Tigris River. It and outgrowths from it were the fabulously opulent Baghdad that is often mentioned in the *Thousand and One Nights.* Nothing whatever remains of this early Baghdad, although the big Shia shrine at Kazimayn marks the location of a cemetery on its outskirts, and the present "old city" originated as an extension from the outskirts of the original city on the east bank of the river.

This emphasis on a long history of changes in Middle Eastern cities is necessary for the gaining of a proper perspective on what is generally happening in them now. Most observers of modern Middle Eastern cities are struck by the contrasts between their old and new parts. The visual and other sensory impacts are very great indeed. As a result, many observers understandably jump to the conclusion that the old cities have remained unchanged since time immemorial and now are suddenly being changed out of recognition for the first time. Furthermore, the sensory contrasts between old and new are so great that one is inclined to assume that the differences in values and cultural patterns between the inhabitants of the old and the new parts of the city must also be as great as the differences in architecture and street patterns. This assumption contributes to the idea that the Middle East as a whole is undergoing total transformation. The views from the airport, from one's room in a modern high-rise hotel, or from an air-conditioned bank lobby are likely to reinforce this impression. Yet it is a very superficial one, and the characteristics of the various behavior patterns of the inhabitants cannot be assumed from such superficial impressions; they must be studied. There certainly are behavioral changes, but there also seem to be behavioral continuities from the past.

In most modern Middle Eastern cities the following parts are likely to be found, parts that are discernibly different, one from another:

1. The "old city." Hereafter I shall refer to it as the madina. As mentioned in an earlier chapter, this is the generic Arabic word for "city," but it is now being rather widely used to refer to the specific city morphology that, though it has not been the same since time immemorial, did become stabilized and rather standardized in many ways during the latter part of the Conservative Islamic time frame.

2. A western-style business district with streets designed for automotive traffic, hotels, cinemas, and office buildings housing western-style businesses and governmental agencies. In the case of seaports it is likely to include the port facilities and in general is likely to include the railroad and bus stations as well as machine shops serving transportation facilities.
3. Modern residential areas, characteristically including retail commercial establishments serving everyday domestic needs.
4. Industrial areas. Heavy iron and steel industry is not characteristic of Middle Eastern cities, but light industries—such as textile mills, food and beverage processing plants, construction companies, and electrical appliance assembly plants—are typical, often located along the main highways leading into and out of the cities.
5. Squatter settlements.

The newer parts are generally adjacent to each other, growing out from the madina; and factories, squatter settlements, and middle class areas are often close together. Annexed villages occur here and there, often appearing as neighborhoods older than their surroundings. On the far outskirts are satellite villages that may still be predominantly agricultural or may have factories built next to them. In the heavily brick-using areas, such as Iraq and Iran, farthest out on the cities' peripheries are the brick kilns, with their tall smokestacks. Conspicuously absent (with some exceptions of very limited size) are the great sprawls of commuters' suburbs that are so important a feature of American and European cities. True, many Middle Eastern cities have grown so large that public transportation (formerly trams but now mostly buses and taxis) is provided, but long-distance commuter services, and their many problems, are not part of the Middle Eastern scene to the extent that they are in the West.

In most places this growth and morphological differentiation out from the madinas has occurred in the twentieth century, although in Cairo, Istanbul, Beirut, and a few other cities where European influence was particularly heavy it began somewhat earlier. As a result, the populations of many cities have increased enormously, as have their built-up areas. The population growth has been due to natural growth in general (about 3 percent per year) in most Middle Eastern countries, which has accelerated migration of village people to the cities, plus relatively high rates of natural increase in the cities themselves. Cairo grew from 590,000 in 1897 to an estimated 6,170,000 in 1972 (Waterbury 1973b, p. I–2); Casablanca from 20,500 in 1897 to 965,000 in 1960 (Adam 1972, p. 149). Baghdad grew about 800 percent between 1904 and 1965

(Gulick 1967a, p. 248), Tehran about fifteen-fold from 1922 to the present (Planhol 1968, p. 445), and Beirut about ten-fold since 1932 (Khalaf and Kongstad 1973a, p. 18). While the effects of all this change, and of city sizes of unprecedented proportions, must be felt in the lives of the inhabitants, we do not have very much good descriptive data on them. Some people have become "modernized," but this is not solely due to the effects of city growth. Other people, living in the same huge agglomerations, appear not to have been so greatly modernized.

Nor have many large Middle Eastern cities been totally transformed in their building styles and street patterns. In most of them, in fact, the old city survives and is densely populated.

THE MADINA IN MODERN CITIES

Many of the features of the madina are probably far older than the later centuries of the Conservative Islamic time frame. However, it was certainly during the latter time that the specific forms of madinas as they have survived to the present day took shape and became standardized to such an extent that from Fez, in Morocco, to Herat, in Afghanistan, the same features can be observed.

Madinas are of obvious historical interest in themselves, and events in cities are important in the conventional historical accounts of the Middle East in the past. Present-day madinas, if in nothing else than their physical forms, are direct continuations from an earlier cultural time frame when many conditions of life were different from what they are now. Consequently, efforts have been made to reconstruct the cultural patterns of Conservative Islamic cities and to see whether any of those patterns survive in the remaining madinas. The results of those efforts are important for the modern urban anthropology of the Middle East.

The general characteristics of the madina are: (1) very densely built up area with no plazas or parks and with very few straight through-streets; (2) inward-oriented dwellings, with courtyards and/or walled enclosures, access to which is gained by narrow, twisting, often dead-end, alleys that are sometimes overhung by the upper stories of the houses; (3) the souq, or bazaar, a network of roofed-over streets along which shops and workshops are arranged, often grouped by specialty. Repeatedly, observers report the strong impression of a labyrinth of alleys, cul-de-sacs, and tunnels; (4) important, but often rather inconspicuous, buildings, are: mosques, churches, and synagogues, the mosques including a Congregational or Friday Mosque adjacent to the souq or bazaar; Quranic schools (madrassas), many of which have recently ceased to be used for their original purpose; khans or caravanserais—large structures with gates and a courtyard—originally designed to be caravan terminals, serving as warehouse for the goods, stable for the animals, and inn for the caravaneers, now often converted to other purposes, such as tenements for indigent people; a citadel which may or may not contain the residence and headquarters of what was until recently the chief magistrate of the city; and public bath houses (hammams), the form being that known as "Turkish bath" in the West; and (5) one or more cemeteries.

All these features survive more or less intact in many cities, as we shall see, but a few important changes have occurred that must be emphasized. First, virtually all Middle Eastern nations have adopted, during the Machine-Age Islamic period, European-style governmental organizations, from the national to the municipal levels. This has meant an enormous proliferation of agencies and offices, so that the citadel and former chief magistrate's residence have long since been outgrown. Some residual governmental functions may still be carried out in them, but most governmental functions (municipal and provincial in most cases, plus national and international in a few others) are now carried out in newer buildings outside the madina. Second, in many cases, strips of the madina have been demolished in order to make room for wide vehicular traffic streets and avenues. Third, the city walls that surrounded many of the madinas have, in many instances, been demolished in Machine-Age Islamic times, and often the only reminders of them are the names of former gates applied to neighborhoods or to major intersections of streets on the edges of the madinas. The madinas of Jerusalem and Fez are exceptions in that their city walls have been fairly completely preserved.

Another important characteristic of the madina that is usually not in any way visible is its division into a large number of named quarters, commonly used Middle Eastern terms for which are hayy, hara, and mahalla. A very important question is whether each of these quarters can always be assumed to be a self-aware, self-contained community. I shall discuss this question further a little later in reference to specific cities. The evidence, such as it is, suggests a variety of situations both now and in the past. Lapidus warns against making the above assumption as far as the thirteenth to sixteenth century cities of Egypt and the western Fertile Crescent are concerned (Lapidus 1967, pp. 85–86). Apropos of the changing city in the past, incidentally, he notes that the frequently mentioned ghettolike closing off of these quarters from one another, by means of walls and gates that could be locked, developed later on, under changed conditions during Ottoman times (1967, pp. 94–95). Certain quarters, during certain periods of time, appear very definitely to have been self-contained communities-in-depth. For example, there have been many quarters inhabited by minority sectarian groups or quarters newly established by recent migrants belonging to a particular tribe or coming from a particular region. Many names of quarters, however, appear to have lost their original significance as identifiers of the inhabitants. They have become, instead, geographical labels that are very much needed because of the absence of house numbers and the uncertainty about the names of specific alleys and streets. Scholars seem to have been impressed by the large number of named sections of madinas, for instance 217 in early twentieth century Bukhara (Sjoberg 1960, p. 100); 50 in fifteenth century Aleppo and 100 in sixteenth century Damascus (Lapidus 1967, pp. 85–86); 53 in eighteenth century Cairo (Gibb and Bowen 1950, p. 279); 25 in the present-day madina of Tripoli, Lebanon, whose area is about one-sixth of one square mile (Gulick 1967b, pp. 154–155); and 75 in the madina of present-day Baghdad (Susa 1952, p. 21). The very frequency of these named sections should induce caution about assuming that every one of them necessarily was once, or still is, a complete "community" with its own mosque, hammam, shops, and cozy (or embattled) identity. However, even though many, and possibly most, of the names of quarters that appear in various lists and on various maps may not be, or may not have been, "total communities" in the above sense, they are probably indicative of the strongly parochial character that most observers feel is typical of residential behavior in madinas, at least in the past (see Lapidus 1973, p. 56).

As to the present, there are so few pertinent studies that we do not have enough information to make any general statements on how the named quarters correspond with true neighborhoods (restricted territories with territorially aware inhabitants). There are two recent studies, both done in towns, that are valuable contributions, however. One is in a Moroccan town where the networks of personal interaction in one quarter are analyzed and shown to result in a sense of "closeness" (Eickelman 1974, p. 283). The other is Magnarella's observation of the "defended neighborhoods" in Susurluk, Turkey, that was mentioned in Chapter Three. An assumption that such neighborhoods are typical of the madinas, past and present, is safer than one that they are not, but we have no evidence that madinas are completely subdivided into these neighborhoods, on the analogy of beehive cells. Indeed, with the turnover of inhabitants that is currently occurring in the madinas, there may well be much unneighborly behavior among people living close together. As to the names, we can only guess that some of those referring to small quarters may identify true neighborhoods, or what were once true neighborhoods. The larger the named quarters are, the less, of course, they are likely to be true neighborhoods.

It is clear enough that Middle Eastern cities are divided, overall, into large named districts. One of these, nowadays, is likely to be the madina itself. Depending on its age and population density, each district is subdivided into a variable number of named quarters. These may or may not be formal administrative precincts. Depending on their size, and other considerations, these quarters may have a distinctive communal identity or functions (such as having their own mosque, bath, shops). Or such quarters may simply be named localities in which there are different neighborhoods. At any rate, scholarly attention to these matters has been devoted largely to city madinas, or their equivalents in towns, although some pertinent studies have been made on and in newer districts of a few cities.

The most detailed study of a madina as a living city, in relatively recent times, is Le Tourneau's on Fez, Morocco (Le Tourneau 1949). This book is a reconstruction of the madina of Fez as it was shortly before 1912, when France assumed its protectorate of Morocco. Le Tourneau's task was easier than it might have been because the French decided to leave the madina intact and build the modern part of Fez entirely separate from it. One of the many consequences of this was that the madina was not dissected by modern streets as most other madinas have been. Without firsthand knowledge of Fez one finds it difficult to judge how much of what Le Tourneau discusses was still true when he published his monograph and how much may still be true today. As far as morphology is concerned, a recent aerial photograph (Brown 1973, p. 20) would presumably be an appropriate illustration for his book. The madina consisted of two districts on opposite sides of the small river running through the site (Andalous Bank and Kairouan Bank), subdivided into a total of eighteen quarters, plus Fez Jedid (New Fez), which was founded in the thirteenth century, about 500 years later than the original founding of the city (Le Tourneau 1949, p. 154). Fez Jedid included (and still includes) the sultan's palace and its precincts and the Mellah (Jewish quarter). Le Tourneau says that the populations of the quarters were otherwise generally heterogeneous, hence most of the quarters were not very distinctive, although recent migrants from certain regions of the country were more numerous in some than in others (p. 219). There were plenty of mosques in the central quarters, and each quarter had notables to whom the inhabitants could turn for help if necessary. The quarters had miniature souqs, smaller than the main ones. Fez had, and definitely still has, its patron saint founder, Moulay Idris, whose birthday is a major festival and whose shrine is a major focus of pilgrimage. Moulay Idris was a descendent of Hassan, grandson of the Prophet, and Hassan's descendants, plus those of Husayn, constituted the shorfa (singular: sherif) of Fez, that is to say, the religious aristocracy descended from the Prophet. (The actual designation of the present nation of Morocco is "The Sherifian Kingdom of the Maghrib," owing to the fact that the members of the royal family are shorfa.) Saints, saints' brotherhoods, and guilds (a subject of some scholarly controversy) are other topics dealt with at some length by Le Tourneau.

Paul English's study of the madina of Herat, Afghanistan, though not equal in scope to Le Tourneau's on Fez, provides some important comparable details. The madina is divided into four large, named sections, each of which is an official administrative district. But these are too large to constitute communities in themselves, and those smaller ethnic, sectarian, or occupational quarters that have commonly been observed in other Middle Eastern cities are "apparently absent." However, English notes that neighborhood activity focuses around small mosques and shrines (English 1973, pp. 82–83). This last point broaches a subject that has hardly been studied at all: whether the small mosque (of which there are many in all Middle Eastern cities) is the active center of what might be called, for want of a better term, a parish. English's observations in Herat, and the observations of others that have recently been made in Iran, suggest that at least some small mosques serve this function.

One of the most famous madinas in the whole Middle East is that of Isfahan, Iran. It has all the general features of madinas that have been mentioned, including the Friday Mosque adjacent to (actually at one end of) the bazaar. A map that attempts to reconstruct the names and locations of the quarters of the whole area of the present-day city of Isfahan (including annexed villages) shows seventy-four quarters (mahallat). About thirty of these—some of which are districts rather than quarters—coincide with the madina (Iran, Empire of, p. 12). The madina of Isfahan is famous principally because it contains several of the outstanding masterpieces of Islamic architecture and related arts. Ardalan and Bakhtiar's plan showing the 105 buildings and other features ranged along the bazaar and the maydan includes most of these (Ardalan and Bakhtiar 1973, pp. 98–99). The maydan (an enormous rectangular plaza with two monumental mosques, a royal pavilion, and the entry to the bazaar on its four sides) is highly exceptional for a madina, where, as I have said, organized open spaces are rare.

While the various monuments of the Isfahan madina will probably be preserved because of their exceptional fame, other parts of the madina are threatened by demolition under various pretexts. Such threats, and much actual demolition, are typical of Middle Eastern cities, and this is a controversial matter of some importance. Some Middle Eastern architects (for example, Fathy 1963 and Shiber 1963) have noted the great ecological value of certain aspects of madinas: the enclosed courtyard houses allowing privacy in the midst of high population density; the narrow covered streets beautifully adapted to providing protection from the harsh elements of the desert-oasis climate, as well as to facilitating pedestrian traffic. In the last connection, incidentally, English notes that the 5,500 shops of Herat are within easy walking distance of the 80,000 residents (English 1973, p. 80). On the other hand, many Middle Easterners regard the madinas as slums that are shameful remnants of the "medieval backwardness" that they know many Westerners think is typical in general of them. Consequently, while many madina residents move to new styles of housing outside the madina, their places very often being taken by poor people recently moved to the city, there are continuing government efforts to demolish the madinas. Where they are demolished, or where they are outgrown and surrounded by new districts, the new street plans and buildings are copied from European and American models, including wide streets designed for automotive traffic and not at all well suited for walking in the desert-oasis climate. Building materials feature heat conductors like concrete, steel, and glass, and while the new dwellings can be—and sometimes are—designed to preserve the traditional values of domestic privacy (see Fathy 1963, p. 332, and Gulick 1974) they also require energy-consuming utilities. In short, the newer parts of Middle Eastern cities are being built for increasingly high energy consumption—gasoline for vehicles and electricity for air conditioning and other utilities. In the future, when the now-abundant energy resources of some Middle Eastern countries are exhausted, perhaps new madinalike areas will be built to replace the "modern" cities whose present growth is so conspicuous.

There is an important aspect of city life, involving the interrelationships of madina living and modern city living, that has often been overlooked. This is the bourgeois culture of the merchants, shopkeepers, and craftsmen who work in the souq or bazaar (and elsewhere) and are the people who actually operate the symbioses of agriculture, animal husbandry, and commerce. Serious attention to them has been neglected, for most observers have been more attracted to the peasants and nomads or to the highly westernized professional city people.

An important element among these "traditional-urban" madina-living people are the bazaar merchants and artisans. In Fez, Le Tourneau noted the piousness of these people (1949, p. 266), as has Thaiss (among others) of the "bazaaris" of Iranian cities (Thaiss 1971). These are the people who are one of the cores of the "traditional urbanites" of Cairo and who, Abu-Lughod estimates, predominate in quarters of the city that have at least 30 percent of its population (Abu-Lughod 1969, p. 175). These are people the more prosperous of whom (presumably) listed themselves in the Tripoli, Lebanon, telephone directory simply as tujjaar (merchants) and indicated their places of business to be largely in the souq (Gulick 1967b, p. 106). These are the people who traditionally formed the memberships of the various guilds (asnaf; singular: sinf).

The controversy about Middle Eastern guilds, to which I alluded earlier, has to do with whether or not they were, in Conservative Islamic times, the very strong and autonomous organizations that guilds were in medieval and Renaissance Europe. Massignon asserted that they were, but apparently he had no evidence for his assertion, and it has recently been contradicted, with the concurrence of a number of historians (Stern 1970). The crucial difference was that the asnaf were always under the direct supervision of the muhtasib, one of the few specific Conservative Islamic municipal officers, whereas the European guilds became largely autonomous of government control (Stern 1970, p. 46). In Egypt urban guilds were in operation until the latter part of the nineteenth century—even for a brief time incorporating early "modern" occupations—but they eventually disappeared, largely due to the competition of European goods (Baer 1969, p. 153). In Iran, however, asnaf are still in operation among some bazaaris, though their functions seem to be related to sociability and to sectarian interests at least as much as to production and marketing interests.

At any rate, two field studies have recently been done in Iranian cities (Rotblat 1972 and Thaiss 1973) that shed light not only on the economic structure of the bazaar itself but also on the culture of the bazaar merchants. A major element in that culture is the sectarian and religious orientation and activities of these people. (Consideration of the bazaaris' religious interests leads, in turn, to a consideration of the modern ulama of Iranian cities. This subject will be dealt with in more detail in Chapter Six. The ulama is the body of religious doctors that constitutes the principal institutional structure of Islam in general and of each major Islamic city in particular.)

Qazvin is a city in northern Iran, not far from Tehran. Like that of most Middle Eastern cities, its history is a succession of prosperous and disastrous periods. Its population in 1970 was about 92,000 (Rotblat 1972, p. 32). Rotblat's study includes lengthy analyses of the components of the bazaar, mainly (1) produce commission agents, jobbers, retailers, and traders, and (2) the various craftsmen and other retailers. In brief, he thinks that, as a whole (the components' problems differ), the bazaaris are having difficulties adapting successfully to the political and economic changes in Iran. His detailed discussions are a very realistic portrayal of the many things that "modernization" means, and those interested should read his presentation itself. A basic problem, which exemplifies the peril-and-refuge mentality, is the restriction of friendships among Qazvin bazaaris (Rotblat 1972, p. 175) and the general state of mistrust among them (p. 219), this in combination with much social interaction. This lack of trust inhibits their forming new types of association designed to cope with new collective problems, a type of activity that is not encouraged by the government, either. One could generalize from this particular case and conclude that traditional social patterns in the Middle East cannot survive "modernization." While some of them, indeed, may not, others may. An example of those that do survive is provided by Miner's study of craftsmen in Fez, which includes one family history over the past 100 years. While some people decide, and are able, to carry on the older crafts, others of their relatives may decide not to. Miner's point is that neither the "traditional" nor the "modern" options are decided on blindly, but rather are based on calculations as to which of the options will be more advantageous (Miner 1973, p. 35). Members of the same family decide differently.

Thaiss says that the bazaaris of Tehran are organized in networks of dyadic (two-person) relationships (Thaiss 1973, p. 26). This observation seems basically similar to Rosen's among merchants in a moderate-sized Moroccan city (Rosen 1972), and it seems consistent with Rotblat's impression of limited ties in Qazvin. Put another way, none of these authors has observed urban merchants who carry on their business through highly organized multiperson associations. In Tehran (but not in Qazvin) the asnaf are active, but Thaiss is very careful not to call them guilds. They are associations of fellow workers or fellow professionals in the same specialty (hamkaari) who feel a sense of closeness because of similar values and religious beliefs and are mutually supportive in this regard (Thaiss 1973, p. 44). The asnaf serve this supportive function and are not active primarily for business purposes. Thaiss has much to say about the alliances of the bazaaris with the ulama, but most of his study is concerned with their religious observances, in which the asnaf play a central part. The basic observance is the meeting known as rozeh khani. This is a prayer meeting and memorial service for one of the Shia martyrs, especially Imam Husayn. It allows for the expression of very powerful emotions, but it also provides opportunities for gossip and sociability. In Iran, participation in rozeh khani is not by any means restricted to bazaar merchants, but Thaiss's concern is to show how its themes continually reinforce the bazaari subculture.

Whether all of the bazaar merchants actually still live in the madina or not, they are an important element in the "traditional urbanite" population. One of the functions of that population, as I have said, is to make the agricultural-animal husbandry-commercial symbiosis work. The wholesaling of products and the manufacture and distribution of goods are obviously involved in this. Also involved is the extending of credit by bazaaris to rural clients, a rather bitter subject to which Rotblat gives some attention (1972, p. 189).

Kerman, another moderate-sized Iranian city, is the subject of a book by Paul English (1966). Though he gives considerable attention to the morphology of the city itself, with detailed consideration of the Zoroastrian quarter in the madina (pp. 48–49), his main concern is with the controls that Kerman merchants exercise over the village hinterland of the city. This is one of the few detailed studies of this regional phenomenon, whose significance in Middle Eastern culture I have already noted, and the book's importance has been duly recognized by a critical review article (Spooner and Salzman 1969). Kerman and its hinterland depend upon qanats (subterranean aqueducts) for water, and the forms of ownership and control are very much influenced by this fact. Consequently, the forms of regional controls emanating from cities may not be the same in places where there are no qanats (Spooner and Salzman 1969, p. 111).

This discussion of the traditional bourgeoisie has relied heavily on Iranian materials because most of the more recent and detailed anthropological studies were done in Iran. This should not be taken to indicate that there has necessarily been less change in this type of urban subculture in Iran than in any of the other Middle Eastern countries. We really do not know whether there has been or not. I have mentioned some suggestions of its presence in other countries, and studies elsewhere of the continued importance of kinship alliances among modern businessmen suggest that there may be an on-going process of *adaptation* of the traditional patterns of behavior to fit new conditions.

PROFILES OF FOUR CITIES

Four contemporary Middle Eastern cities have been given lengthy and comprehensive attention by single authors, with important additional sources in several cases. These cities are Beirut, Cairo, Casablanca, and Tripoli (Lebanon). These studies are comprehensive because, on the whole, they discuss many subjects that will be analyzed later in this book (social classes and family structure, for example) as well as the forms of the cities themselves. At this point I shall mention only some of the more general highlights of these studies.

Beirut

Beirut has the reputation of being the most "westernized" of all Middle Eastern cities. European and American cultural patterns and ongoing interests are certainly very strong there. It is a major seaport, airport, and center of international trade. Its glittery facades also attract many foreign tourists, including people from other Middle Eastern countries, for its casinos, night clubs, and restaurants offer many diversions not so easily found in the more austere ethos of most other Middle Eastern cities.

These qualities have been developed over the past century or so, along with the complete demolition of the old madina. However, the city is far from being homogeneously modern. Beyond the downtown business and entertainment district (located where the madina used to be), there are several large districts that are felt by residents to be culturally distinct from each other: Ashrafiyah, Basta, and Ras Beirut. Basta is supposed to be inhabited primarily by Sunni Muslims, but since it only roughly coincides with two administrative districts with different names, and since there has been no sectarian (or any other) census in Lebanon since 1932, we can only state what its reputation is. The other two districts do coincide pretty much with administrative districts with the same names, but the available statistics on them do not help to clarify their reputations either. One of the major studies done in Beirut (Churchill 1954) reports on a large-scale household survey, but, apart from showing that it sampled all the twelve administrative districts, it does not for the most part cross-tabulate its findings with district residence. Chehabe-ed-Dine (1960) briefly describes the various administrative districts (pp. 240–273), and from his discussion a careful reader can deduce some of the cultural characteristics that give special reputations to some of the districts. Basta is, as I have said, supposed to be predominantly Sunni Muslim in the composition of its residents and therefore supposedly less "westernized" in a number of respects. Ashrafiyah is supposed to be predominantly Maronite (Lebanese Roman Catholic) in residential population and therefore westernized in specifically French ways. Ras Beirut, adjoining the campus of the American University of Beirut, is "international" in character, American influences being especially noticeable. Abou reports on observations of the languages in which signs along the streets of Beirut are written. Arabic signs alone were especially frequent in Basta, Arabic-French signs in Ashrafiyah, Arabic-English signs in Ras Beirut, and Armenian or Armenian-Arabic-French signs in another area where Armenian refugees are common (Abou 1962, pp. 120–121). The reputations that the districts have are based on many observations of this kind plus personal experiences of the inhabitants, but there have been no other large-scale systematic studies of the city as a whole.

However, Khalaf and Kongstad have done a geographical-sociological study of Ras Beirut. Hamra is the name of the major thoroughfare that runs through the cluster of blocks they studied, a mostly residential area immediately south of the American University campus. Part of the study is devoted to a meticulous reconstruction of the area's phases of development. In 1919 it consisted of a few scattered houses (including farmhouses) and open fields and orchards adjoining the then much smaller university campus. In 1967 it had become solidly built-up, many of its buildings being over five stories high and a few of them skyscrapers (Khalaf and Kongstad 1973a, pp. 34–41). In addition to the small local groceries and similar shops that have always been present, more intensive commercialization has recently taken place on Hamra street itself—cinemas, restaurants, clothing stores, stereo bars, and others.

What are the people like who live in this obviously very "modern" and "westernized" area? In some respects they are very much what one would expect in a Western university or college town. They are mostly middle class, with emphasis on professionals, clerks, and small business people, among the household heads, in addition to students. Almost half of the household heads have university educations. These people probably can be likened to the edari of Tehran (office workers, clerks, and bureaucrats in businesses or university or government offices) who consciously contrast themselves with the bazaaris (Thaiss 1973, p. 22), and it is certainly among them that consciousness of conflicts in regard to changing cultural patterns can be found in perhaps more intense form than among less westernized city dwellers.

It is important that almost 80 percent of the households are composed of nuclear families (Khalaf and Kongstad 1973a, p. 62) and that they exhibit a high level of intensity of contacts with other relatives and of neighborhood ties (p. 133–134). This is wholly consistent with Farsoun's study of households in various parts of Beirut (Farsoun 1970). Khalaf and Kongstad interpret the high intensity of social networks outside the nuclear family as indicating the retention of rural or village social patterns (1973a, p. 130). Another interpretation, however, is entirely possible, especially in view of the fact that the great majority of household heads were born in cities (p. 101). Studies in Middle Eastern cities (including this one of unusually "modern" people) generally confirm the fact that extensive social networks are characteristic of city dwellers, and that therefore they are not "incompatible" with urban life. This notion of incompatibility was for a long time assumed to be true of Western industrial cities, but it is now being challenged even in regard to them. As was emphasized in Chapter Two, social alienation and feelings of mistrust are certainly present also (in villages as well as cities), but they should not be assumed to imply social isolation. Indeed, they may well be intensified by contacts.

Cairo

While Beirut was an unimportant town in Conservative Islamic times, Cairo grew to greatness early in that period and has continued to be one of the most important cities in the Middle East. At the present time it is definitely the largest, and it has few rivals in prestige as a long-time center of Islamic art, learning, and power.

Many books have been written about Cairo. Among them, E. W. Lane's *Manners and Customs of the Modern Egyptians*, first published in 1836, was one of the first Westerner's accounts of

Middle Eastern social life ("traditional," urban, upper class). Of the numerous recent books, the most informative and best illustrated is that of Janet Abu-Lughod (1971). Much of her discussion consists of historical reconstruction, but I shall draw on that part of it that focuses on contemporary Cairo, especially the chapter entitled, "The Anatomy of Metropolitan Cairo." This is probably the best systematic social science description of any modern Middle Eastern city. The sources of information include the author's long residence in, and detailed knowledge of, Cairo, plus vital statistics on each of the 216' census tracts that are subdivisions of the fourteen administrative districts of the city. Some of the census tracts in the older parts of the city coincide with what once, at any rate, were quarters in the sense of community-in-depth. In addition, the large number of statistical units makes possible the plotting of quantifiable cultural characteristics (education of men and women, for example), this being informed by qualitative observations made throughout the city. Abu-Lughod's analysis leads her to describe Cairo in terms of thirteen "subcities". This term is greatly preferable, I think, to the word "communities," which she also uses in this connection. The subcities are essentially the same as what I have been calling districts, as opposed to smaller quarters.

In the following outline I have rearranged Abu-Lughod's thirteen subcities and put them under headings that she does not use. The names and numbers of the subcities, however, are unchanged so that the reader can easily refer to what is said (and shown with photographs) about them in the original (Abu-Lughod 1971, pp. 182–220).

A. Madina and Squatter Settlements.
>   XII. Old Cairo. The first settlement site of Cairo, on the river south of, and separate from, the main madina, which is slightly inland from the river.
>   X. Medieval Cairo Unreconstructed. Contains the citadel, al-Azhar University, and other famous landmarks of the old city.
>   IX. The Funereal Quarters of the Eastern Fringe. The so-called "city of the dead," which is actually very much alive, with about 100,000 residents who live in and around the mausoleums that adjoin Subcity X.

B. The Nineteenth Century European Business District in Transition.
>   XI. The Transitional Zone of Osmosis. Scene of much demolition and rebuilding, seen by Abu-Lughod as an area that will provide cultural osmosis between the extremes of traditional (X) and modern (VII) cultural patterns.

C. Old Lower-Class Slum.
>   I. The Baladi Slum of Bulaq. Outgrowth from an old set-

tlement on the river. Highest residential densities in the city.

D. Modern Districts.

VII. The Gold Coast. Includes upper-class residential areas along the east bank of the Nile and on the island of Zamalik. Also includes the newest "downtown" area of business and governmental institutions.

VIII. A Parallel "Silver Coast." New middle-class residential area on the island of Ruda.

II. Shubra, a lower-middle class mélange. East of Bulaq.

IV. A Strip City of the urban working class. East of Shubra.

E. Rural Fringe Areas.

XIII. The Southern Rural Fringe. Extends from Old Cairo to the satellite town of Halwan and geographically includes Cairo's "only true suburb," the British-built town of Ma'adi.

VI. Imbabah and the Western Rural Fringe. Includes annexed villages and new housing projects financed by waqf funds.

III. A Northern Agricultural Wedge.

F. Urban Residential and Institutional Fringe.

V. A Sector City of the Old and New Middle Class. This includes the old foreign-oriented suburb of Heliopolis—no longer foreign or suburban—a university campus, and new housing projects. It also includes Nasr City, where many government ministries have been relocated, and that was also intended to be the home of those working in the ministries. However, according to Waterbury (1973b, p. II–16), this has not worked out, and most of the ministry employees commute daily from the center of the city where they live.

The rural fringe areas of Cairo, as of all Middle Eastern cities, include people who are still engaged in agriculture, though they are faced with industrial developments surrounding them. There are also migrants of rural origin living in various parts of the city. Abu-Lughod sees the rural as one of the three types of life that coexist in Cairo, the others being the traditional urban and the modern or industrial urban (1971, p. 218). I would interpret these three as being large categories of urban heterogeneity.

Casablanca

Toward the end of his book, Adam says, "The hell of Casablanca is not wholly in the squatter settlements" (Adam 1972, p. 777), and this is accompanied by other general remarks about the destructive effects of the city environment. It is not easy to find any clear substantiation for this point of view in his long presentation that relies rather heavily on aggregate statistics. The feeling-tone is certainly different from that of Abu-Lughod's book, which is clearly a labor of love, and from that of Waterbury's serious, yet at times hilarious, report on public transportation in Cairo (Waterbury 1973b, part 2). One of Adam's main concerns is the squatter settlements (bidonvilles) of Casablanca, this type of residential area being far more important in Casablanca than in Beirut or Cairo. Adam was one of the first scholars to study Middle Eastern squatter settlements with any thoroughness (see Adam 1949), yet he is also the author of a monograph on rural housetypes in Morocco (1951), and it may be that the huge sprawls of artlessly built and insalubrious tin-can shacks are particularly distressing to him. At any rate, it is interesting how he interprets some figures on crime rates in his chapter called "Social Pathology." He cites figures indicating lower crime rates in the squatter settlements than in the madina. He seems inclined to explain this as due to a generally evil influence of the city, but he points out that the majority of the culprits were not born in Casablanca and that therefore the crime rate may be due to difficulties of adapting to city life (Adam 1972, p. 668). One wonders if these same facts could not be interpreted in different terms, terms similar to those used by Patch in his study in Lima, Peru. Patch says that crime rates, and other ills, are far greater in the old in-town slums than in the squatter settlements, due basically to contrasts in general attitude between hopelessness in the slum and hopefulness in the squatter settlement (Patch 1968, p. 178). Perhaps the same is true in Casablanca. However, conditions may be different in different Moroccan cities, for Crapanzano notes that in Meknes, bidonville residents expressed a preference for living in the more peaceful, quiet, and civilized madina of that city (Crapanzano 1973, p. 105).

In addition to making such qualitative judgments, Adam presents a rather thorough, and very well illustrated, picture of the various parts of Casablanca, which are:

1. The old madina. The madina as described and discussed in this book. This particular madina, however, dates back only to the early nineteenth century.
2. The European-style section, originally built in the early twentieth century, with diverse parts, now including a downtown business area with skyscrapers.
3. The "new madina." A Muslim residential area originally established by Muslims in order to separate themselves from the Jews, who were taking over the old madina, and from the Europeans, who constituted a substantial proportion of the city's population in the 1920s and 1930s.

4. Three very large agglomerations of squatter settlements.
5. New low-cost housing projects intended to replace the squatter settlements.

Adam relies heavily on aggregate statistics, and he does not provide the same depth of feeling concerning these districts of Casablanca as does Abu-Lughod in regard to the various districts of Cairo. The subtitle of his book, "The Transformation of Moroccan Society in Contact with the West," makes one wonder if Casablanca should not be considered more "westernized" than Beirut. However, the heterogeneity of both cities militates against such a sweeping comparison. Waterbury's study of a Sousi merchant who has lived and worked in Casablanca for many years gives some depth of perspective on these matters. The man is a migrant from the Sous Valley, an area of tribes structured in the ways described in Chapter Three. He has also been active in Moroccan politics and is head of the Moroccan Union of Wholesalers of Food Products, a "modern" organization. The people from Sous are famous, as also noted in Chapter Three, for having migrated to all parts of Morocco, becoming shopkeepers and merchants. However, Waterbury concludes that their personalities have not become dominated by that very "modern" trait called "high need for achievement." Those who, like his protagonist, moved to Casablanca took advantage of a situation created by huge French investments, but now, under conditions that have changed, they may abandon the city (1972, p. 197). They certainly cannot be assumed to be the people who will transform Moroccan society in some predictable fashion.

Tripoli

Tripoli (Lebanon), with a population of about 200,000, is not only much smaller than Beirut, Cairo, and Casablanca, it is also less important than the others in all respects. As Churchill points out, it is too close to Beirut to be able to compete with it as a port or a commercial center (Churchill 1970, p. 651). Nevertheless, it has grown rapidly during the past 150 years. Though severely damaged by street widening and other clearance projects, the madina is still intact. It contrasts sharply with six modern districts surrounding it: (1) European-style business and residential; (2) wholesale-produce and lower-class residential; (3) predominantly Christian middle-class residential; (4 and 5) two predominantly Muslim residential; and (6) a light-industry district on the outskirts. The city also has a predominantly Christian port section that is separate from the rest. The new dwellings are mostly four- to six-story apartment buildings. The city is extremely compact, and the transitions between the built-up parts and the open country (mostly orchards) are abrupt.

Like most, if not all, Middle Eastern cities, Tripoli has a reputation: conservative and austere. This is a stereotype, and one that Beirut people readily give expression to when the subject of Tripoli comes up. Nevertheless, a recent study has indicated that in regard to family matters and gender, a sample of Tripoli people was indeed somewhat more conservative than a comparable sample of Beirut people, the differences being matters of degree, however, and not extreme (Prothro and Diab 1974). Among the points that I emphasize in my own study of Tripoli are (1) consciousness among the inhabitants of the importance in daily life of the districts and quarters of even this rather small city (Gulick 1963)—a sense of parochialism within a provincial urban setting; (2) the felt need for protection and privacy of the family that is expressed not only in the madina but also in the newer districts as well (Gulick 1967b, Chapter 7); and (3) the presence of a personal (rather than "impersonal") style of life that is not rural in origin, together with a sense of wariness of others—"alienation" some would call it —that is not a latter-day result of the recent influences of modern industrialism. Similar observations have been made by others elsewhere in the Middle East, and they constitute some of the support for the hypothesis of the peril-and-refuge mentality.

The data on which these four city profiles are based were gathered by different scholars working independently of each other, choosing their research sites for very different reasons and certainly not according to any master plan for the best possible sampling of Middle Eastern cities for in-depth studies. Data from other cities could have been added to this set of profiles, but the presentation has been limited to these particular examples because each is based on extensive in-depth studies to which the reader may refer for more details.

Taken together, the four profiles accentuate some of the general characteristics of Middle Eastern cities and the problems of satisfactorily identifying what the relative importance is of each of those characteristics that were discussed at the beginning of the chapter. Cairo is, without any question, a classic case of the city as a place with all of those special qualities that were listed. None of the others is such a case. Beirut and Casablanca are not shrine cities at all, but they do have the (recently attained) prestige of political and economic power concentrations. Their histories are, however, very different, as illustrated by their old quarters. Casablanca's "old" madina was being built *de novo* in the early nineteenth century, not long before Beirut's truly old madina, complete with encircling wall, was demolished to make room for new European-style business and residential areas that are now the old parts of the city. Tripoli, it could be argued, lacks all of the special city qualities, and is therefore not really a city at all, but rather a large town. Certainly it lacks the traditional prestige of Aleppo and Damascus, its inland rivals, and the modernized prestige of Beirut. Nevertheless, in a small way it is attractive to the residents of its hinterland (for marketing, jobs, and schooling), and it is the locus of political and sectarian power in its region.

While the morphological growth patterns of each of the four cities are different in details, they all exhibit certain similarities: (1) retention, for the time being at least, of old residential-commercial areas that accommodate high-density living with minimum dependence on vehicular transportation for everyday needs, including traditional markets of the bazaar-souq type; (2) the growth of western-style business districts; (3) the growth of new residential areas where differentiation by various ethnic and class criteria is evident; and (4) the absence, or minimal growth, so far, of far-flung suburban settlements inhabited by commuters.

No one knows where the trends implied in these features may lead, but they will presumably involve accommodation of, and adjustments in, present-day urban life styles such as those to which we now turn.

RELIGION AND SECTARIANISM IN CITIES

Most Middle Eastern cities are predominantly Muslim in population, but all of the larger ones, as far as I know, and many of the smaller ones, have non-Muslim populations also. (Two important exceptions are Madina and Mecca, which non-Muslims may not even visit, let alone reside in.) The clustering of non-Muslims into their own quarters or districts is one of the conspicuous features of Middle Eastern cities. To put it another way, those quarters that are inhabited by sectarian minorities are, for this reason, among the more distinct and clear-cut quarters. I have already mentioned the old Jewish quarter in the madina of Fez, and there are others elsewhere. I have also mentioned the relatively new Maronite Christian, as opposed to Sunni Muslim, districts of Beirut. A few other examples should be added. The madina of Damascus has a Christian and a Jewish quarter (Thubron 1967, maps between pp. 18–19; and pp. 167–174). In the madina of Cairo there are two clearly Jewish-named quarters that had 84 percent and 73 percent non-Muslim (presumably Jewish) populations (Abu-Lughod and At-tiya 1963, pp. 62–63) in 1947. The madina of Jerusalem has a Jewish and two Christian quarters, as distinct from the Muslim one. The madina of Baghdad until fairly recently had Jewish and Chaldaean Christian quarters distinct from the Sunni Muslim ones. With the influx of Armenian Christians, followed by the departure to Israel of most of the large Jewish population, the remaining Jews and various Christians have regrouped in the new Sadoun district just south of the madina, while the Sunni Muslims have expanded into the new Azimiyah district just to the north of it. Cultural differences between these two districts were, in 1965, noticeable in such matters as women's clothing styles and whether or not alcoholic beverages were available in restaurants (Gulick 1967a). Baghdad also has a major Shia Muslim district, Kazimayn, whose center is the great double-domed shrine-tomb of the Seventh and Ninth Imams, Musa al-Kazim and his grandson, Muhammad al-Taqi. Isfahan, a predominantly Shia Muslim city, has a Jewish quarter in the madina, an Armenian Christian quarter that was originally a separate town, and (like all the other cities) a small "foreign" quarter where non-Muslim cultural patterns are particularly in evidence, as, for example, in clothing styles and types of goods sold in shops. These are only a few of the examples that could be adduced. Lest there be any misunderstanding, I repeat that while minority sectarian quarters and districts are among the more definite and distinctive sociocultural spatial clusterings in cities, they are not the only ones. There are quarters and districts among the majority, too, these being Muslims in most cities. However, in three Israeli cities (Tel Aviv, Haifa, and Jerusalem), where Jews are in the majority, they, too, are to some extent residentially clustered in terms of groups with Western, as opposed to Middle Eastern, origins combined with social-class differences (Klaff 1973, p. 180).

In most Middle Eastern cities Muslims are in the majority, and Muslim institutions are still of great importance, although they were probably of relatively greater importance prior to various changes that have taken place in Machine-Age Islamic times. Those institutions will now be considered. Muhammad established the original Muslim community (umma) in Madina, and shortly thereafter other Muslim communities were established in most of the other towns and cities throughout the Middle East. Muslim canon law (sharia) was developed in order to define and adjudicate all conceivable civil and criminal issues in ways considered consistent with the revelations of the Quran. Gradually, during the earlier part of Conservative Islamic times, administrative procedures were developed that seem to have become fairly standard everywhere. The canon law judge (qadi) decided criminal and civil cases in terms of sharia law. Where interpretations of sharia law, or modifications of it in terms of the Quran, were necessary, the qadi could turn to the ulama of his city for assistance. The ulama were an aggregation of "learned ones," learned in the Quran, in the traditions of the Prophet, and in sharia law. Somewhat differentiated from the qadi (a judge who heard cases) were the muftis (among the Sunnis) and the mujtaheds (among the Shias), who were the spokesmen (issuing legal opinions on cases), and sometimes the leaders, of the ulama in their respective cities. One of the most important responsibilities of these officers was (and still is where the new forms of government have not assumed it) the administration of the awqaf (plural of waqf). The awqaf (pronounced "evqaf" in Turkish and widely called "habous" in the Maghrib) are the properties that private donors made over to the religious establishment as acts of piety. The usufruct, in kind or money, is used for the support of the establishment, and that includes the upkeep and staffing of mosques and madrassas (Quranic schools where the ulama—and many others—receive their scriptural education), although these institutions are supported by direct donations as well.

Every large city had, and most still have, its own establishment of these officers and institutions. Indeed, the sectarian structure of Islam is a multimunicipal, city-by-city system. The cities have their sectarian (as well as political and economic) hinterlands, too, so that village people must go before a qadi in the city, and whole villages may consist of waqf property administered by the city's ulama. Every city also has, among its many mosques, a Congregational or Friday Mosque (masjed al-jami) where all members of the Muslim community, in theory, gather on the sabbath (Friday) for group prayers and a sermon delivered, very possibly, by a member of the ulama. In fact, of course, only a very small proportion of the population of a large modern city can actually gather at one time in the Friday Mosque, but the concept and the prestige of this institution remain intact.

In Conservative Islamic times the sectarian structures of Islam and important elements in the municipal authority structure of each Islamic city were the same. However, each city also had a limited structure of "secular" authorities, such as the market supervisor and a governor (often the governor of the province, too, in the chief provincial cities) or other chief magistrate who had armed force at his disposal. While all of these, in theory, operated under sharia law, conflict between the ulama and the secular powers has been a major theme in the history of many cities. For example, in Cairo, al-Azhar, the ancient university (until recent curricular changes, essentially a super-madrassa), has served as a physical as well as a spiritual refuge for the common people against the outrages of secular rulers in the city (Dodge 1974, p. 91).

The major changes that have occurred in Machine-Age Islamic times are (1) that the old "secular" governmental forms have been completely replaced by far more complex European-style bureaucracies, and (2) that sharia law (where it has not been abrogated entirely) is now restricted in application to domestic and family relations, and, correspondingly, the qadis, where they still judge cases, have jurisdiction only over domestic relations and family issues. An extensive description of the kinds of cases involved can be found in an article on the current responsibilities of ulamas (all town- and city-based) in Israel (Layish 1971). Ulamas are still active, although their authority has clearly been diminished, and waqf properties are still extensive and important even where administration of them has been taken over by secular authorities.

These changes are important and may have further consequences. In the meantime the influence and impact of Islam on city life remain important in many ways. First, there is the close association of many "traditional urbanites" with the ulama. This has already been discussed. Then there is the fact that many cities have shrines to which pilgrimages are continually being made. Mecca has the most important of them, the Bayt Allah (House of God), whose enclosure contains the Ka'aba, to which all Muslims should make one pilgrimage in their lifetime if possible. But there are many other pilgrimage centers. Among those that I have not already mentioned are the tomb of Muhammad himself at Madina. Burton's firsthand description of it is long out of date in some details but is still worth reading (Burton 1885, Chapter 16). Another is Najaf in Iraq, where Ali, the first Imam, is buried, and where the bodies of many Shias are brought over long distances for burial. In Iran there are hundreds of greater and lesser shrines, the two most important being that of Ali al-Reza, the Eighth Imam, in Mashhad, and that of Fatima the Immaculate (Ali al-Reza's sister) in Qom. Most important of all for Shias is the shrine of Imam Husayn at Karbala, in Iraq, where he was killed. His martyrdom day (the tenth day of Muharram, or Ashura) is noted for intensely emotional street processions of flagellants, and these are especially intense in Karbala itself. Non-Muslims are not welcome on these occasions and are at all times forbidden entry into the shrines, and so available firsthand descriptions are few. One of them, however, is Elizabeth Fernea's account of rites at Karbala. She did not go into the shrine but, veiled and gowned and accompanied by Muslim women, did mingle in the crowds outside (Fernea 1969, Chapter 18). In similar disguise, but on a quiet, dark night, Freya Stark visited the tomb chamber of the two Imams at Kazimayn (Stark 1938, pp. 228–236).

Not all of these shrines are Shia. In Cairo, for example, there is the tomb of Sayyida Zaynab, sister of the martyred Husayn, that is the focal symbol of Haqqi's story, "The Saint's Lamp." And in the Maghrib, especially, there are the shrines of the many saints' brotherhoods. In the case of the Hamadsha, who have a cult of two saints, the shrines themselves are in the open country, but in the city of Meknes the brotherhood has lodges in the madina, (as well as teams of devotees in the bidonvilles) that have been described in detail by Crapanzano (1973, pp. 75–113).

In Baghdad there is the tomb-shrine of Abdul-Qadir al-Gilani (1077–1166), a Sunni saint and founder of the Qadiriyyah Brotherhood. In 1965 I was guided through it by one of the saint's descendants. An impressive complex of buildings, it is not flamboyant in the same way that the Shia Imams' shrines are. (They typically consist of a central mosque structure, containing the tomb chamber, surmounted by a huge gold dome and minarets, all embellished with exuberant displays of polychrome ceramic tilework and surrounded by a separate building several stories high. The enclosing structure of Imam Husayn's tomb in Karbala has storefronts on the outside and pilgrims' quarters inside, non-Muslims being allowed to look down into the interior open space from its roof.) Abdul-Qadir's shrine is a large but more rambling and modest structure, its parts built at different times, containing around its courtyard two or three prayer halls, a library, a Quranic school, a kitchen that serves daily free meals to the poor, and the saint's tomb chamber. The interior of this room is very similar to what has been described for various Shia Imams' tomb chambers. Crystal chandeliers (donated by the faithful) hang in profusion from the ceiling. The ceiling and walls are covered with small mirrors set at various angles and in complex designs so that the room sparkles with light. The tomb is covered with brocaded cloth and enclosed in a cage of ornamental polished-silver grillwork to which many locks have been attached by the faithful. It was not a crowded day, and so I was able to observe one pilgrim with some care. He stood close to the grillwork facing into the tomb and grasped the grillwork with both hands so tightly that his knuckles were white, and his mouth opened and closed in silent prayer or entreaty. Every few moments he would release his grasp, step backwards a couple of paces, run the palms of his hands all over his body, and then step forward grasping the grillwork again. To this man, it would seem, the baraka of the saint was a palpable though invisible substance, applicable to his body like an ointment. This was no "superstition-ridden" peasant or laborer. He was dressed in a western-style business suit, with shirt and necktie, and he had set his briefcase on the floor beside him.

In addition to shrines, which convey a special aura to those cities that have important ones, there are a number of festivals throughout the year, such as the birthdays of the Prophet and other holy figures, that involve street processions and intensified social activities, such as visiting, among the faithful. Furthermore, Ramadan, the thirty-day month of dawn-to-sunset fasting, causes noticeable alterations in the daily routine. Coffeehouses and restaurants are empty or closed during the day, and shops may be closed for longer periods than usual. In the early evening, however, there is far more commercial and social activity than usual.

Various authors have suggested that in modern Middle Eastern cities there are fewer clubs and associations, and less variety of them, than there are in Western industrial cities. This may be true.

Nevertheless, such organizations are certainly present, and those that have been observed are frequently sectarian in nature. For instance, typical of Iranian cities, especially the madinas, is the heyat. Heyats are clubs that meet in private homes. Religious instruction or inspiration is the formal purpose, but it is believed that other group interests are served as well (Spooner 1971, pp. 171–172). Heyats are also involved in the organization of festival observances, such as the processions that move through the streets carrying great banners and other symbolic objects. Brotherhood lodges, or zawiyas, serve the same functions elsewhere.

Another type of group in cities consists of voluntary associations that are also generally sectarian but have apparently been recently inspired by Western models. In some cases their activities are recreational, but child care and assistance to the needy are also important purposes. Berger notes the existence of 1,117 of these associations in Cairo alone (Berger 1970, Chapter 4), and I have discussed the Christian and Muslim ones in Tripoli, Lebanon (Gulick 1967b, pp. 61–65).

KINSHIP, GENDER, AND SEX

One of the truisms about cities is that "the family" in "the city" is smaller than "the family" in rural areas. Like all such generalizations, this one ignores the cultural heterogeneity of cities, and of rural regions, too. Another reason why it should not be accepted without supporting evidence is that "smaller" is often used in ways that confuse two very different dimensions of "family size." One of these is the number of children per married couple. Since parents and dependent children constitute the personnel of the majority of households (in cities and in villages), and since households are the domestic units typically enumerated by censuses, "household size" tends to be equated with "family size," and the largest factor in these sizes is the number of children living with their parents. Most measures of central tendency, however, are likely to mask the fact that some households include relatives other than, or in addition to, parents and their dependent children.

To calculate one average household size for an entire city or for a whole rural area, a figure that blends together and confuses fertility and structural factors, would seem to be an exercise in oversimplification. Nevertheless, it has been done, and the results have been used as the basis for discussion. Not surprisingly, when such figures from various rural and urban samples are compared, they do not seem to point clearly in any direction. My own efforts in this regard show that some village figures are higher than city ones and vice versa (Gulick 1969, pp. 132–133). If nothing more, this should at least serve as a warning against accepting the old assumptions as axioms.

Further details about individual cities reveal the possibility of differential household sizes linked to other cultural factors. For example, in a sample of households in Tripoli, Lebanon, I found the Christian average to be 5.7 persons and the Muslim average to be 6.7 persons (Gulick 1967b, p. 122). This sample was so small that it could well be disregarded, yet it is consistent with other Christian-Muslim figures, including Hacker's findings in Amman, Jordan: Christian households, 5.6 persons; Muslim households, 7 persons (Hacker 1960, p. 75).

Religious or sectarian influences on fertility (hence, to some extent, on family size) are suggested in the following figures (Yaukey 1961, p. 183) on total fertility rates of samples of Lebanese women:

> Village, uneducated
>   Muslim: 7.43
>   Christian: 8.16
> Beirut, uneducated
>   Muslim: 7.35
>   Christian: 4.14
> Beirut, educated
>   Muslim: 5.56
>   Christian: 3.44

However, it is not clear what sectarian-specific influences are at work, if indeed they can be separated from the possible influences of education. Abu-Lughod (1964, p. 243) has demonstrated correlations between relatively high education and relatively low fertility in urban Egypt, and similar findings have come from Shiraz, Iran (Paydarfar and Sarram 1970). The reasons for the correlations, however, are not at all clear. In any case the fact that highly educated people in the Middle East are largely city dwellers suggests that their presence is an important factor in low fertility (hence small nuclear family size) among some city dwellers. However, the proportion of highly educated people is small, even in cities.

Level of education is one of the criteria of social class in the Middle East, and so what has just been said about it can be extended to the figures in Table 1, which are derived from interviews

Table 1. Average Sizes of Families of Orientation per Household

City	Total N	UPPER CLASS Husbands	Wives	MIDDLE CLASS Husbands	Wives	LOWER CLASS Husbands	Wives
Amman	129	7.8	6.6	7.3	6.8	7.0	7.4
Damascus	66	4.0	4.3	6.4	6.0	4.6	7.9
Tripoli	189	5.5	5.7	6.8	7.5	6.8	6.9
Beirut	112	4.9	4.2	5.4	5.2	7.6	6.6

Source: Terry Prothro and Lutfy N. Diab, *Changing Family Patterns in the Arab East* (Beirut, Lebanon: American University of Beirut, 1974), pp. 105–106.

among Sunni Muslims in four western Fertile Crescent cities. The figures represent the average sizes of the "families of orientation" of husbands and wives married in the 1960s. ("Family of orientation" is a technical term for the nuclear family in which a person is born and raised. The data do not indicate how many of these nuclear families had constituted independent households, or had been, by contrast, parts of households more complex in structure.)

Differences between social classes in the same city, and differences between cities, are suggested by these figures, but the many variations should make one hesitant to generalize except to say that most of these figures suggest the presence of nuclear families that are very large by Western industrial city standards.

This brings us to household-structure types other than the simple nuclear family. Among the highly educated middle-class people of the Hamra section of Ras Beirut (Khalaf and Kongstad 1973a, pp. 61–62), 78 percent of the households consist of nuclear families with occasional additional relatives, and 3 percent of the households consist of extended families, by which is presumably meant grandparents, married children and spouses, and grandchildren. A smaller sample of households of far less educated working-class people in Isfahan had 10.45 percent consisting of parents and married children with and without grandchildren (Gulick and Gulick 1974, p. 455). There are data from other cities, but frequently they are presented in ways that make meaningful comparisons very difficult Consider the information from Casablanca in Table 2.

Table 2.   Percentages of Types of Family in Casablanca

Type of family	Middle Class (percentage)	Proletariat (percentage)
Couples	7	10
Nuclear families	33	46
Large families	20	20
Grouped families	13	8
Defective families	6	14
Polygamous families	21	2

Source: André Adam, *Casablanca: Essai sur la transformation de la Société Marocaine au contact de l'Occident,* 2 vols., 2nd ed. (Paris: Editions du Centre National de la Recherche Scientifique, 1972), p. 744.

The distinction between large and grouped families is not clear, but the full extended family is included, apparently, only among the latter. The study by Gulick and Gulick in Isfahan records 66.2 percent of the households consisting of parents and unmarried children. These, plus one-person households and married couples without children, constitute the "simple households" of the sample, average size 4.38 people. The complex households

(15.68 percent of the sample) average 7.44 persons and range from a household of three (husband and wife and husband's brother) to a household of nineteen (two married brothers, their wives and children, plus the brothers' parents and ten brothers' siblings). This largest household is a full-fledged extended family, and there is one other in the sample that consists of eleven persons. Most of the complex households, however, consist of one nuclear family with one or both parents of the husband, or less commonly but not infrequently, one or both parents of the wife (Gulick and Gulick 1974, pp. 455–457). Paydarfar (1974b, p. 50) reports similar frequencies of nuclear and complex households in the Iranian city of Shiraz. Only more and sufficiently detailed studies can put these fragmentary findings into a generalizable perspective.

Linkages with, and ties to, kinsmen outside of the household (whatever its size or structure) in Middle Eastern cities appear to be numerous and frequent, according to the few studies that have been done. In Isfahan only 9 percent of the married couples studied in the Gulick sample did not have daily or regular contact with relatives outside the household (Gulick and Gulick 1974, p. 462). In a number of cases some of these relatives lived around the same courtyard though not in the same household. In Ras Beirut, 12 percent of the households had daily contacts with relatives living in the same building (mostly high-rise apartments), 44 percent outside the building but in Ras Beirut, and 43 percent in other parts of Beirut. Over a third of these people used contacts with relatives in order to find a place to live in Ras Beirut (Khalaf and Kongstad 1973a, p. 84). This is only one of the kinds of assistance among relatives that occur in urban Lebanon. Farsoun (1970) and Khalaf (1972) have dealt in detail with the many financial and mutual aid alliances that are involved. If this is true of the highly "westernized" situation in Lebanese cities, it must surely be at least as true, if not more true, of other Middle Eastern cities.

Among the many aspects of this subject that require more investigation is the extensiveness of these kin ties beyond the nuclear family or the household. The involvements of adult brothers and first cousins seem entirely clear, but there is no evidence, one way or the other, as to the concerted action of lineages that include more distant cousins. That ties with relatives on the mother's, as well as the father's, side are involved seems evident, but no specifics are available as far as I know. Beyond this we have reason to believe that Middle Eastern city dwellers are as familiar with the common ancestor metaphor as everyone else. In Iran the "unions of families" in Tehran that apparently make decisions about marriages (Vieille and Kotobi 1966, pp. 97–98) are apparently the same as the taifehs that occur both in villages and cities (Touba 1972a, pp. 19–21), and these appear to be groups with lineage structures. However, common descent is one, but apparently not the only, factor in the identification and structure of these groups.

Sex and gender differences will be discussed more fully in Chapter Seven, but their urban dimension requires discussion in itself. In cities women are more likely to encounter strangers than they are in villages or pastoral camps, and for this reason the women of urban traditional or conservative families are more carefully and thoroughly veiled and gowned in public than are women in villages and among nomads. Veiled and gowned women are still very frequent in many sections of many Middle Eastern cities. However, there is a directly contrary influence—with accompanying styles—that is also found in cities, more than it is in villages and among nomads. This is modern styles of dress, not only unveiled and ungowned but also frequently accentuating the sexuality of the wearer. These differences result in sharp, sometimes startling, contrasts, and there is no doubt that they represent conflicting values. For the time being, it is important to keep in mind that *both* are present in Middle Eastern cities, that *both* are aspects of the heterogeneity of the cities.

In villages and among nomads the women typically work outside of their houses or tents as well as inside them. Because this work is largely manual—such as gardening, caring for livestock, and hauling water—it is basically lacking in any prestige. Some observers have noted that rural women who migrate to cities may become more secluded in their homes than they were before and that they may welcome this because it suggests higher status. It may also be a consequence of the relative lack of opportunity for outside work that is interrelated with the seclusion ethos.

Some opportunities for nondomestic occupations for women are available in Middle Eastern cities, and the opportunities are expanding with the increasing number of new types of jobs and the increasing levels of women's educational attainments. However, women's participation in nondomestic activities in Middle Eastern cities is still very slight compared to what it is in Western Europe and North America. It is even slight compared to what it is in the less-industrialized Latin American countries, as has been described and analyzed at length by Nadia Youssef (1974). In six Latin American countries, for example, female participation in the nonagricultural labor force ranges from 28 percent to 34 percent, whereas in seven Middle Eastern countries it ranges from 7 percent to 17 percent (Youssef 1974, p. 27). Touba has examined census figures for employed women in Iranian cities between 1956 and 1966. There are some interesting differences among the cities. In Abadan, the new city that exists because of the oil refineries, the employment rate of women is the lowest of all (3.6 percent in both years). In Tehran, with its supposedly ultramodern liberated sectors, the rate was 8.5 percent in 1966, as compared with 9.2 percent in Isfahan, with its reputation for being provincial and conservative (Touba 1972b, p. 33). The point is that most of the employed women are in low-status manufacturing and service jobs.

Apart from studies of prostitutes in Beirut (Khalaf 1965) and Tehran (Farmanfarmaian 1970), there are no detailed studies of which I am aware that are concerned with women working outside domestic enclosures in Middle Eastern cities. However, there is one study, at least, of city women not employed outside their homes that considers them in other terms than the sex-bound wife and mother functions. This is Fox's study of women in Ankara, Turkey (1973). Fox suggests four personality types among these women that are recombinations of characteristics that are distributed along two axes: free-constrained and traditional-modern. This is an attempt to portray different combinations of attitudes and behavior. Thus, for example, one type is the "constrained modern": modern in attitudes but constrained in behavior. The descriptive material is brief, but the model is very suggestive for future research.

SOCIAL INEQUALITY

At the beginning of this chapter I pointed out that Middle Eastern cities are nodes of communication in the agricultural-animal husbandry-commercial symbiosis and that, in connection with this, people with political and economic power are concentrated in the cities. Obviously, however, only a few city dwellers are powerful people, and this introduces the matter of social inequality. Many details of cultural differentiation and social inequality have already been presented, and they will not be repeated or summarized. Rather, I will conclude this chapter by focusing on two contexts of cultural differentiation and social inequality that have received considerable attention. One of these is the delineation of social classes that includes both the traditional and the modern (originally foreign and largely Western) cultural patterns that are highly visible in Middle Eastern cities. The other is the migration of large numbers of people from elsewhere to Middle Eastern cities, which reflects social inequalities and also reminds us of cities in the context of regional ecological systems.

James Bill has developed a model of the social class structure of Iran that shows how the so-called "modern" groups are interrelated with the others. With one major modification, his model can serve rather well as a model for these phenomena in other parts of the Middle East. The major modification is that the royal family at the top of the Iranian upper class would either be absent or would have to be replaced by approximate counterparts almost everywhere else. Except for the "peasant and tribal masses" lumped together by Bill at the bottom, most members of most of the categories he delineates live in the cities.

Bill's categories (1972, p. 8), the majority of which are characteristic primarily of cities, are:

Upper Class
Shah and royal families
Tribal nobility
Native landlords
Economic elite*
Military elite
High ulama
Foreign capitalists*
Landless, rentier elite*

Middle Classes
Bureaucratic
Bourgeois
Cleric
Professional*

Working Classes
Traditional
Industrial*

The starred categories are the "modern" ones. Bill's main interest is in the members of the professional middle class, who he sees as having entered the traditional "web-system," as he calls it, but who often feel themselves in conflict with it (p. 71). Many of the things that they feel themselves in conflict with are those aspects of culture that I have mentioned as being both reactions to, and parts of, the peril-and-refuge mentality. Bill divides the professional middle class, many of whom have civil service jobs with the government, into four "ideal-types": technocrats, uprooters, maneuverers, and followers (p. 71). It is the first two that are the most concerned with, or vocal about, innovation and the changing of traditional patterns of behavior. A comparable non-Iranian example, incidentally, would be the left-wing social scientists and technicians in Tunis—members of the "national elite"—mentioned by Hopkins (1974, p. 433). It is with the professional middle class that foreign visitors to the Middle East are especially likely to interact, and those foreign visitors must recognize that these people, who are often highly educated in Western or Western-style institutions, constitute only part of the present-day urban social scene.

Bill's diagram of this model presents the middle and working classes not as "strata," with one on top of another, but at tilted angles to suggest that there are status differentiations within them and also that, as aggegates, they are not clearly arranged in a hierarchy.

Prominent among bourgeois and cleric middle-class people are the bazaaris and tujjar, whom I have discussed earlier. Though many of the professional middle class are bureaucrats, many bureaucrats are not professionals in the Western-style educated sense that is emphasized by the term. Whether "professional," "modern," or neither, bureaucrats are functionaries of bled al-makhzen, and several Middle Eastern authors have emphasized what an affliction those functionaries can be. Yusuf Idris' short story "Farahat's Republic," focuses on a sardonic and obtuse desk sergeant in a Cairo police station (Idris 1967). Esfandiary's novel *Identity Card* (1968), set in Tehran, is a nightmare of victimization by buckpassing, and the short plays by Ali Salem are allegories in the style of Kafka that deal especially harshly with the "modern" professional middle-class bureaucrats (Waterbury 1973a).

These new elements in the structure of urban social inequality are being reflected in the physical growth of Middle Eastern cities. Formerly, in the madinas, while there was spatial differentiation in terms of other cultural criteria, there was apparently little such differentiation in terms of wealth and poverty. People of different social prestige lived mixed together. Of course this did not reflect any democratic theme, for the social distance between these people was maintained, despite their close proximity, by the inward-turned walled-enclosure style of house. Nevertheless, the old quarters tended to be diverse, rather than homogeneous, in terms of social class.

Recently, wealthy and/or Western-oriented people have been moving out of the madinas, where there are correspondingly greater concentrations of poor people. In the newer districts there are now sections or quarters that do attract wealthy people. In Baghdad, under the socialist-inclined regime of the country, housing projects for various groups of government-employed, professional, middle-class people are among the new residential areas, but it is too early to tell whether these are the beginning of new forms of internally homogeneous quarters (Gulick 1967a; Hakim 1973).

New directions, in terms of nonkinship groups, are being taken by members of the new classes. For instance, many of the voluntary benevolent societies, including the sectarian ones, are the creations of professional middle-class or modern-educated elite people. Among the organizational innovations are labor unions and political parties. They are primarily urban and are concerned with various aspects of social differentiation and inequality. Adam discusses them in regard to Casablanca (1972, pp. 513–584), and Khalaf discusses unions in Lebanon (1972, pp. 589–595), but they have not received very close study as systems of behavior. In addition to the studies of bazaar people that I have mentioned, one of the most notable behavioral studies of the Middle Eastern working aggregation is Berger's study of Egyptian bureaucrats, wherein the importance of personal ties—in contexts that are continuous with traditional cultural patterns—are emphasized (Berger 1957). Dubetsky's study of social relations in a Turkish factory (1972) has a similar theme with very different details.

However, compared to the industrial West, neither unions nor political parties are strong, and most of the attention that has been paid to them has been ideologically oriented. This emphasis may exaggerate the impression that the people most involved are extremely and totally "modern." Only more detailed studies of actual behavior in these organizations can bring the needed perspectives on the subject. Commenting on Hopkins' paper on the city of Tunis, Larson suggests that Tunisian institutions of this general sort, though still incipient, may in time link the individual to the national society in a way that lineage groups (now apparently declining) never did (Larson 1974, pp. 438–439). Probably there are others who would agree and would extend the idea to other Middle Eastern countries.

MIGRANTS

Hopkins writes of the "ruralization" of modern Tunis—that is, the growth of peripheral quarters that look rural and have a majority of household heads who were not born in the city (Hopkins 1974, p. 432). He uses the word in quotation marks, perhaps because he has misgivings about its connotations, as I do. The migration of people to cities, mostly (but not exclusively) from villages, and their initial establishment in their own city quarters, is a very ancient occurrence in Middle Eastern history (Hourani 1970, p. 22). This being the case, one can say that Middle Eastern cities have continually been "ruralized" throughout history and that "ruralization" has been a continuous process in the dynamics of the cultural heterogeneity of cities. One specific example that may put into perspective observations like that of Hopkins (as well as Abu-Lughod's on the rural fringe districts of Cairo) is the names of three of the small quarters in the madina of Baghdad. They are clearly tribal names (Albu Mufarraj, Albu Shabal, and Bani Said), and they are located on what was the periphery of the city up until the early part of the twentieth century. They probably represent nineteenth-century "ruralizations." More recently, farther out from these quarters, beyond the flood protection dyke that replaced the old city walls, other rural settlements have been established, most especially those of the squatters who, in the 1950s, retained intact their several tribal structures: shaykhs, guesthouses, and applications of tribal codes (Gulick 1969, p. 149). Most of these squatters were, in the early 1960s, moved to housing developments still farther out from the center of the city.

In the late 1940s Adam observed the use of tribal names in, and the retention of senses of tribal identity among, some of the inhabitants of Ben Msik, one of the very large squatter settlements of Casablanca (Adam 1949, pp. 72, 189). The general picture he presents is of great poverty and trashy surroundings but not of social disorganization or anarchy. Ramadan observances were important (p. 155), the women had adopted a new saint whose tomb was nearby (p. 156), and, as mentioned before, the crime rate was lower than in the old parts of the city. The birth rate was quite low, too (pp. 119–120), and there were even some women shop-keepers, which is very unusual in Middle Eastern cities.

Some people settled in Ben Msik who had lived in other parts of Casablanca previously, their reasons being that rents were lower or that they could build their own houses or an additional one that they could rent to others (Adam 1949, p. 110). This sort of entrepreneurial activity has also been observed in squatter settlements in Latin America. Evidence of adapting successfully to the urban situation is accompanied by evidence of continued contacts with villages.

Over half of the people Adam studied in Ben Msik maintained ties with the villages from which they had migrated, and most of those who maintained village ties also continued to own property there (Adam 1949, pp. 110–111). Among squatters in Istanbul the supportive functions of the village-of-origin group have also been documented and analyzed (Suzuki 1964).

This same combination of characteristics has been noted by Levine among residents in squatter settlements (gecekondu) in Ankara, Turkey (Levine 1973, p. 356). Levine carries his analysis further, however, to suggest that migrants who maintain village ties and do *not* live in the squatter settlements, but rather live elsewhere in the city, promote their adaptation to city life rather than inhibiting it. The people in question were a sample of apartment-house janitors who were physically isolated from fellow villagers in the city (unlike the squatters who are often clustered by village of origin) and therfore were assumed to be particularly vulnerable to disorientation due to loss of primary contacts. This assumption is shown by Levine's study to be false.

The point is that these and other studies of migrants to Middle Eastern cities do not bear out the widespread image of vast hordes of desperate, rootless squatters surrounding the cities, or of less-visible but equally desperate migrants living in the older quarters. This is not to deny that there are personal problems of adjustment or massive problems of bad sanitation. There are such problems, but what is challenged by the literature is the notion of disoriented and dangerous people who in every case were driven to the city as a last resort. Indeed, Harrison, in his study of migrants in Tripoli, Libya, specifically mentions the attractions of city life *over and beyond* the greater job opportunities there (Harrison 1966, pp. 404–405). Many of these migrants, as usual, live in bidonville clusters according to region of origin, and migrants from one village tend to attract more migrants from the same village.

The rapidity and large scale of twentieth-century migration to cities may be unprecedented, but the phenomenon itself is not. The squatter settlements are the most striking display of the rapid and large-scale migration, but there are many migrants who are absorbed into older housing, such as people like the janitors in Ankara studied by Levine.

There have been other studies of migrants to cities who do not live in squatter settlements. One is Abu-Lughod's in Cairo, first published in 1961. She found evidence indicating that migrants from the Delta tend to settle in the northern parts of the city, while those from Upper Egypt settle in the southern parts, nearness to the appropriate bus terminals being an important deciding factor. Moving in with relatives, or settling near them, is a common practice, sometimes resulting in village enclaves. The mutual aid societies of the northern migrants are located in family residential areas, possibly because the Delta people tend to move to the city in family groups. The mutual aid societies of the Upper Egyptian migrants are generally located in rented office space in commercial areas, possibly connected with the fact that single males—rather than families—are much more frequent among them. There are other adaptational—subcultural—differences between these two aggregates of migrants (Abu-Lughod, 1970, pp. 670-671). Petersen (1971) has pointed out that Abu-Lughod's main points are really hypotheses requiring test, rather than conclusions that can be generalized, and she has presented a partial test of them using a sample of migrants in Cairo, who were not the same people on which Abu-Lughod's conclusions were based. Petersen confirms the importance of relatives in helping the migrants (p. 571), but she raises cautions about the frequency of village enclaves (p. 567) and the importance of assistance societies (p. 571).

It seems evident that migration to cities, though involving large numbers of people and assuming "mass" proportions under some circumstances, consists of many different behavioral patterns and situations that should discourage facile generalizations. For example, while kinsmen are obviously important in the migrants' making adjustments, they are not the only agents of adjustment, as a study of a political power broker among Shia migrants to Beirut shows (Early 1973) and as another study among Shia migrants to Beirut shows in regard to their own political behavior (Khuri 1972). The latter study was done in two new districts of Beirut that are outgrowths from an annexed village. Khuri's main point is that rather than perpetuating the kin-dominated alliances and feuds of village life, these Shia migrants are becoming involved in more intense and obvious *sectarian* affiliations. As to the matter of village enclaves, one clue to the variations that have been reported is suggested by another study by Khuri in Beirut (1967): Working-class migrants may tend to cluster together more than middle-class migrants do. Of course, rental conditions and the availability and style of housing are very important factors in the processes of settlement that may, or may not, promote the establishment of village enclaves.

The emphasis in migration studies is on the movement of the poor "masses" from rural areas to cities. The movement, or migration, of middle- and upper-class people has been neglected. Middle- and upper-class Middle Easterners are now usually highly educated, and highly educated people far more frequently live in cities than in villages. Consequently, middle-class migrants to a particular city are likely to be moving from another city rather than from villages. In Shiraz, Iran, most of a sample of migrants studied by Paydarfar (1974a) were, in fact, from other cities, and apparently most of the urban migrants were middle-class people, judging from the sociocultural indicators (for example, high in job status, high in education, low in "fatalism") by which Paydarfar compares them with the native Shirazi subsample (p. 514). Paydarfar recognizes that the situation may be unusual. Shiraz is a cultural, intellectual, and medical center, rather than a commercial and manufacturing one, and so it may attract more professional middle-class migrants than it does less-educated people looking for nonprofessional employment. It is a little surprising, but not in the least at variance with what we know about Middle Eastern cities generally, to find that the urban migrants to Shiraz, as an aggregate, are more "modern" than the native Shirazis, as an aggregate (Paydarfar 1974a, p. 516).

Nor is it at variance with what we know about Middle Eastern cities generally to find a different type of comparison between migrants and non-migrants in a city like Alexandria, Egypt, which is very commercial and has many light industries. In Alexandria the migrants (largely from villages) appear to be somewhat less modern than the nonmigrants. In their leisure time they tend to stay at home, rather than go out; they read newspapers and go to the cinema a little less regularly (el-Saaty and Hirabayashi 1959, pp. 117–127). The differences are not very great, however, and this suggests, once more, the very important point that has been made earlier: On the whole, cultural continuities between most city dwellers and most rural people are many, normal, and usual. The processes of migrants' adaptation to living in cities are, and always have been, continuous. They can be viewed as an integral part of the heterogeneous cultural patterns of cities rather than as processes that are in some way set apart from the essentials of urban life.

City planning (or lack or insufficiency of it) is a government activity that is mentioned in a number of publications on Middle Eastern cities. It is the major theme of Shiber's book about Kuwait (1964), of Dethier's article on Morocco that is chiefly concerned with Casablanca (1973), of Waterbury's reports on Cairo (1973b), of Hakim's dissertation on Baghdad (1973), of Micaud's article on Tunis (1974), and of many other works. Of course, conscious decisions and projects to alter the layout of Middle Eastern cities are nothing new. The original "round city" of Baghdad and the maydan of Isfahan were constructed at the express commands of specific monarchs, and there are many other such examples, including some rather recent ones. Nor is planning for major mundane problems such as water supply and waste disposal wholly new. However, planning departments and ministries—like other "services" of government—are new. Entirely apart from such issues as the "politics" of low-cost housing projects, for example, there is the perhaps more anthropological issue of whether or not to take cultural patterns, such as the need for privacy, into account in large-scale plans. Some Middle Eastern architects and planners, such as Hakim, Fathy, and Shiber, are very much aware of this as an issue, but many others appear not to be. Should *new* plans be made for facilitating the retention of *old* cultural patterns?

In Europe and the United States there is widespread agreement that twentieth-century industrial cities have become highly undesirable as places in which to live. There is great controversy, to be sure, on the causes of this situation, on which undesirable features are most in need of reform, and, of course, on what reform measures should be taken.

In the Middle East the typical city of the early twentieth-century was a madina, and I have suggested that the morphology of the madina was well adapted to the prevailing ecological patterns. It was, in short, eminently livable. What has subsequently happened is that the largest cities especially have undergone great changes, many of which have been copied directly from Western models. If those Western models themselves have resulted in unlivable conditions, what will be the fate of Middle Eastern cities that seem to be set on a course of complete modernization?

The paramount questions are (1) whether the growth trends now in evidence will lead to the various "unlivable" characteristics that many observers perceive in Western industrialized cities (such as "empty" central business districts, enforced containment of poor minorities in deteriorated in-town quarters, and the manifold problems of suburbia) or (2) whether hitherto successful Middle Eastern patterns of high-density living will be adapted to the new conditions of modernization, resulting in specifically Middle Eastern forms of modern urban life.

Abou, Selim. *Le bilinguisme Arabe-Français au Liban.* Paris: Presses Universitaires de France, 1962.

Abu-Lughod, Janet. "The Emergence of Differential Fertility in Urban Egypt." *The Milbank Memorial Fund Quarterly* 43(1965): 235–253.

Abu-Lughod, Janet. "Varieties of Urban Experience: Contrast, Coexistence and Coalescence in Cairo." In *Middle Eastern Cities,* edited by Ira M. Lapidus, pp. 159–187. Berkeley: University of California Press, 1969.

Abu-Lughod, Janet. "Migrant Adjustment to City Life: The Egyptian Case." In *Readings in Arab Middle Eastern Societies and Cultures,* edited by C. W. Churchill and A. M. Lutfiyya, pp. 664–678. The Hague: Mouton & Co., 1970.

Abu-Lughod, Janet. *Cairo: 1001 Years of the City Victorious.* Princeton, N.J.: Princeton University Press, 1971.

Abu-Lughod, Janet, and Ezz el-Din Attiya. *Cairo Fact Book.* Cairo: Social Research Center, American University in Cairo, 1963.

Adam, André. *Le "Bidonville" de Ben Msik à Casablanca: Contribution à l'étude du prolétariat musulman au Maroc.* Algiers: Annales de l'Institut d'études orientales 8 (1949): 61–199.

Adam, André. *La maison et le village dans quelques tribus de l'Anti-Atlas.* Paris: Collection Hespéris; Institut des Hautes-Etudes Marocaines, 8, 1951.

Adam, André. *Casablanca: Essai sur la transformation de la société Marocaine au contact de l'Occident.* 2nd ed. Paris: Editions du Centre National de la Recherche Scientifique, 1972.

Ardalan, Nader, and Laleh Bakhtiar. *The Sense of Unity: The Sufi Tradition in Persian Architecture.* Chicago: University of Chicago Press, 1973.

Baer, Gabriel. *Studies in the Social History of Modern Egypt.* Chicago: University of Chicago Press, 1969.

Berger, Morroe. *Bureaucracy and Society in Modern Egypt: A Study of the Higher Civil Service.* Princeton, N.J.: Princeton University Press, 1957.

Berger, Morroe. *Islam in Egypt Today: Social and Political Aspects of Popular Religion.* Cambridge: at the University Press, 1970.

Bill, James Alban. *The Politics of Iran: Groups, Classes and Modernization.* Columbus, Ohio: Merrill, 1972.

Brown, L. Carl. Introduction to *From Madina to Metropolis: Heritage and Change in the Near Eastern City,* edited by L. Carl Brown, pp. 15–46. Princeton, N.J.: Darwin Press, 1973.

Burton, Richard F. *Personal Narrative of a Pilgrimage to al-Madinah and Meccah.* New York: Dover, 1964. (First published in 1855.)

142   Chehabe-ed-Dine, Said. *Géographie humaine de Beyrouth.* Beirut: Imprimerie Calfat, 1960.

Churchill, Charles W. *The City of Beirut: A Socio-Economic Survey.* Beirut: Dar El-Kitab, 1954.

Churchill, Charles W. "Fertile Crescent Cities." In *Readings in Arab Middle Eastern Societies and Cultures,* edited by C. W. Churchill and A. M. Lutfiyya, pp. 643–663. The Hague: Mouton & Co., 1970.

Clarke, John I. *The Iranian City of Shiraz.* Durham, England: University of Durham, Dept. of Geography. Research Papers Series, no. 7, 1963.

Clarke, John I., and B. D. Clark. *Kermanshah: An Iranian Provincial City.* Durham, England: University of Durham, Dept. of Geography, 1969.

Connell, John, ed. *Semnan: A Persian City and Region.* University College London Expedition to Iran, 1969.

Crapanzano, Vincent. *The Hamadsha: A Study in Moroccan Ethnopsychiatry.* Berkeley: University of California Press, 1973.

Dethier, Jean. "Evolution of Concepts of Housing, Urbanism, and Country Planning in a Developing Country: Morocco, 1900–1972." In *From Madina to Metropolis: Heritage and Change in the Near Eastern City,* edited by L. Carl Brown, pp. 197–243. Princeton, N.J.: Darwin Press, 1973.

Dodge, Bayard. *Al-Azhar: A Millennium of Muslim Learning.* Washington, D.C.: Middle East Institute, 1974.

Dubetsky, Allen. "Kinship, Primordial Ties and Factory Organization in Turkey: An Anthropological View." Paper presented at Annual Meeting of Middle East Studies Association, Binghamton, N.Y., November 2–4, 1972.

Early, Evelyn A. "The Emergence of an Urban Za'im: A Social Analysis." Paper presented at Annual Meeting of Middle East Studies Association, Milwaukee, Wisc., Nov. 8–10, 1973.

Eickelman, Dale F. "Is There an Islamic City? The Making of a Quarter in a Moroccan Town." *International Journal of Middle Eastern Studies.* 5, no. 3(1974): 274–294.

English, Paul W. *City and Village in Iran: Settlement and Economy in the Kirman Basin.* Madison: University of Wisconsin Press, 1966.

English, Paul W. "The Traditional City of Herat, Afghanistan." In *From Madina to Metropolis: Heritage and Change in the Near Eastern City,* edited by L. Carl Brown, pp. 73–89. Princeton, N.J.: Darwin Press, 1973.

Esfandiary, F. M. *Identity Card.* New York: Grove Press, 1968.

Farmanfarmaian, Settareh. *Piramun-e Ruspigari dar Shahr-e Tehran. (The Prostitution Area in the City of Tehran.)* Tehran: Tehran School of Social Work, 1970.

City, edited by L. Carl Brown, pp. 51–72. Princeton, N.J.: Darwin Press, 1973.

Larson, Barbara K. "Discussion of Hopkins's Traditional Tunis." In *City and Peasant: A Study in Sociocultural Dynamics*, edited by Anthony La Ruffa, Ruth S. Freed, Lucie Wood Saunders, Edward C. Hansen, and Sula Benet, pp. 437–440. New York: Annals of the New York Academy of Sciences, vol. 220, article 6, 1974.

Lassner, J. "The Caliph's Personal Domain: the City Plan of Baghdad Re-Examined." In *The Islamic City: A Colloquium*, edited by A. H. Hourani and S. M. Stern, pp. 103–118. Oxford: Bruno Cassirer & University of Pennsylvania Press, 1970.

Layish, Aharon. "Qadis and Shari'a in Israel." In *The 'Ulama in Modern History*, edited by Gabriel Baer. Jerusalem: Annual of the Israel Oriental Society, 1971.

Le Tourneau, Roger. *Fès avant le Protectorat*. Casablanca: Société Marocaine de Librairie et d'Edition, 1949.

Levine, Ned. "Old Culture–New Culture: A Study of Migrants in Ankara, Turkey." *Social Forces* 51(1973): 255–268.

Lézine, Alexandre. *Deux Villes d'Ifriqiyya: Sousse, Tunis*. Paris: Librairie Orientaliste Paul Geuthner, 1971.

Mahfouz, Naguib. *Midaq Alley, Cairo*. Beirut: Khayats, 1966.

Micaud, Ellen C. "Belated Urban Planning in Tunis: Problems and Prospects." *Human Organization* 33(1974): 123–137.

Miner, Horace M. "Traditional Mobility among the Weavers of Fez." *Proceedings of the American Philosophical Society* 117(1973): 17–36.

Patch, Richard W. "La Parada: Lima's Market." In *City and Nation in the Developing World*. New York: American Universities Field Staff Readings, vol. 2, pp. 177–223, 1968.

Paydarfar, Ali A. "Differential Life-Styles between Migrants and Nonmigrants: A Case Study of the City of Shiraz, Iran." *Demography* 11(1974,a): 509–520.

Paydarfar, Ali A. *Social Change in a Southern Province of Iran*. Chapel Hill: Institute for Research in Social Science, University of North Carolina, 1974(b).

Paydarfar, Ali A., and Mahmoud Sarram. "Differential Fertility and Socioeconomic Status of Shirazi Women: A Pilot Study." *Journal of Marriage and the Family*, November 1970, pp. 692–699.

Petersen, Karen Kay. "Villagers in Cairo: Hypotheses versus Data." *The American Journal of Sociology* 77(1971): 560–573.

Planhol, Xavier de. "Geography of Settlement." In *Cambridge History of Iran*, vol. 1, edited by W. B. Fisher, pp. 409–467. Cambridge: at the University Press, 1968.

Prothro, E. Terry and Lutfy N. Diab. *Changing Family Patterns in the Arab East.* Beirut: American University of Beirut, 1974.

Rosen, Lawrence. "Muslim-Jewish Relations in a Moroccan City." *International Journal of Middle Eastern Studies* 3(1972): 435–449.

Rotblat, Howard J. *Stability and Change in an Iranian Provincial Bazaar.* Ph.D. dissertation, University of Chicago, 1972.

El-Saaty, Hassan, and Gordon K. Hirabayashi. *Industrialization in Alexandria: Some Ecological and Social Aspects.* Cairo: Social Research Center, American University in Cairo, 1959.

Sebag, Paul. *La Hara de Tunis: L'evolution d'un ghetto nord-africain.* Paris: Presses Universitaires de France, 1959.

Sharon, Arieh. *Planning Jerusalem: The Old City and Its Environs.* Jerusalem: Weidenfeld & Nicolson, 1973.

Shiber, Saba G. "Planning Needs and Obstacles." In *The New Metropolis in the Arab World,* edited by Morroe Berger, pp. 166–188. New Delhi: Allied Publishers, 1963.

Shiber, Saba G. *The Kuwait Urbanization.* Kuwait: Ministry of Guidance and Information, 1964.

Sjoberg, Gideon. *The Preindustrial City: Past and Present.* New York: Free Press, 1960.

Spooner, Brian. "Religion and Society Today: An Anthropological Perspective." In *Iran Faces the Seventies,* edited by Ihsan Yar-Shater, pp. 166–188. New York: Praeger, 1971.

Spooner, Brian, and Philip C. Salzman. "Kirman and the Middle East: Paul Ward English's City and Village in Iran: Settlement and Economy in the Kirman Basin." *Iran: Journal of the British Institute of Persian Studies* 7(1969): 107–113.

Stark, Freya. *Baghdad Sketches.* New York: Dutton, 1938.

Stern, S. M. "The Constitution of the Islamic City." In *The Islamic City: A Colloquium,* edited by A. H. Hourani and S. M. Stern, pp. 25–50. Oxford: Bruno Cassirer & University of Pennsylvania Press, 1970.

Susa, Ahmed. *Atlus Baghdad.* Baghdad: Surveys Press, 1952.

Suzuki, P. "Encounters with Istanbul: Urban Peasants and Rural Peasants." *International Journal of Comparative Sociology* 5(1964): 208–216.

Thaiss, Gustav E. "The Bazaar as a Case Study of Religion and Social Change." In *Iran Faces the Seventies,* edited by Ihsan Yar-Shater, pp. 189–216. New York: Praeger, 1971.

Thaiss, Gustav E. *Religious Symbolism and Social Change: The Drama of Husain.* Ph.D. dissertation, Washington University, 1973.

Thoumin, Richard. "Deux Quartiers de Damas." *Bulletin d'Etudes Orientales* (Damascus) 1(1931): 99–135.

Thubron, Colin. *Mirror to Damascus*. London: Heinemann, 1967.

Touba, Jacquiline Rudolph. *Marriage and the Family in Iran*. Tehran: University of Tehran, Institute for Social Studies and Research, 1972(a).

Touba, Jacquiline Rudolph. "The Relationship between Urbanization and the Changing Status of Women in Iran, 1956–1966." *Iranian Studies* 5(1972,b): 25–36.

Vieille, Paul, and Morteza Kotobi. "Familles et unions de familles en Iran." *Cahiers Internationaux de Sociologie* 41(1966): 93–104.

Waterbury, John. *North for the Trade: The Life and Times of a Berber Merchant*. Berkeley: University of California Press, 1972.

Waterbury, John. "The Phantoms of New Egypt." American Universities Field Staff: Field Reports, Northeast Africa Series, vol. 18, no. 1, 1973(a).

Waterbury, John. "Cairo: Third World Metropolis." American Universities Field Staff: Field Reports, Northeast Africa Series, vol. 18, nos. 5, 7, & 8, 1973(b).

Weulersse, Jacques. "Antioche: Essai de géographie urbaine." *Bulletin d'Etudes Orientales* 4(1934): 27–79.

Yaukey, David. *Fertility Differences in a Modernizing Country: A Survey of Lebanese Couples*. Princeton, N.J.: Princeton University Press, 1961.

Youssef, Nadia Haggag. *Women and Work in Developing Societies*. Berkeley: University of California, Population Monograph Series, no. 15, 1974.

ANNOTATED BIBLIOGRAPHY

The following general books, all of which have been cited in previous chapters, have sections or chapters on the town or city, as indicated.

REFERENCES

Baer, Gabriel. *Population and Society in the Arab East* (1964). Chapter 4, "Ecological Structure"; Part C, "The City," pp. 177–203.

Berger, Morroe. *The Arab World Today* (1962). Chapter 3, "Patterns of Living: The Desert, Village and Urban Communities," pp. 59–116.

Coon, Carleton S. *Caravan: The Story of the Middle East* (1958). Chapter 14, "Town and City," pp. 226–259.

Patai, Raphael. *Society, Culture, and Change in the Middle East* (1971). Chapter 10," The Middle Eastern Town," pp. 303–321.

Planhol, Xavier de. *The World of Islam* (1959). Chapter 1, "The Geographical Mark of Islam: Islam and the City," pp. 1–41.

Van Nieuwenhuijze, C.A.O. *Sociology of the Middle East: a Stocktaking and Interpretation* (1971). Chapter 11, "Units of Common Living; the City," pp. 435–454.

The following anthologies on Middle Eastern cities have been cited in this chapter, and each requires some comment.

REFERENCES

Berger, Morroe, ed. *The New Metropolis in the Arab World*. New Delhi: Allied Publishers, 1963.

The chapters, by different authors, were originally presented at a conference in Cairo in December 1960 that was sponsored by the Egyptian Society of Engineers and the Congress for Cultural Freedom. There is a chapter on each of these cities: Cairo, Baghdad, Damascus, Aleppo, Beirut, Greater Khartoum, and Amman. The emphasis is on growth and its many difficult consequences, viewed largely in statistical terms or on the basis of general observations. There are also some papers on more general topics, including those by Shiber and Fathy, that show some concern about Middle Eastern values and life styles and how they can be accommodated in modern cities.

Brown, L. Carl, ed. *From Madina to Metropolis: Heritage and Change in the Near Eastern City*. Princeton, N.J.: Darwin Press, 1973.

An outgrowth of a conference at Princeton University, this book is magnificently illustrated with 111 photographs and 25 maps, graphs, and drawings in the text. The authors of the chapters include architects, demographers, urban planners, art historians, sociologists, and others. For a quick grasp of the vast subject that is conveyed well by the title, this book is probably the best source at the present time.

Hourani, A. H., and S. M. Stern, eds. *The Islamic City: A Colloquium*. Oxford: Bruno Cassirer & University of Pennsylvania Press, 1970.

Based on a 1965 conference at Oxford University on Islamic urban history, this book does not contribute directly to an understanding of present-day Middle Eastern cities. However, several of its chapters are valuable indirectly by challenging assumptions about madinas in the past and therefore contributing to understanding more clearly the characteristics of madinas that are now under great pressures of change. Another important point that is brought out in various chapters is that in previous eras, Middle Eastern cities were continually subject to change, just as they are now.

Lapidus, Ira M., ed. *Middle Eastern Cities: Ancient, Islamic, and Contemporary Middle Eastern Urbanism; A Symposium*. Berkeley: University of California Press, 1969.

The various chapters provide a conceptual bridging between ancient and modern, and between urban and rural, that has something in common with Brown's *From Madina to Metropolis*. Most of the authors, however, are different.

For a quick plunge into the modern heterogeneity of Cairo, for subjective but sensitive reactions, Naguib Mahfouz's novel, *Midaq Alley, Cairo* (1966) and Vivian Gornick's *In Search of Ali Mahmoud* (1973) are recommended. Mahfouz is generally regarded as the foremost senior modern-fiction writer of Egypt, and *Midaq Alley* is the only one of his novels about "traditional urbanites" that has been translated into English. Gornick's book, by contrast, is an empathetic American Jewish woman's account of her encounters with various sorts of "modern" urbanites in Cairo in the early 1970s.

There are some books and monographs, cited in the list of references but not in the text, that provide a wealth of detail on the madinas of several cities. Brown (1973, p. 29) has a sketch map of the madina of Tunis, with the modern city immediately adjacent, that epitomizes the sharp differences between the two, and Lézine's discussion is especially good in regard to small details on the dead-end alleys and the private, in-turned house plans (Lézine 1971, p. 131). An anthropologist, Nicholas Hopkins, has recently discussed the culture of the madina of Tunis as it was in the nineteenth century. He emphasizes its relative homogeneity, the traditional bourgeois class known as the *beldi*, and the patron saint's shrine (Hopkins 1974, p. 428). The Jewish quarter of Tunis is the subject of a special study (Sebag 1959).

Several studies in urban geography are important among those discussions of madinas that describe the existing reality either in spite of, or in conjunction with, recent changes. Among these are Thoumin's study of two quarters of Damascus (Thoumin 1931), and Weulersse's of Antakya (Antioch) in the Hatay province of Turkey (Weulersse 1934). Also valuable are three studies of Iranian cities: Shiraz (Clarke 1963), Kermanshah (Clarke and Clark 1969), and Semnan (Connell *et al.* 1969). In each of these the madina is discussed—usually with emphasis on the bazaar and the types of shops still located in it—in relation to the rest of the city and its ecological characteristics.

In sharp contrast to the studies of madinas are a few studies that concentrate wholly on new sections of cities. Several works on squatter settlements have been mentioned in the text. Here, special comment on Fuad Khuri's *From Village to Suburb* (1975) is in order. This is a major contribution to Middle Eastern social anthropology. It begins with an incisive critical review of the literature. Then it presents the data that Khuri and associates gathered in Chiyah and Ghobeire, which are two adjacent suburbs of Beirut. These suburbs grew out of the village of Chiyah, largely by the migration of Maronite and Shia villagers to them. Khuri stresses their relative independence from Beirut despite their proximity to it. They are not "bedroom" suburbs; the great majority of their wage-earners work in them.

Khuri's data were gathered by two methods: a general survey in 1967–1969 and intensive qualitative studies in 1968–1972. They are remarkably rich and detailed and cannot be adequately summarized here. Khuri is interested in showing how class, kin-group, and sectarian values and behavior, brought from village settings, are reformulated in this suburban setting that he differentiates from the in-town sections of urban Beirut. Given particular attention are occupations, family and household life, and political and sectarian leadership, especially as they are intermeshed with manipulations of the genealogical metaphor of social relations.

This is not another "urban village" study, but a far more informative and sophisticated analysis of migrant-and-native adaptations than most of those to which we have become accustomed. I think it may become a milestone in Middle Eastern community studies.

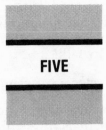

FIVE

CULTURAL AGGREGATES AND INDIVIDUAL IDENTITIES

The Middle East has been described as a conglomerate of nine cultural-ecological subregions in each of which the desert-oasis-commercial symbiosis makes life possible for pastoralists, villagers, townsmen, and city folk. A hypothesis has been advanced to the effect that during the long history of these ecological patterns in the Middle East a pervasive ethos, or mentality, of peril-and-refuge has evolved. This seems to be expressed in various of the characteristics of the major settings of daily life (pastoral camps, villages, towns, and cities), each of which has been discussed at length. In the chapters to follow some of the important concerns of everyday life will be discussed. All of them have already been mentioned, but in the context of larger territorial, communal, or mental settings. The focus in the remaining chapters will be on these concerns more from the perspective of the individual.

In this chapter we must consider three broad aggregates of Middle Eastern culture—religion, language, and nationality. All three have already been mentioned in various connections, but we have not considered the cultural correlates of these aggregates that may affect individuals in significantly different ways.

Virtually every Middle Eastern person has a religious and a linguistic identity. That is certain. Most Middle Eastern persons have a national identity, too, but since most of the Middle Eastern states are new as functioning political entities, this type of identity is perhaps more ambiguous than the other two are. Enthusiastic patriots would probably disagree with this, at least in regard to their own nations, but the alienation from their national governments that many Middle Easterners feel must surely dilute their sense of national identity. It has certainly done so in the past, though the situation may be changing now in some cases. Furthermore, religious and linguistic identities often compete with nationalistic ones, thus further diluting them.

But beyond the matter of identities, what effects may these three aggregates have on individuals, regardless of the cultural-ecological region they may live in or whether they are pastoralists, villagers, townsmen, or city folk?

AGGREGATES AND SUBREGIONS

First, let us review the cultural-ecological subregions and how languages, religions, and nations are distributed among areas:

The Fertile Crescent
  Languages: Arabic (majority), Armenian, Hebrew, Kurdish, Persian, and Turkish.
  Religions: Christianity (various sects), Sunni Islam, Shia Islam (various sects), Judaism.
  Nations: Iraq, Israel, Jordan, Lebanon, and Syria; small portions of Iran and Turkey.
Anatolia
  Languages: Turkish.
  Religions: Sunni Islam.
  Nations: Turkey (western half).
The Kurd-Azeri Mountains
  Languages: Turkish (majority), Armenian, Kurdish, Persian.
  Religions: Shia Islam, Sunni Islam, Christianity (various sects).
  Nations: portions of Iran, Iraq, and Turkey.
The Alborz-Zagros Mountains and Plateau
  Languages: Persian (majority), Turkish, Armenian, Arabic, Baluchi.
  Religions: Shia Islam, (small minorities: Sunni Islam, Judaism, Christianity).
  Nations: most of Iran.
The Hindu Kush-Helmand System
  Languages: Indo-Iranian (various languages including Persian and Pashto), Turkic (various languages).
  Religions: Shia Islam, Sunni Islam.
  Nations: Afghanistan.
The Arabian Peninsula
  Languages: Arabic.
  Religions: Sunni Islam, (in Yemen: Jews, Zaydi Shias).
  Nations: Bahrain, Kuwait, Oman, Qatar, Saudi Arabia, South Yemen, United Arab Emirates, Yemen.
The Nile
  Languages: Arabic.
  Religions: Sunni Islam, Coptic Christianity, Judaism.
  Nations: portions of Egypt and Sudan.
The Sahara
  Languages: Arabic, Berber.

Religions: Sunni Islam.
Nations: Libya; portions of Morocco, Algeria, Tunisia, Egypt, Sudan, Senegal, Mali, Mauritania, Niger, and Chad,

The Maghrib
Languages: Arabic, Berber.
Religions: Sunni Islam, Judaism.
Nations: portions of Morocco, Algeria, and Tunisia.

AGGREGATES AND IDENTITIES

It should be clear that the major aggregate identities do not neatly coincide but rather crosscut or overlap with one another. Yet most individuals have all three identities, and the result is many different permutations of identity affecting individuals. Consider religion. Being a Sunni Muslim is a keenly felt identity, differentiated not only from non-Muslims but also from Shia Muslims. Sunnis have much in common, yet they are also divided. There are, for example, Moroccan and Iraqi Sunnis who, typically, can barely understand each other's dialects of Arabic; there are Turkish and Arab Sunnis whose disdain for each other is famous; and so forth. The individual must try to act in accord with priorities made advisible by the particular circumstances in which he finds himself.

As an example of nationality, let us consider Anatolia, where Turkish nationality, Turkish language, and Sunni Islam apparently coincide closely. However, the Turkish nation also includes portions of the Fertile Crescent and the Kurd-Azeri subregions, and these inclusions reveal Turkish nationality to be far more heterogeneous than it may appear to be when one considers Anatolia alone. And the linguistic and religious homogeneity of Anatolia is not of long standing. It is the result of the expulsion of a large number of Greek-speaking Christians in the early 1920s, an episode that contributed to the bitterness of the troubles between the Greek and Turkish Cypriots.

This brings up the matter of grievances, which is the predictable concomitant of these aggregate identities in specific, local, or regional instances. Repeatedly, aggregate identity carries with it traditions of grievance. The following examples illustrate the various permutations involved:

1. Arabic-speaking versus Berber-speaking Sunni Muslims in the Maghrib
2. Arabic-speaking Christians versus Arabic-speaking Muslims in Lebanon
3. Turkish-speaking Shia Muslims versus Persian-speaking Shia Muslims in Iran

4. Kurdish-speaking Sunni Muslims versus Arabic-speaking Sunni Muslims in Iraq
5. Arabic-speaking Sunni Muslims versus Arabic-speaking Shia Muslims in Iraq

Possibly the most bitter of all are the Middle Easterners who feel themselves to have a national identity but do not have, and consider themselves to have been deprived of, a homeland that is rightfully theirs. Notable among them are the Armenians, the Kurds, and the Palestinians.

The broadest linguistic aggregates are probably the least important of the three identities as foci of mobilized effort, but nevertheless they need to be given some consideration in their own right. I am referring to the three families to which almost all of the Middle Eastern languages belong. They are the Afro-Asian, the Indo-European, and the Ural-Altaic. The Afro-Asian family includes Arabic, Hebrew, and the other Semitic languages, as well as Berber and the other Hamitic languages. The territory of the Afro-Asian family includes all of the Maghrib, the Sahara, the Nile, the Fertile Crescent, and the Arabian Peninsula. Arabic predominates almost everywhere in this territory, with the important exceptions of (1) the islands of Berber speech in the Maghrib and the Sahara and (2) Israel, in which Hebrew is the national language. There are several Berber languages, and they are very different from Arabic and Hebrew, yet the prevailing opinion among linguists at present is that they all probably had a common origin. Arabic and Hebrew, on the other hand, are recognizably similar to each other (although their alphabets look very different).

The Indo-European languages include Armenian, Kurdish, Persian, Pashto, Urdu, and some others. In basic structure they are so different from the Afro-Asian languages that they are considered to be of entirely separate origin, but they have various remarkable resemblances to the Celtic, Germanic, Romance, and Slavic languages of Europe and are believed to have had remote common origins with them. Armenian is unique, whereas the other four have greater similarities among themselves. Spoken by Christians, Armenian has its own alphabet, and its speakers have not, unlike the others, who are Muslims, borrowed words extensively from Arabic. The Middle Eastern Indo-European languages predominate in eastern Turkey, Iran, Afghanistan, and Pakistan.

The Ural-Altaic language family, entirely different from the other two, was brought from Central Asia by the Turkish tribes who invaded the Middle East in the early centuries of Islam. They include Turkish proper (the national language of Turkey) and several other Turkic languages spoken by various groups living mostly in Iran.

This is an oversimplified picture of the linguistic diversity of the Middle East, and for further details readers are referred to Sebeok (1970).

When our focus shifts from language families to specific languages and their various dialects, the importance of language as a marker of identity becomes more apparent. Several different examples are in order here: (1) In the Maghrib, speakers of Arabic and Berber care nothing about the linguists' theories about the remote common origins of their languages. Their concerns are that the languages are mutually unintelligible and that they are often cues for hostilities between mountaineers and plainsmen and between the land of government and the land of dissidence. (2) That Arabic and Hebrew are quite similar (for instance, "salam" and "shalom" both mean "peace") does not in the least ease the hostilities between the Arabs and the Israelis. (3) During the centuries of the Ottoman Empire, Turkish-speaking elites were resident throughout most of the Arabic-speaking areas, and Turkish words were added to the Arabic vocabulary. With the attainment of independence, first from the Ottomans and then from European rule, in the twentieth-century concerted efforts have been made to purge Arabic of these foreign words that are symbols of a hated, alien occupation. (4) Conversely, Turkish and Persian contain many words of Arabic origin, introduced primarily in connection with Islam. With the crystallization of concepts of modern Turkish and Iranian nationalism in recent decades there have been various attempts to purge Turkish and Persian of Arabic words.

Unlike India, where English is a lingua franca that is very useful despite its association with British imperialism, the Middle East has no lingua franca. None of the native languages would be acceptable to all. English and French, and to a lesser extent German and Russian, are spoken as second or third languages by many Middle Easterners, but their primary purpose is communication with non-Middle Eastern people or about Western or international business and professional matters.

AGGREGATE IDENTITIES AND CULTURAL CORRELATES

Language and religion can and do operate separately from each other as markers of identity in alliances and conflicts. Can they also be viewed as markers of distinctive cultural characteristics? Do Turkish speakers have cultural characteristics that are distinctive from Arabic speakers, Persian speakers, or Berber speakers? Do Sunni Muslims behave differently from Shia Muslims in nonreligious aspects of life?

Although these are difficult and controversial questions, there are those who readily give very simple and definite answers to them. Such answers are usually expressed vehemently and in conclusive terms, such as "Turks are ... but Persians are just the opposite." Implied in "Turk" and "Persian" are not only the two different languages but also Turkish and Iranian nationalities and probably Sunni in contrast to Shia Islam as well. Language (or nation or religion) alone may serve as an identity marker, but as a set of behavioral patterns it cannot be considered separately from other behavioral patterns, for in no living person does it exist apart from them.

There are a number of attempts in the literature to characterize "Arabs" or "the Arab," and they all include particular uses or influences or characteristics of the Arabic language itself. Hamady, for instance, emphasizes the great verbal expressiveness of the Arabs, their love of their language, and its beauty (1960, Chapter 5). Patai devotes a chapter in his book, *The Arab Mind*, to the language. The chapter's title is "Under the Spell of Language," and the titles of three of its sections are indicative of commonly held ideas on the subject: "Rhetoricism," "Exaggeration, Overassertion, Repetition," and "Words for Actions" (Patai 1973, pp. 41–72). Al-Marayati, at the beginning of his book on Middle Eastern governments and politics, refers to "love of and talent for words" as a characteristic of Arab personality (1972, p. 62). However, language is only one aspect of these characterizations that seem to become more complex as they become longer. Al-Marayati's sketch, which is very brief, attempts to summarize the Arab personality in terms of two contradictory impulses: egotism and conformity (p. 61). Patai's book-length treatment, on the other hand, ranges very widely, bringing in pastoral-nomadic, urban, Islamic, and other components. The question remains: Would not a book on the "Turkish Mind," or the "Persian mind" involve just the same components, and what, if any, of the detailed characterizations would be substantially different?

The assertion of sweeping characterizations is itself a feature of Middle Eastern behavior. For example, Wilbur refers to the reputed differences between the Persians and the Afghans, the former reputed to be "cultivated and somewhat effete" while the latter are reputed to be "hardy" and "rougher" (Wilber 1962, p. 60). The same sort of invidious comparison is made among all of the other Middle Eastern aggregates. These are stereotypes, of course, and they are typically asserted in total disregard of the differences *within* such large aggregates as Persian or Afghan—in particular, differences in ecological adaptations and differences connected with social inequalities. The examples that I have heard used in many discussions of the subject are always anecdotal, never taking account of these internal differences—never, in other words, meeting the criteria of controlled comparison. Unless and until studies are made that do meet these criteria, any broad behavioral characterizations of these cultural aggregates of the Middle East should be viewed with great caution.

As far as I know, there is only one major published study that makes systematic comparisons among the different linguistic and national aggregates in the Middle East. This is Lerner's study (1958) of exposure to the mass media based on interviews in Egypt, Iran, Jordan, Lebanon, Syria, and Turkey. The same set of questions was asked of samples of people in these six countries (representing speakers of Arabic, Persian, and Turkish) and so to some extent the research meets the criteria of controlled comparison among these aggregates. Lerner rank orders these countries in terms of "modernization," the index of which is a composite of percentages of people living in cities, literacy and voting rates, media consumption, media production, and education. The people interviewed were, on the basis of their responses, classified as traditionals, transitionals, or moderns. Table 3 shows one example of Lerner's comparative findings.

Table 3. Personal Impotency

Country (in descending order of modernity)	Traditional (percentage)	Transitional (percentage)	Modern (percentage)
Turkey	35	33	33
Lebanon	51	35	40
Egypt	63	73	51
Syria	90	92	37
Jordan	52	57	45
Iran	63	100	72

Source: Daniel Lerner, *The Passing of Traditional Society: Modernizing the Middle East* (Glencoe, Ill.: The Free Press, 1958), p. 100. Copyright 1958 by The Free Press, a corporation. Reprinted by permission of Macmillan Publishing Co., Inc.

"Personal impotency," as used in Table 3, is the feeling of being unable to go against religion or fate in efforts to solve problems. Lerner accounts for the differences among the countries in terms of their modernity as of 1950, modernity being a combination of characteristics resulting from governmental policies and foreign influences. Nowhere, I believe, does he attribute the relative modernity of Turkey to "Turkishness" or the relative unmodernity of the Iranians to "Persianness." It is possible, of course, that a cross-religious, or cross-linquistic comparative study within each of the categories (traditional, transitional, or modern) might reveal some significant differences in terms of those cultural aggregates. That would certainly be a further step in the direction of controlled comparison, but as far as I know, it has yet to be taken in Middle Eastern research.

Does national citizenship in itself have effects on the behavior of individuals? Does citizenship in nation A have effects on its individual citizens that are substantially different from the effects that citizenship in nation B has on its citizens? As far as the Middle East is concerned, these are controversial questions because there is not likely to be much consensus on the answers.

Citizenship means, among other things, recognition of a government that has jurisdiction over a national territory. Government per se, with its power base in cities, is very old in the Middle East, and Middle Eastern individuals typically have a set of attitudes toward government that has been referred to as the land of dissidence in the mind. This is an aspect of the hypothesized peril-and-refuge theme in Middle Eastern culture, and it carries the implication that Middle Eastern people are likely to be reluctant to identify themselves with a national culture to the extent that this culture is the creation of the national government.

Though government per se is very ancient in the Middle East, the present-day nations are all very new. For example, the five states of the Fertile Crescent are all twentieth-century creations. At the beginning of this century the land of government in the Fertile Crescent consisted of several provinces of the Ottoman Empire, and most of the present boundaries derive from those of the British- and French-mandated territories into which this part of the empire was divided after World War I. The territory of Turkey itself was the core of the Ottoman Empire, but the Turkish Republic is a consciously and deliberately new and different entity. It is true that some present-day national governments, such as those of Egypt and Iran, invoke glories of the past in order to give time depth to a hoped-for sense of national identity, but these seem primarily to be latter-day invocations rather than expressions of traditional feelings that are deeply internalized among the people in general.

In some areas—generally the better-favored cultural-ecological regions—there has for a long time been *relatively* continuous centralized government. Some examples are Morocco, the Lower Nile, Anatolia, and the Iranian Plateau. But even here the continuities have involved perpetual dynastic rivalries and overthrows and have not been strongly expressed in terms of traditional national consciousness. In areas like the Arabian Peninsula, by contrast, the land of government has, during most of history, been limited to small, individual city-states in the vast desertic hinterland. The Saudi monarchy is the result not of some ancient royal tradition but of the twentieth-century tribal conquests of the Saudi lineage. The national hegemony the Saudi lineage is, of course, related to the twentieth-century discovery and production of petroleum in eastern Arabia.

To what extent have all these essentially new national entities of the Middle East changed the state of mind that we call the land of dissidence? Ideally, the question should be pursued in reference to each country or in a good sample of them. However, to do this would involve full, free, and open appraisals of each government by its citizenry, and this is generally impossible at the present time. Only the Lebanese and Israeli governments regularly allow open dissent (Landau 1972, p. 6), and these countries are so exceptional in various ways that findings on this subject from them probably could not be applied to others. It is well known that the governments of Middle Eastern countries in general are characterized by secret police, ready use of military force, systematic censorship, and limited electoral participation.

One can argue that all this is prima facie evidence of the continuation of the ancient contention between bled al-makhzen and bled al-siba. However, it is also true that there are activities of the modern national governments that affect the daily lives of individuals in other ways than the traditional exercise and evasion of power. For example, new codes concerning the legal status of women presumably will in time substantially change some of the patterns of family life that have been accepted as unchangeable. Emphasis on vocational or technical education, too, may radically alter attitudes toward manual labor. Then there is the fact that government bureaucracies have greatly expanded, which means that far more people are now working for governments than ever before. This has already affected the social-class structures of many, if not all, Middle Eastern countries, as was pointed out in Chapter Four. Will this lead to diminution of the confrontation between land of government and land of dissidence, or will it only mean that a greater proportion of the population will be co-opted by the land of government? The outcome may well be different in different countries depending on the quality of leadership, the equitability of the distribution of national resources, and the effectiveness of national services to the people.

How much difference does it make in the daily lives of people if the government is an absolutistic monarchy or a socialist republic? There is no easy answer. Saudi Arabia, an absolutistic monarchy, has the reputation of being very conservative in such matters as family law and penal codes. This, however, is not due to the monarchy as such, but to the powerful influence of the fundamentalist Wahhabi sect of Islam, which antedates the Saudi kingdom by a considerable period of time. Algeria, a socialist republic, achieved its independence from France under extremely traumatic circumstances, and Fanon's passionate account of those events asserts that among the results will be a radical transformation of the role of women in Algerian culture (Fanon 1967, pp. 64–67), hence a radical transformation of the culture as a whole. However, other observers point to a postindependence reassertion of traditional patterns in this regard precisely, though ironically, because they are native rather than European (Gordon 1968, p. 74). So far, nationhood itself seems to have made little difference, though the issue is hardly settled in either country. Another aspect of the subject has been examined in a study of the modern educational systems of three major Middle Eastern governments (Egypt, Iran, and Turkey), which the author differentiates one from another as reformist, radical, and adaptive. The author's conclusion is that in spite of the differences the results have been similar: reinforcement of ruling elites and the hindering of the "achievement of modernity" by the nonelite majorities of the countries' populations (Szyliowicz 1973, p. 448). There may well be cultural correlates, beyond simple identity, that are specific to certain nationalities as such, but, if so, their precise nature still eludes us.

The elusiveness of national cultural correlates can be illustrated in the case of Egypt. This is a particularly striking example because the ancient Pharaonic culture of Egypt was very distinctive in many important respects, and there are still strong reminders of it despite two thousand years of Hellenistic, Coptic-Christian, and Arabic-Islamic infusions. What are the essential Egyptian character, identity, and self-concept that make Egyptians distinctive from other Middle Easterners? Laila el-Hamamsy, an Egyptian anthropologist, has recently published on this subject (1975), and her conclusion narrows down to the delineation of those Egyptians known as "awlad al-balad." Literally, this means sons of the country (in the general, not the "rural," sense) or sons of the town. "Ahl al-balad," people of the country (or town), is an alternate phrasing of the same concept. The literal translations are awkward; what the term really means is native as opposed to foreign. El-Hamamsy points out that it has long been used to differentiate native Egyptians from foreigners like the Mamluks and Turks who ruled them for centuries and always kept themselves apart. Native, then, meant speaking the Egyptian dialect of Arabic, and, as foreign influences became apparent among the rulers, the retention of traditional patterns of behavior in dress, family life, and religion. In more recent times these connotations of "traditional person" have been maintained, the contrasting mode being that of the modern, Westernized sophisticates who can be so alienated from their native surroundings that they speak foreign languages better than Arabic (el-Hamamsy 1975, p. 297).

The characteristics of these baladi people include those features of traditional Middle Eastern culture that have so far been discussed as well as those that will be discussed in the ensuing chapters. El-Hamamsy does not discuss them in detail, concentrating more on the ways in which baladi people are (1) not foreign, (2) behave in non-European ways, and (3) are likely to be found among lower-middle-class and lower-class urban residents who practice the "old ways." I find it difficult to see how this characterization differentiates Egyptians from other traditionally oriented Middle Easterners. What distinctiveness is there between these Egyptian baladi people and the beldi people of Tunis, for example, who were mentioned in the Annotated Bibliography at the end of Chapter Four? Baladi and beldi are, incidentally, not two different words, but the same word pronounced in accordance with two different Arabic dialects.

El-Hamamsy recognizes that the baladi person is an idealized concept of what a "real Egyptian" is, excluding the westernized part of himself. The characteristics of this ideal type—evidently male—are that he is gay and jovial, with an acute sense of humor; he lives for the moment and is cheerfully fatalistic; he shares joys and sorrows with others and is hospitable; he is intelligent and adjusts readily to realities; he personifies *shahama*, being gallant, noble, bold, generous, and manly; and he personifies *fahlawa*, being quickly adaptable, sharp, shrewd, and sometimes polite on the surface (to cover up his real feelings); and he bluffs, sometimes to the extent that he overplays his hand (el-Hamamsy 1975, p. 300).

I do not question el-Hamamsy's assertion that this is a strongly felt characterization of real Egyptian identity. The problem is that I have heard the "real" ideal type of Iranian described in very similar terms, and I suspect that these terms are not confined to Egypt and Iran.

Distinctive cultural correlates that differentiate among Middle Eastern nationalities may well exist, or, if they have been indistinct in the past, they may now be taking new and clearer forms as the various nationalisms of the Middle East become more distinctive. However, for the present, our limited anthropological perspectives on the subject do not allow us to assume that there are very many clear-cut national differences in the patterns of behavior that will be considered in the chapters that follow.

REFERENCES

Fanon, Frantz. *A Dying Colonialism.* New York: Grove Press, 1967.

Gordon, David C. *Women of Algeria: An Essay on Change.* Cambridge, Mass.: Harvard Middle Eastern Monographs, vol. 19, 1968.

Hamady, Sania. *Temperament and Character of the Arabs.* New York: Twayne, 1960.

El-Hamamsy, Laila Shukry. "The Assertion of Egyptian Identity." In *Ethnic Identity: Cultural Continuities and Change,* edited by George DeVos and Lola Romanucci-Ross, pp. 276–306. Palo Alto, Calif.: Mayfield, 1975.

Landau, Jacob M., ed. *Man, State and Society in the Contemporary Middle East.* New York: Praeger, 1972.

162 Lerner, Daniel. *The Passing of Traditional Society: Modernizing the Middle East.* Glencoe: Free Press, 1958.

al-Marayati, Abid A., et al. *The Middle East: Its Governments and Politics.* Belmont, Calif.: Duxbury Press, 1972.

Patai, Raphael. *The Arab Mind.* New York: Scribner's, 1973.

Sebeok, Thomas, ed. *Linguistics in Southwest Asia and North Africa.* The Hague: Mouton & Co., 1970.

Szyliowicz, Joseph S. *Education and Modernization in the Middle East.* Ithaca, N.Y.: Cornell University Press, 1973.

Wilber, Donald N., et al. *Afghanistan: Its People, its Society, its Culture.* New Haven, Conn.: HRAF Press, 1962.

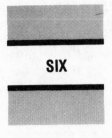

SIX

RELIGION AND SECTARIANISM

Judaism, Christianity, and Islam originated in the Middle East and evolved there, one growing from another. They differ greatly, however, in the degree to which they can now be considered native Middle Eastern religions. There are some Jews who are native to Middle Eastern culture, but they are far less numerous than the Jews in other parts of the world. Many of them have recently migrated to Israel where they confront other Jews who have brought with them non-Middle Eastern cultural patterns, including those of orthodox European Judaism and radical Jewish secularism. It is too early to say what new forms of Israeli-Middle Eastern Judaism may evolve from this situation.

There are native Middle Eastern Christians, too. I referred to several of their sects in the historical sections of Chapter One. However, it is well known that the great expansion and diversification of Christianity took place outside of the Middle East. In a number of cases the native Middle Eastern sects are now affiliated, in one way or another, with larger non-Middle Eastern Christian sects.

Islam, by contrast, is the predominant Middle Eastern religion. The vast majority of Middle Easterners are Muslims, and though there are many millions of Muslims in sub-Saharan Africa and Indonesia, the main features of Islam evolved in the Middle East. They were not imported from elsewhere.

For these reasons, this chapter will be devoted primarily to Islam. There is another reason, too. Caricatures of Islamic religious behavior are among the most vivid of Westerners' misconceptions of the Middle East. This chapter is intended to redress the balance by discussing details of the more familiar and the less familiar aspects of Islam as parts of a complex, vital structure of normal, everyday Middle Eastern life.

A recent description of the social and political difficulties that face archaeologists who want to dig in Jerusalem ends with the plaintive suggestion that Judaism, Christianity, and Islam, rather than being considered three different religions, ought to be regarded by their believers as being three denominations of the same religion. Each claims to be the true religion of the God of Abraham. However, each rejects the claims of the other two (Libassi 1974, p. 12) This is a religious debate, a disagreement about the essentials of human beings' relationships with God. The difficulties facing the archeologists, however, are not religious in this sense. Rather, they are connected with disputes as to who has jurisdictional priorities in Jerusalem, specifically in the Haram al-Sharif, where the Western Wall and the mosques of al-Aqsa and the Dome of the Rock are supremely sacred places to Jews and Muslims respectively. Though certainly anchored in religion, this dispute is social, political, and military. If it is ever resolved, the means will not be theological or religious but social, political, or military. This is, in other words, a *sectarian* dispute, as distinct from a religious one. As defined here, a religion is a system of beliefs and symbolic acts concerned with the superhuman and with human beings' beliefs about their relationships with the superhuman. A sect, on the other hand, is a group of people that has a religious identity but also has its own internal social structure and its own external political relationships with other sects and groups. Sectarian behavior, therefore, though it may be given religious identity or justification, is social behavior—as, for example, behavior related to internal and external power struggles—and is quite distinct from symbolic behavior concerning the superhuman.

This distinction between religious and sectarian is not the same as the commonly made distinction between sacred and secular and between sacred and profane. These are polar-opposite concepts that force our thinking about behavior into one category or the other—often with the lurking implication that sacred is "good" and secular, or profane, is "bad." The distinction between religion and sect is also quite different from a commonly used classification in which a "religion" (for example, Christianity or Islam) is divided into "denominations," and these are either subdivided into "sects" or are seen as being opposed by dissident sects that are heretical and belong to none of the denominations. In this usage "sect" is a belittling or contemptuous word. My usage of it is, however, neither judgmental nor polarized. Rather, it represents a spectrum of behavior in which the nonreligious concerns of group dynamics are, in a great variety of ways, combined or connected with religious concerns.

Sectarianism, as I have been discussing it, has been extremely important in Middle Eastern history, and it is a core element in the peril-and-refuge theme of Middle Eastern life today. In saying this I am *not* saying that religion "permeates" all aspects of life among Middle Eastern peoples, though this is one of those sweeping generalizations that occurs very frequently in the literature, often with the intention of asserting that each act of daily life is regarded by the actors as being some sort of sacrament. More precise and better informed observations do not support this view, which is often accompanied by the idea that Muslims are religious fanatics. While there certainly are Middle Eastern examples of religious fanaticism, it cannot be said to be ordinary behavior. Sectarianism, too, is not immune from fanaticism, particularly fanatic leadership. Sectarianism as a feature of everyday life is, however, quite another matter from fanaticism, and it is here that its importance primarily lies.

The Judaic and Muslim sects are very distinct from each other, yet they have in common some of the same religious rituals. For example, circumcision is practiced by both, and both Muslims and Jews believe that it establishes the boy's sectarian membership. Roman Catholicism and Shia Islam are also very distinct sects, and they, too, share a complex of religious beliefs that seem very similar, to some outsiders at any rate, even though they may not be so regarded by their respective believers. I refer to the faith in a sacred mother whose sacred son's martyrdom assures the salvation of humankind. This theme is far older than either Christianity or Islam, yet it is shared by sects that are so divergent that no Christian is allowed anywhere near Madina, where Fatima is buried, nor within the shrine enclosure of Husayn at Karbala. Nevertheless, in little shops around the outer walls of that enclosure, where prayer "stones" of pressed Karbala earth are sold to pilgrims, pictures of a haloed mother with haloed infant are (or were in 1965 when I saw them) also on sale. There was nothing to distinguish this image—presumably of Fatima and Husayn—from an image of Mary and Jesus, and this is not all there is to parallels between the beliefs concerning these two holy pairs.

These religious convergences are not accidental. Each represents the same set of religious concerns, but embedded in a different mix of religious themes and espoused by different sects. Belief in the one God of Abraham is another such convergence, of course, but though it is a grand unitary religious conception in theory, it has not deterred Middle Eastern and other people from proliferating into a great variety of sects.

Christianity originated as a Judaic sect, and Jesus was opposed and killed largely for sectarian reasons. The subsequent persecutions of the early Christians by the Roman authorities were largely motivated by sectarian, rather than religious, concerns. Christianity then became a sectarian establishment itself, and it split, as the Roman Empire did, into Western (Roman) and Eastern (Byzantine) major sects. The Eastern Christian sect's authorities had to deal with a number of religious heretics (from their point of view) in the early centuries. Prominent today among the descendants of these are the Copts in Egypt, the Armenians (originally concentrated in Asia Minor), and the Maronites in Lebanon. The original religious differences had to do with such issues as Monophysitism (one "nature" of Christ as opposed to two) and Monothelism (one "will" of Christ as opposed to two). One wonders how concerned the main body of these sectarians really were with such issues, for they were diverse in other cultural ways, too. The Copts were Hamitic speakers facing Greek-speaking elites in the cities; the Armenian speakers were likewise distinctive linguistically, territorially, and politically; and the Maronites were Semitic-speaking mountaineers facing Greek-speaking central authorities in the lowland towns. It seems likely that ethnic and regional political concerns were equally as important as religious ones in the formation of these sects, and that is precisely the point of the differentiation between sect and religion.

At the time of the spread of Islam throughout most of the Middle East, in the seventh and eighth centuries A.D., the Eastern Orthodox sect was itself divided into a number of different patriarchates with regional jurisdictions, this being one of its major sectarian differences from the Roman Catholic centralization of power in the papacy. In addition, there not only were the three other Christian sects mentioned above, but there were also more, such as the Jacobites and Nestorians. Each of these had its own sectarian structure and its own system of community regulations. Moreover, there were Jewish congregations scattered throughout the area —congregations linked by cultural and religious bonds but decentralized in general social structure. In some contrast to this was the Zoroastrian establishment in Iran, the state church of the Sassanian kings. This establishment was apparently highly centralized, and its priesthood is thought to have become, by that time, so oppressive that its overthrow by the invading Muslims was welcomed by the Iranians.

How much of the rapid spread of Islam was facilitated by such sectarian considerations? There seems to be no clear answer to this question. Nor does there seem to be any answer to the question of how many conversions to Islam were desperate life-saving crisis decisions on the part of the converts. Mass conversion at swordpoint is the traditional Western image of the process, partly because there *is* an aggressive, militant element in Islam and partly, too, because it may have been difficult for Western Christians to believe that so many other Christians could be genuinely converted to Islam so rapidly. The initial Muslim conquerors established garrisons at strategic points, took over the secular governments very much as they found them (co-opting many of the functionaries in the process), exacted tribute, and levied taxes. As in all military adventures, there were massacres and much abuse of defeated people, but wholesale slaughter as the only alternative to *pro forma* mass conversion to Islam does not appear in fact to have been the standard procedure. One demonstration of this is the survival to the present time of a wide variety of Christian sects, a large number of Jewish communities, and a few small Zoroastrian communities in Iran (Fischer 1973; Loeb 1970). Altogether these non-Muslim sects constitute a very small minority in the total population of the Middle East, and they have often suffered because of their minority status. The fact of their existence as communities, however, disproves the fanatic "holy war" stereotype as applied to all Muslims.

Islam itself recognizes Jews and Christians as being, like Muslims, "People of the Book"—that is to say, people with their own prophetic scripture. Christians and Jews living in areas conquered by Muslims were technically designated *dhimmi:* non-Muslims whose relations with the Muslim ruler were theoretically governed by *dhimma*, or contract (Gibb and Bowen 1957, p. 207). While many Christians and Jews were obviously converted to Islam, the status of *dhimmi* was sometimes advantageous, and Jewish and Christian sects not only survived but at times prospered.

When the Ottomans achieved their first major conquests in the fourteenth century, they were actually outnumbered by the Orthodox and Armenian Christians in Asia Minor and the Balkans, and they established a formal sectarian system that gave the non-Muslims control over their own internal affairs. These included religious behavior, family law, and related matters. Known as the millet system (from an Arabic word connoting "religious community"), the Ottoman system was not, in principle, new. It was a logical extension of the *dhimmi* concept and had roots going back to Roman times, when subject peoples were allowed to retain their own laws provided they paid taxes and fulfilled other obligations.

The millets were formalized sects, and this formalization has unquestionably affected the sectarian structure of the present-day Middle East. Sometimes the millets were especially favored. For example, consider what happened when the beginnings of the Ottoman Empire coincided with the expulsion of Muslims and Jews from Spain and Portugal at the end of the fifteenth century. The Ottomans welcomed these Sephardic Jews, who joined the Jews already resident in lands conquered by the Ottomans, and this favorable atmosphere attracted more Jews: Ashkenazi Jews from Germany. These were added to such native Middle Eastern Jews as the Karaites, a sect that rejected rabbinical authority. The Jewish millet in the early Ottoman Empire was not a single homogeneous group but a sect of diverse subgroups (Gibb and Bowen 1957, pp.

217–219). Such subsectarian diversity continues in the modern state of Israel, where there is a small but distinctive group of Karaites in the city of Acre (Rubin 1974, p. 70).

Long before the Ottoman Empire was established, with its formalization of non-Muslim sects, Islam itself had divided into many sects, of which Sunni and Shia are the two major categories. Within the Sunni category developed numerous sufi, dervish, and saints' brotherhoods, all devoted to intense religious emotionalism. Most of these had strong internal sectarian loyalties and were in more or less open opposition to the ulamas of the cities in the various regions. Being decentralized, these ulamas themselves came to follow four different "schools" of Quranic interpretation (Hanafi, Hanbali, Maliki, and Shafi'i). In addition, there have been several fundamentalist movements in Sunni Islam whose religious purpose was to return Muslim practices to their supposedly original form. Three of these are represented by the Mzabites of Algeria, the Wahhabi movement of Arabia (both already mentioned), and the Sanusiyya of Libya, who will be discussed shortly. All three became political movements, in other words sects, as much as, if not more than, religious movements.

Sectarian divisions within the Shia category are related chiefly to disputes about who the rightful Imam was at any given time and about whether the Imams are merely bearers of baraka or are themselves emanations of the divine. The great majority of Shias believe in the legitimacy of all twelve of the Imams, beginning with Ali (died 661 A.D.) and ending with Muhammad al-Mahdi, who went into "occultation" in 873–874 A.D. The official state religion of Iran is Ithna ashari ("Twelver") Shi'ism. The Mitwalis of Lebanon and the Shias of Iraq are also "Twelvers." The Ismailis, however, are spiritual followers of Ismail (died 760 A.D.), whom they regard as the Seventh Imam. The "Twelvers" do not recognize Ismail as the Seventh Imam but recognize, instead, his brother, Musa al-Kazim. The Ismailis are an important sect in Syria, Afghanistan, and Pakistan (where their sectarian head, the Agha Khan, resides). The Zaydis are devotees of Zayd, brother of Muhammad al-Baqir who is recognized by all other Shias as the Fifth Imam. They are the major sect of Yemen. The Druze, an important sect in Lebanon, Syria, and Israel, derive their religious legitimacy from Muhammad, the son of Imam Ismail, thence through a series of "hidden Imams" whose holiness became "open" with the rise to power of the Fatimid Caliphate in Egypt (Makarem 1974, p. 116). With the decline of the Fatimids in Egypt itself, missionaries established the Druze sect among Lebanese mountaineers adjacent to the Maronites. The sense of divine emanations resident in the Imams, which is featured in Druze beliefs, reaches its extreme among the Nusayris, or Alawites, of Syria, for whom Ali is not merely the first Imam but is himself divine. The

Alawites, whose tribal structure was referred to in Chapter Three, are another mountaineer sect whose founders capitalized on their followers' opposition to lowland power centers. There is some dispute as to whether the Druze and the Alawites should be considered Muslims at all.

These sects are known today as cultural communities long after the processes of their founding have really become mythical and the circumstances under which they were founded have very much changed. There is, however, a large amount of detailed historical information on the relatively recent founding and expansion of the Sanusiyya sect in Libya, a subject that has been studied by an anthropologist, E. E. Evans-Pritchard (1949). The Sanusi order was founded by Muhammad bin Ali al-Sanusi (1787–1859), an Algerian scholar and a marabout (that is, a living saint and worker of miracles). Known as the Grand Sanusi, he decided to convert the pastoral nomads of Libya to what he regarded as a pure form of original Islam. Though already considering themselves to be Muslims, these nomads were extremely lax in their observance of the so-called "Five Pillars," which will be discussed later. In this respect they were similar to most other pastoral nomads in the Middle East, at least according to the accounts of many observers. The Libyan nomads were, however, very familiar with deceased saints, marabouts, and saints' brotherhoods, and Evans-Pritchard emphasizes that the Grand Sanusi's success among them was greatly facilitated by the fact that he and his organization conformed perfectly with these established patterns. During the nineteenth century the Sanusiyya founded many lodges (zawiyas) in Libya that were placed strategically in, or on the borders between, tribal or subtribal territories.

Apart from conforming to the traditional patterns of a saint's brotherhood, the Sanusiyya provided the focus for increasing cohesion among the nomads in confrontation with the governmental authorities in the towns, where nominal Turkish rule was replaced by that of militaristic Italian invaders early in the twentieth century. Eventually defeated by the Italians, the Sanusiyya order, which originated with a religious idea, grew in strength because it became a sectarian, essentially national, movement. In 1951, after the defeat of the Italians in World War II and the recognition of the independence of Libya by the United Nations, the head of the Sanusiyya, a grandson of the founder, was elected king of Libya, but the Libyan pastoral nomads had little knowledge of, or interest in, the religious teachings of the order (Evans-Pritchard 1949, p. 5). In fact, one wonders whether sectarian concerns have not often been far more important than purely religious ones in the on-going Middle Eastern experience.

Lebanon exemplifies many of the issues of Middle Eastern religion and sectarianism. True, this nation is not typical of the

Middle East in a number of respects. It is very small, Western influences have been very strong and have had all the more impact because of the country's small size, and its population includes an unusually large proportion of non-Muslims (on the whole, a cause, rather than a result, of the Western influences). However, its population represents a wide variety of Middle Eastern religions, and its political structure is consciously and deliberately organized along sectarian lines.

The last official census of Lebanon was taken in 1932, and its sectarian enumerations were used as the basis for the proportionate representation of the sects among the elected members of parliament and the other, mostly appointed, governmental offices. The 1932 census established an official ratio of five Muslims for every six Christians in the country. No census has since been taken in Lebanon, partly out of fear of what might be the consequences of upsetting this delicate balance. The situation is complicated by the fact that Christians and Muslims are, in this matter of the ratio, aggregate populations, each consisting of several sects. Table 4 gives a somewhat more detailed idea of them.

Table 4. Estimated Population of Lebanon by Sect (1951)

Sect	Number
Western Roman Catholics ("Latins")	4,000
Roman Catholic Uniates:	
Maronites	377,000
Greek Catholics	82,000
Armenian Catholics	14,000
Syrian Catholics	6,000
Chaldeans	1,000
Total Roman Catholics	*484,000*
Eastern Orthodox	131,000
Syrian Orthodox (Jacobites)	5,000
Armenians (Gregorian)	67,000
Protestants	13,000
Total Non-Catholic Christians	*216,000*
Total Christians	*700,000*
Muslims:	
Sunnis	272,000
Shias	237,000
Druze	82,000
Total Muslims	*591,000*
Jews	6,000
Others	7,000
Grand Total	*1,304,000*

Source: Raphael Patai, *The Republic of Lebanon* (New Haven, Conn.: Human Relations Area Files, Subcontractor's monograph, 1956), p. 385.

Table 4 specifies thirteen separate sects, not counting the "Others" and the Protestants, who are actually an aggregate of several "denominations." Each of the thirteen is internally organized, and each is largely responsible for the domestic relations of its members. Even the *small* sects have their own educational establishments, for example. On the whole, this sectarian structure is directly derived from the Ottoman millet system, but it has been adapted in various ways to the republican regime of Lebanon. Since all of the sects are minorities, they must continually make and remake alliances with each other for various purposes, and these alliances sometimes cross Muslim-Christian lines. Elaborate public courtesies are exchanged by their leaders on important religious holidays, such as Easter and Eed al-Fitr (end of the Muslim month of Ramadan), but, on the whole, cross-sectarian social relations are wary. All of the sects are endogamous on principle—marriages between them are discouraged if not forbidden altogether. One result of this social distance, combined with the general norms that protect family privacy, is that the members of one sect seem to know very little about life in the others. Stereotypes abound, but there is little knowledge, and this includes little knowledge of, or interest in, each other's religions. Consequently, it is difficult to discover whether there really are important cultural differences among the sects beyond some obviously distinct ritual practices and certain aspects of marriage and family law. One thing is clear, however: Each sect is felt by its members to be a refuge in a perilous heterogeneous cultural environment (Gulick 1965, p. 181), and, in this respect, Lebanese sectarianism is a microcosm of that of the Middle East as a whole.

GREAT TRADITION AND LITTLE TRADITION

In 1954 an anthropological seminar on the village cultures of India was held at the University of Chicago, under the direction of Robert Redfield and Milton Singer. One of its accomplishments was the formulation of two important heuristic concepts: "great tradition" and "little tradition." The basic problem was how to relate the cultures of Indian villages, inhabited almost entirely by illiterate people, to the literary tradition of Indian culture as a whole. In particular, there was the problem of how to relate the "great tradition" of the Hindu scriptures, written in the archaic Sanskrit language, to the "little traditions" of Hindu belief and ritual as practiced in the villages. Each diverges from the other, yet each also influences the other. Marriott, in an article that first set forth these ideas, discusses the "parochialization" of great tradition beliefs at the village level, and the "Sanskritization" (also "universalization") of some little tradition features (Marriott 1955, pp. 197 ff.).

The great- and little-tradition concepts are helpful in the understanding of religious and sectarian behavior in the Middle East, where there is a city-based literate elite, just as in India. Instead of Sanskrit, however, the language of the great tradition is Classical Arabic, the language of the Quran and the Hadith (the "Traditions" of the Prophet). The Quran is the scriptural base for *all* Muslims, and the Hadith is accepted by most of them as the sacred supplement to the Quran. These are the foundation of the *religious* great tradition of Islam, and their recognized custodians and interpreters—the ulama—are the *sectarian* personnel of that great tradition. As we have already seen, however, there is much more to the religious and sectarian reality of Islam than this, and it is in this connection that the concept of little tradition is helpful. Figure 1 indicates the major phenomena that are to be considered.

GREAT TRADITION	LITTLE TRADITION
The "Five Pillars" RELIGION	Reverence for saints Dhikr Zar and Evil Eye prophylaxis
jinn life-crisis rituals	
SECT Ulama and specialized functionaries	Marabouts Brotherhoods

Figure 1. Great Tradition and Little Tradition.

The four cells of Figure 1 are intended to indicate different emphases of great and little tradition, religion, and sect, rather than sharp boundaries. Indeed, life-crisis rituals and jinn must be spread across two cells. However, there are those who *do* think in exclusive terms about these matters. In particular, they characteristically reject or denigrate little-tradition phenomena, dismiss them contemptuously as superstitions, and do not recognize them at all as being aspects of religion.

Shia and Sunni ulama have in common an inclination to look askance at some of the more extravagant emotional expressions of the little tradition. However, they differ significantly in their attitudes toward saints. The Sunni ulama, possibly influenced in recent times by Wahhabi fundamentalism, reject the saints and rituals concerning them. The Shia ulama, on the contrary, are the custodians of an establishment whose power is predicated on the immanent sacredness of the Twelve Imams and many other saints. As a matter of fact, an argument as to whether reverence for saints

should be included in both the great- and little-tradition cells of
the matrix in Figure 1 would go to the heart of what is perhaps the
major bone of contention between Shia and Sunni Islam.

In the remainder of this chapter I shall discuss the religious
great and little traditions of Islam first and then, reversing the
order, the sectarian little and great traditions.

THE RELIGIOUS GREAT TRADITION

In the beginning was the written word—or so it would seem to be
in the minds of many Muslims. Although the Quran was, as the
word itself denotes, recited by Muhammad, its written form has
taken on a sacred character of its own. Furthermore, the Quran
itself asserts that writing is "pre-eternal" and of divine origin
(Schimmel 1970, p. 1). This is an Arabian version. A Persian vision
of the origin of writing is similarly primordial but quite different in
details. According to Ferdowsi's *Shahnameh*, writing was revealed
early in the course of human existence to Tahmuras, son of
Hushang (the discoverer of human uses of fire). Tahmuras defeated
some demons in battle and spared their lives in return for their
giving him some useful knowledge, namely knowledge of several
alphabets (Welch 1972, p. 96).

These mythological accounts are, of course, completely different from the known history of the origins of writing that was
outlined earlier in this book. However, the fact that mythology
distorts history is not the important point. What is important is
that these particular mythologies symbolize the feeling of great
power that is inherent in writing. This symbolism is consistent
with other patterns of a culture in which knowledge of writing
—control of it—is possessed by only a few people, prominent
among whom are sectarian authorities, both of the great and the
little traditions. The Quran and the Hadiith are in an archaic form
of the Arabic language, and written in the Arabic alphabet. All the
forms are fixed, for change would threaten the validity of the
scriptures. While the Arabic alphabet has been adapted for writing
non-Arabic languages such as Turkish and Persian, and is used to
write a standard form of non-Quranic Arabic, important changes in
it have been resisted partly because they would alter the forms that
in themselves have taken on sacred significance. One of the most
compelling illustrations of that sacredness is the widely reported
little tradition practice of writing a prayer or charm for the sake of
an afflicted person, dissolving the ink in water, and having the
patient drink the water with the ink dissolved in it. Another
practice that emphasizes the power of writing per se is the writing
of prayers or wishes on small bits of paper, which are rolled into
balls of earth that are deposited in places imbued with baraka. I
have watched such objects being prepared, for a fee, by an old
woman at a shrine in Isfahan. She dropped the hope-laden missiles

into a "well" believed to be suffused with the baraka of the Twelfth Imam.

These are extensions of the power that is administered by the sectarian authorities of the great tradition. It is they who, until well into the twentieth century in some places, conducted the only schools in the Middle East, the kuttabs or maktabs. There, reading and writing were taught for the purpose of being able to read the Quran. In this tradition the major defect of the Arabic alphabet, its lack of letters for most of the Arabic vowels, was enshrined. This defect was perpetuated—even though other minor changes were made—in the adaptation of the alphabet for writing Turkish, Persian, and other languages spoken by Muslims, with the possible exception of rarely encountered writings in Kurdish (Naim 1971, p. 140).

Makal notes the strong feeling among Turkish villagers—largely illiterate—that anything worthwhile that is written must be religious, and that writing that is not religious is not to be believed (Makal 1954, p. 104). Furthermore, these villagers considered charms written in Turkish, using the Arabic alphabet, to have been effective, but they did not accept charms written in the Roman-style phonetic alphabet that was adopted by Turkey in the late 1920s (Makal 1954, p. 172).

The Five Pillars

Most important among the religious duties that are prescribed by this writing-conscious religion are the so-called Five Pillars of Islam. There are many descriptions and discussions of them in the literature, including a lively anecdotal one by Carleton Coon (1958, Chapter 7). While it is easy to state what they are, it is not at all easy to assess their importance in the everyday lives of ordinary Muslims, which is our primary concern.

The first Pillar consists of the recitation of what is called the Shahada: *La ilaha-illa-llah, wa Muhammad rasul Allah.* ("There is not god but Allah, and Muhammad is the messenger of Allah.") This is the essential credo of Islam. Muslims apparently assume that no one would say it who did not believe it, and therefore anyone who says it is presumed to be a Muslim. There is far more to being a Muslim than simply reciting the Shahada. However, it is repeated as part of many prayers and invocations and is featured in countless inscriptions, old and new, including the modern national flag of Saudi Arabia.

The word Allah is often translated as "God," capitalized, signifying the same one-and-only God of Abraham as that worshipped by Jews and Christians. However, Allah is also the Muslims' own name for this deity, although it is not to be considered a personal name like Jupiter or the names of all the other anthropomorphic classical deities. "Allah" has power of its own, is repeated in many

everyday contexts, and in written form is so commonly encountered that it is probably easily recognized by the many illiterate
faithful. Being repeated so often, however, it seems often to have
the *pro forma* quality of "God" in "goodbye" (God be with ye).

The second Pillar is prayer. There are several kinds and occasions, but the most frequent and important are the five daily
prayers. As Abd al-Ati explains (1963, pp. 34–35), each of these is
to be said within certain time periods as follows:

1. The early morning prayer (as-salatu-l-fajr), first light to
   sunrise.
2. The early afternoon prayer (as-salatu-z-zuhr), noon to the
   midpoint between noon and sunset.
3. The late afternoon prayer (as-salatu-l-'asr), midpoint between noon and sunset until sunset.
4. The early after-sunset prayer (as-salatu-l-maghrib), sunset
   until the disappearance of light.
5. The late after-sunset prayer (as-salatu-l-'isha), disappearance
   of light until first light the next morning.

Rather than requiring all Muslims to say their prayers in
unison—as seems to be enjoined by the public call to prayer (al-
adhan) that is such a familiar sound in Muslim communities—the
rules allow for considerable personal latitude in timing. In addition,
prayers can be, and are, said in any location that is not polluted by
corpses, blood, or any natural discharges of the body. Moreover, no
prayers are required during the main part of the working day
(sunrise to noon), and prayer can be delayed for an hour or two after
noon, when many people quit work for the day or retire for a long
siesta. Thus it becomes clear why the five daily prayers do not
obtrude as much as one might expect into the visible activities of
the day. Furthermore, the second and third prayers may be offered
together, as may the fourth and fifth, thus reducing the total
number of daily sessions from five to three.

While many of the prayers can, in fact, be offered in the
privacy of the home, it is not unseemly to pray in more or less
public places, provided they are not ritually unclean. Inasmuch as
the prayers involve specified actions of the body, praying individuals can usually be easily recognized and left undisturbed. Sometimes, however, one is surprised. In Isfahan I once walked into a
small stationery store where I was a regular customer. The time
was about one P.M. The storekeeper was standing behind his
counter, but instead of greeting me in his usual friendly fashion, he
showed no sign of being aware of my presence and stared fixedly
away to my left. Before there was time for me to do or say anything, he disappeared below the top of the counter. I then realized
what he was doing and withdrew. I had intruded on him while he
was in the wuquf position (standing upright, with hands folded

over the waist, and facing the qiblah, or direction of Mecca, which, in Isfahan, is southwestward). When he disappeared, he was assuming the ruku' position: upper body bent over at right angles to the legs, hands on knees. This is followed by the sujud position: full prostration with toes, knees, hands, and forehead touching the ground. In each of these positions set formulas—in Arabic—are recited, sometimes inaudibly, and the whole series of positions and recitations is repeated a specified number of times.

As with the other basic ritual requirements of Islam, there are various circumstances under which a person may be excused from praying, and there are also ways in which prayers may be abbreviated. An essential condition is that a person may pray only when he or she is in a state of ritual purity, and this is normally attained by ablutions that consist of washing various parts of the head, the hands and forearms, and the feet. The feet must remain uncovered until after prayer, and shoes or other coverings that may be contaminated must be removed. For ablutions, mosques always provide a fountain, pool, or spigots in the courtyard or outside the prayer hall. Symbolic ablution—in the absence of water—may be performed with sand, but if sand is not available either, one is presumably excused. Ritual purity is violated primarily by contact with natural products of the body: feces, urine, vomit, bowel gas, semen, vaginal discharges, and blood—especially menstrual blood. Indeed, women who are menstruating or are confined after childbirth may not offer the formally prescribed prayers at all, and they must take a full bath before resuming formal prayers after these periods are over. Both men and women are required to take a full bath—not just the standard ablutions—after having had sexual intercourse and before their next prayers.

These great tradition stipulations raise two major issues that can only be resolved by further studies. The first has to do with sexuality and religion. One interpretation is that Muslims feel that sex and religion are incompatible or antithetical. This may be lacking in insight, however, for Islam as a behavioral and attitudinal system is free of two of the antisexual themes that are prominent in Christianity, namely the veneration of celibacy and the lurking fear that sexual pleasure is a sinful indulgence.

The other major issue has to do with the extent to which people actually observe the required prayers. The subject is delicate and has largely been avoided by scholars, except for those who repeat the old assumption that pastoral nomads are not only lax in observance but also fundamentally ignorant of what is required. However, there are two studies that are explicit on the subject and are based on close observation. One is that of Alberts, who says that the majority of the women in the Iranian village of Davarabad are faithful in the performance of their prayers but that most of the men probably are not. The latter include self-excused irregular performers and a few who never pray at all yet consider themselves to be good Muslims (Alberts 1963, p. 838). Mansur, in her study of the Turkish coastal town of Bodrum, reaches a similar conclusion. The faithful performers are mostly older men and, especially, older women, and most of the rest of the population ignore the daily religious requirements (Mansur 1972, p. 114). An important but neglected aspect of this behavior is that the prescribed prayers are in Quranic Arabic, a language totally foreign to Turks, Persians, and other non-Arabic-speaking Muslims and quite different from the Arabic dialects spoken today. The meaning of these prayers, which of course can be memorized, consists essentially of impersonal formulas that assert the believer's submission to God (the basic meaning of "Islam") and faith in God as a refuge. More individual and personal matters are not accommodated. Do Muslims have no need for prayers concerned with such matters? This hardly seems likely. Apparently, improvised prayers, in the language of the actor, are often inserted at various points in the standard prayers. Much of the praying associated with the little tradition of the saints is probably of this nature, as has been dramatically described in connection with a new brotherhood in Egypt (Gilsenan 1973, pp. 50–51).

On Fridays, Muslims have the opportunity to offer the early afternoon prayer in a mosque, in congregation with others, and under the leadership of a prayer leader or preacher. Mosques are always open, and one can say prayers there whenever one wishes. However, the Friday afternoon prayer is a special occasion that is usually embellished by a sermon. Nevertheless, though sectarian authorities may insist otherwise, the Friday congregational prayers are not felt by most Muslims to be obligatory. The mosque provides ablution facilities and a niche to orient one toward Mecca in case there is doubt about the matter, but prayers said in a mosque and in company with others are no more effective than those said in solitude in any ritually clean place. Hearing the sermon—which may be theologically abstract or in hellfire-and-damnation style (Makal 1954) or political or aimed at some community sinner (el-Kayyali 1968, pp. 212–218)—is not essential for salvation. Unless the mosque is also a saint's shrine, or part of one, no baraka inheres in it as a place. One of the words for mosque is "masjed," which means place of prostration (sujud), but any ritually clean place will serve that purpose. The other commonly used word for mosque is "jami'," which means a place of gathering. This refers especially to the Friday congregation, but mosques are also gathering places for other purposes, such as study. In other words, though the mosque is one of the most distinctive types of building, the Friday congregational prayers are not directly equivalent to the various Sunday church services that are obligatory for many Christians. The call to prayer that is chanted five times a day from the mosque (either by a live muezzin or by an amplified recording) is not a summons to come to the mosque, but simply a reminder that it is prayer time.

Friday congregations in mosques are frequently composed of an obviously small proportion of the people living in the vicinity of the mosque. It should now be understandable why this in itself cannot be taken as evidence of lack of interest in religion, the decline of religion, or secularization due to modernization. A further consideration is that for the most part it is primarily males who frequent mosques. Though no systematic study has been done on this subject, it is evident that practices differ in different parts of the Middle East, and on different occasions. Women may not ordinarily go to mosques at all, they may be separated from the men when they do go, or they may be mixed (Fernea and Fernea 1972, p. 389). Here we are considering the formal great tradition, of course. In contrast, women, as well as men, are very active in the public rituals of the little tradition.

The third Pillar is the regular giving of alms or charity (zakat) to those in need. The theory is that giving away part of one's worldly goods purifies the rest. While beggars appeal to the zakat principle, especially on major holy days such as Eed al-Fitr, zakat is supposed to be given inconspicuously. However, community pressures do get applied, as in the case of Davarabad, Iran. Here Alberts observed several kinds of "voluntary" giving, zakat proper being a standard measure of wheat (or equivalent) per family per year collected by the akhund (backed up by the mayor) and distributed to the poor in kind (Alberts 1963, p. 840). There are also cash collections by the akhund, supposedly for the support of the poor and of religious education in general, and there are kheyrat, which are individual donations of cash to needy people. Alberts is forthright about the fact that though giving alms is a pious act that earns the giver credit in heaven, it is also induced by persuasive pressures and by the expectation of local esteem and approbation (p. 840).

In Chapter Four, benevolent and charitable societies were mentioned as being part of urban social organization. These societies can be seen as direct outgrowths of the injunctions in regard to zakat. They have been given very little attention, but Berger has a rather extensive discussion of them in present-day Egypt. Their major expenditures are for medical and health care, cash assistance, and cultural and educational benefits (Berger 1970, p. 110). In part, these are continuations of old types of charity that existed in times long before there was a socialist welfare-oriented government in Egypt. The voluntary benevolent societies in Egypt are also involved in innovative activities, such as supporting nursery schools and child-care centers. They may, in this connection, be the cutting edges of cultural changes that will become increasingly important in the future.

The fourth Pillar is fasting (sawm) from sunrise to sunset during the month of Ramadan (pronounced "Ramazan" in Turkish and Persian). The fast is supposed to be absolute—no oral intake whatever—rather than selective, as is Christian Lenten fasting. Eating and drinking from sunset to sunrise during Ramadan is supposed to be moderate, in keeping with the fasting spirit. Observance of these proprieties results in noticeable differences in public behavior during Ramadan. Restaurants are empty or closed, food and drink peddlers are nowhere to be seen, smokers refrain from indulging their habit, at least in public. Consequently, there is an impression that Ramadan may be observed more faithfully than many of the requirements of the other Pillars. Mansur does in fact cite statements by her informants that this is indeed true in Bodrum (1972, p. 102). Ramadan is a time for reflection, repentance, and good resolutions. It is also a time of long naps and short tempers, especially when it comes in the summer, when being forbidden to drink water during the long hot days can be a serious hardship. While hard-pressed travelers, the sick, and pregnant and nursing women may be exempted, the fast generally puts strains on people, and compensatory behavior results. The iftar—the break-fast meal after sunset—is often a highly festive and indulgent affair. In preparation for the climactic ending of Ramadan (Eed al-Fitr), new clothes are purchased for display and mountains of sweets are arranged in the food stores for consumption on the same occasion.

The fifth Pillar is the pilgrimage (hajj) to Mecca. Every Muslim is supposed to make it once in his or her lifetime if he or she can afford to do so. This proviso raises a number of interesting questions. What differences are there in the significance of the pilgrimage for a Moroccan and a resident of Mecca? A rich person may be able to afford several pilgrimages in his lifetime; is he more meritorious than the poor person who is unable to go at all? How much effort and sacrifice should a poor person make to save enough money in order to make the pilgrimage?

The truth apparently is that, while a few people make the pilgrimage more than once, many (and probably most) Muslims never make it at all, and if the latter feel a great sense of deprivation, no note has been taken of this in the literature. One reason may well be that the opportunities for substitute pilgrimages are abundant in all parts of the Middle East, this being one of the major features of the little tradition. Contrary to what one might conclude from much of the literature, persons calling themselves hajji and wearing green turbans are *not* notable in community life generally, and those who are entitled to these symbols of having made the pilgrimage to Mecca are not necessarily the subjects of special regard or veneration. Indeed, they may be viewed with definitely mixed feelings (see Alberts 1963, p. 843).

Even though only a very small proportion of Muslims make

the pilgrimage to Mecca in any one year, a major festival occurs during this time that is supposedly celebrated by all Muslims wherever they are. This is Eed al-Azha, the Feast of Sacrifice. It is also known as Bayram or Eed al-Kabir—which means the great feast, in contrast to Eed as-Saghir (the little feast), which is another term for Eed al-Fitr. On Eed al-Azha, sheep are ritually slaughtered and ceremonially consumed. The occasion commemorates Abraham's willingness to sacrifice his son on God's order. However, the son is often said to have been Ishmael (mythical ancestor of all Arabs) rather than Isaac, and the substitute sacrifice is believed to have taken place near Mecca.

In discussing the Five Pillars, which are generally presented as being the core of the great tradition of Islam, I have drawn attention to variations in actual practice and to the fact that the Five Pillars are only part of a larger system of belief and practice. This larger system becomes even more apparent as we consider other features of Islam that are anchored in the great tradition.

The Jinn

One feature of Islam that is anchored in the great tradition is the belief in beings known variously as jinn, jnan, or jnun (singular: jinni). This may be a matter of embarrassment to some Muslims who are aware of such Western images of the Middle East as the wish-fulfilling jinni released from imprisonment in a bottle who subsequently does great feats at the whim of his liberator. While this particular version of belief in the jinn may seem a bit childish, the general belief cannot be dismissed as a silly grotesque. For one thing, the jinn are mentioned in the Quran along with angels and other superhuman beings. Therefore, their reality is to be acknowledged by all Muslims. The facts are that while some Muslims scoff at, or ignore, the idea, others believe in it to an extent that goes far beyond what is said in the Quran. It may well be that what the Quran says is essentially an acknowledgment of beliefs that were important in pre-Islamic times and that have continued to be important. Evidently, however, they were not felt to be incompatible with belief in Allah, unlike the polytheistic idolatry of the pre-Islamic Meccans, which is condemned outright in the Quran.

Be this as it may, the jinn, in the minds of those to whom they are real, seem essentially to be projections and objectifications of strong human feelings—mostly dangerous or disturbing ones such as aggression and hostility. There are ways one can try to avoid them, such as staying away from the dark, damp places they are supposed to frequent, and there are rituals intended to placate them or counteract their influence. Although they have human emotions, the physical conception of them is polymorphous. They are reported to appear sometimes in natural animal forms, sometimes in fantastic animal forms, and sometimes in various fantastic-to-nearly-normal human forms. When most human in appearance, there is always a giveaway that they are jinn, namely that they have animal feet (usually hooves) rather than normal human ones.

Vincent Crapanzano's study of the Hamadsha Brotherhood in Morocco elevates this subject from the level of miscellaneous folk-lore to that of complicated motivational analysis. The Hamadsha are a brotherhood that benefit from the baraka of two saints. They are also believers in jinn in general and in one jinniyya (female jinni) in particular. Her name is Aisha Qandisha. Crapanzano cites earlier publications that place her in a class of female demons that have been widely believed in around the Mediterranean from ancient times until the present (1973, p. 143). Hamadsha rituals are, according to Crapanzano, group therapy in which persons suffering from various psychosomatic difficulties (sudden paralysis or blindness, for instance) or prolonged depression, are freed of jinn possession and imbued with baraka. Aisha Qandisha rituals concentrate on an endemic problem for many men: depression and other ills that result from feeling unable to fulfill the heavy demands of constantly acting out male-dominance expectations (1973, p. 224).

Life Crises

There are three life crises that are occasions for important rituals in the Middle East: getting married, giving birth, and dying. There is also a fourth ritual that is in itself a life crisis, for it does not mark any other obvious transition in the life-cycle of the individual. This is circumcision.

These four rituals, or ritual-complexes, can be considered to be aspects of the religious great tradition because they are universal—that is, practiced everywhere by everyone. However, they are not anchored in the scriptures nearly as deeply as are the Five Pillars. Circumcision, for example, is not even mentioned in the Quran, and most of the details of these rituals, to the extent that they are stipulated in the Quran or the Hadith at all, have non-Islamic (many of them probably also pre-Islamic) elaborations. There are also local variations, amid the similarities, that have been reported from all over the Middle East. It is because of the nonscriptural emphasis and the local variations that these rituals can also be considered part of the little tradition concept.

Circumcision. In an effort at projection into the life cycle of an individual, I shall begin with circumcision. However, we immediately encounter the ambiguities involved in this subject. Circumcision means "cutting around," and in this sense it is a very appropriate word for the surgical removal of the foreskin of the penis. It is an operation performed ceremonially on all Muslim males. However, "circumcision" of girls is also reported, especially from the Nile region. Logically, it should mean surgical removal of the foreskin of the clitoris, but the operation that "female circumcision" refers to is *not* limited to this. It involves excision of the whole clitoris (clitoridectomy) and often excision of the labia minora as well. It may also involve excision of the labia majora and removal of mons veneris tissues (Barclay 1964, pp. 237–240). This is obviously a far more drastic operation than circumcision of the penis. It is extremely painful and prolonged. Fadwa el-Guindi witnessed one operation that took 15 minutes (Callender and el-Guindi 1971, p. 32). The risk of serious infection is far greater than in circumcision of the penis, and one wonders what the mortality rate among genitally excised girls may be, but the literature says nothing on this subject. The operation also results in permanent deformation, including the growth of abnormal scar tissue that may interfere with intercourse to such an extent that another operation is required in preparation for marriage. The main rationalization for the genital excision of girls is that it reduces sexual desire and/or eliminates sexual pleasure, but the factual basis of this rationalization has been denied by persons who were themselves involved (Callender and el-Guindi 1971, p. 32; Barclay 1964, pp. 239–240). These denials interfere with theorizing that the genital excision of girls is a working out of men's fears of women's sexuality. Also interfering with this idea is one fact that seems to be clear: Excision is performed on small girls by women, in the company of women, and in the absence of men. Initiation by ordeal into the sisterhood of women is a motivation that seems plausible—though it is not explicit—in terms of what has been described.

The genital excision of girls is not practiced in the Middle East generally but only in the Nile region for certain, although Arabia has also been mentioned. Unlike the circumcision of boys, it is not sanctioned by the ulama, and in fact it is now illegal in both Egypt and Sudan.

The circumcision of boys is not a puberty ceremony. It is performed at various ages but almost always in early childhood. Traditionally, it has been a public affair and a happy celebration, at least for the onlookers. While a man performs the operation, women watch the procession that precedes it and participate in the celebration that accompanies and follows it.

The boy is frequently prepared, and referred to, as if he were a bridegroom, and the procession is very similar to a wedding procession (Ammar 1954, p. 122; Barclay 1964, p. 241). Indeed, Lane, describing early nineteenth century circumcision processions in Cairo, says that parents often contrived to attach their son's circumcision procession to someone else's wedding procession in order to save the expense (such as hiring musicians) of having their own (Lane 1908, p. 58).

Anticipation of mature sexuality, and of male Muslim adult status, seems to be the theme of circumcision. It is also the occasion for the parents' reassertion that they are father and mother of a boy. Granqvist's description of the ceremonial in the village of Artas, near Bethlehem, makes these multiple symbolic purposes clear (Granqvist 1947, Chapter 7).

People who are the subjects of life-crisis rituals are generally considered to be in acute spiritual danger and more than usually vulnerable to the Evil Eye. In connection with the circumcision procession, Lane reports that in Cairo a boy was dressed in girl's clothes and decorated with women's ornaments in order to attract the Evil Eye "and so divert it from his person" (1908, p. 58). And Granqvist says that in Artas a pitchfork hung with women's clothes was carried in the procession in order to turn the Evil Eye away from the boys to be circumcised (1947, p. 199). Whose envy was being feared the most by whom? Gender differences seem obviously to have been involved, whatever the specific, but possibly unconscious, impetus may have been.

Marriage. All of the descriptions of Middle Eastern weddings that I have read proceed on the assumption that the bride is being married for the first time. Most Middle Eastern women probably get married only once, and while it is legitimate to confine discussion to first-time weddings, we must not forget that widows and divorcees can and do remarry. The discussion here will be concerned only with the wedding as a ceremonial. Other aspects of marriage as the nexus of many social interactions and relationships will be considered in Chapter Seven.

The first-time bride is very frequently, if not typically, in her early teens. The groom is likely to be in his middle twenties, but he may be considerably older, and in the Middle East the marriage of an "old" man and an adolescent woman is more likely to be accepted as unremarkable than it is in Europe or North America. After the marriage has been agreed upon by all parties concerned, the contract is drawn up and signed before witnesses. Its stipulations are governed by sharia law, and its closing is executed either by a registrar who is learned in the sharia or by a cleric (shaykh, hoja, or akhund). It is at this point that the wedding is the most closely linked to the scriptural great tradition. The contract includes the amount of the marriage payment and a statement about the conditions under which it is to be paid. These details vary considerably in practice. According to the Quran, the marriage payment is owed to the bride, or wife, herself, but very often in practice it is paid, when it is paid at all, to her father. Unless the marriage ends in divorce or separation, there may actually be no payment at all, or only a partial one. Recitation of the shahada, at least, is a part of the contract signing. The contract formalizes obligations between the bride and groom and their families. When they are relatives (as they quite often are), it reinforces the bonds of already recognized kinship.

For the bride, and all her relatives, her first wedding is a life-crisis ritual that has another, extreme significance: the celebration of the consummation of the marriage. This may follow immediately upon the signing of the contract or it may be deferred, sometimes for a considerable period of time. Though the details vary greatly in the many descriptions that have been published, there are certain essentials that seem universal. The bride and groom are prepared separately by their friends and relatives. This includes bathing, applications of henna to various portions of the body, extensive shaving of the body, and singing, dancing, and gift exchanges. The bride is then conveyed to the groom's house in a procession that includes various acts symbolizing her separation from her parents and siblings. At the groom's house, feasting, singing, and dancing are standard, but the bride does not participate, or, if she does appear, she does so heavily veiled or in a subdued manner. Wedding dances are likely to include obviously sensual, but not necessarily grossly copulatory, motifs, performed either by amateurs or by hired professionals such as belly dancers. Men may perform such dances as well as women, but whether or not this is in mimicry of the women remains an open question. That sexuality involves far more than copulation is reflected in the suggestion that some of the women's dance movements are effective as post-partum abdominal exercises and may have originated as demonstrations of them. Though frank, the sexual theme is controlled and symbolic. The wedding celebration is attended by people of all ages, including children, and is definitely not an orgy.

Eventually, everyone but the closest relatives of the groom depart and the bride and groom retire to consummate the marriage. They are awaited by relatives and sometimes, apparently, spied upon. Finally a bloodstained cloth is displayed to the relatives as a sign that hymenal rupture occurred, this being taken as proof that the bride was a virgin. Legitimate recognized loss of virginity is the major life crisis for the bride.

Most of the accounts of this series of events that I have seen are not specific eye-witness reports but statements of what is generally expected. The relatives are supposed to be delighted at the sign of the blood token and devastated if it is not produced. But what if no hymenal rupture occurred even though the bride was a virgin? What if the bride was, indeed, not a virgin? Does the groom beat her, divorce her, or kill her on the spot as, supposedly, he has the right to do? What if the groom finds himself unable to have an erection, or to maintain one for a long enough time for sufficient penetration? How many brides and grooms prepare themselves in advance to fake the blood token if that should turn out to be necessary? How many weddings do in fact—as opposed to stereotypic expectation—culminate in the display of the virginity token? I raise these questions because they are reasonable and because the literature now available does not answer them. On the whole, descriptions of expectations of the wedding night emphasize the changing of the bride from virgin to exvirgin strictly in terms of male dominance and female submission. In these terms the groom's impotence would appear to be unthinkable. Occasionally, however, a more balanced image shows through, as for example in accounts of some Turkish villages where worries about both the bride's virginity and the groom's impotence are normal and where there are accepted religious procedures for helping the embarrassed groom overcome his temporary impotence (Makal 1954, p. 131).

Birth. Giving birth, especially when it is for the first time, is a very important ritualized life crisis for the mother. She is secluded for forty days, during which she is extremely vulnerable to the Evil Eye and other spiritual dangers. People who are ritually unclean must not visit her, these people including menstruating women and mourners or others who have had recent contact with corpses. The change to parent status also affects the father, and this is symbolized by a name change for both parents, particularly when the first-born is a son. If the son is given the name Abdullah, for example, the parents are thenceforth called Abu Abdullah (father of Abdullah) and Umm Abdullah (mother of Abdullah) in addition to, and sometimes instead of, their own given names. These are the Arabic forms; there are equivalent forms in the other Middle Eastern languages.

Naming ceremonies have been reported from some parts of the Middle East, but there appear to be no widespread, standard expectations in this matter. However, names of religious significance —usually Arabic in origin and subject to some alterations in pronunciation in other languages—are common and rather standardized everywhere. Fatima, Zaynab, Zohrah, Aisha, and Khadija are among the commonly used names of women. The original namesakes were closely associated with Muhammad. For males, Muhammad itself is frequently used, as are Ali, Hassan, and Husayn. Nonreligious names for females are also very common, such as those referring to flowers, jewels, stars, and planets. Names that are attributes—such as kind, brave, generous, beloved—are bestowed on both males and females. Pre-Islamic names are also common, such as Ibrahim (Abraham), Musa (Moses), Ismail (Ishmael), and Sulayman (Solomon), while among the Iranians the names of Achaemenid and Sassanian kings and of male and female characters in the *Book of Kings (Shahnameh)* are popular.

However, perhaps the most strikingly religious names—all

male—fall into two sets. One combines Abd ("slave" or "servant") with other words, and the other combines al-Din ("the religion") with other words. Taken together, these probably constitute the names of a large proportion of Muslim males. They are essentially theological in nature, and there appear to be no counterparts to them among Christians.

Each of the Abd names combines Abd with one of the ninety-nine names or attributes of Allah that are enumerated chiefly in the Hadith. In addition there is Abdullah, meaning slave or servant of Allah. The ninety-nine attributes are recited in prayers, often with the assistance of rosaries. Among the most common of these names are Abd al-Rahman, Abd al-Malik, Abd al-Aziz, Abd al-Jabbar, Abd al-Wahhab, Abd al-Razzaq, Abd al-Hakim, Abd al-Latif, Abd al-Hafiz, Abd al-Karim, Abd al-Mujib, Abd al-Majid, Abd al-Haqq, Abd al-Hamid, Abd al-Wahid, Abd al-Qadir, Abd al-Nur, and Abd al-Rashid. Respectively, these mean slave (or servant) of: the Merciful, the King, the Mighty, the Repairer, the Bestower, the Provider, the Ruler, the Subtle, the Guardian, the Generous, the Approver, the Glorious, the Truth, the Laudable, the One, the Powerful, the Light, and the Director.

The al-Din set is not as large, but it includes frequently encountered names like Nur al-Din, Shams al-Din, Izz al-Din, and Jamal al-Din (Light, Sun, Glory, and Beauty of the Religion, respectively).

Death. The fourth life-crisis occasion is death. There are no "last rites" for the dying person in the same sense that there are for many Christians. After death occurs the body is washed by relatives or friends of the same sex as the deceased, the orifices are plugged, and the body is wrapped in a shroud. It may be carried to the cemetery on a litter or in a wooden coffin, but it is not buried in the coffin. There is no embalming, and there are no indestructible caskets. The body is buried in its shroud, preferably on the same day that death occurred or, at the latest, as early as possible the next day. There are religious stipulations as to how the body should be placed in the grave (for example, facing toward Mecca), and there are simple graveside prayers that can be recited by any Muslim. That, essentially, is all. However, for a considerable period after the burial, there is a series of visitations to the mourners. There are also what in North America would be called memorial services, and these can take place in the mosque. Of course it can be argued that these observances are social-reinforcement procedures for the survivors rather than life-crisis rituals for the deceased.

Muslim burial practices facilitate complete natural decomposition, and so room can be made for the bodies of newly deceased people among less recent remains. Middle Eastern cemeteries are often quite lively places. Visits on certain holy days such as Eed al-Fitr are major ceremonial occasions. In Iran, Friday afternoon visitations are popular, often taking the form of family outings that combine elements of the picnic with communion with the deceased as if they were physically present or as if their souls were present and conscious of the living.

The most significant manifestation of this lively spiritual communion with the dead—a communion that seems almost physical at times—is the Islamic complex of saints. The foci of this complex are the saints' tombs. There must be thousands of them in the Middle East, ranging from the very humble little unadorned structures that abound in the Maghrib (Berque 1955, pp. 256–260) to grandiose shrines like those of Moulay Idris in Fez and Imam Reza in Mashhad. The saint complex is the core of the little tradition.

THE RELIGIOUS LITTLE TRADITION

The literature on the saint complex is diverse and concentrates on certain aspects as discrete topics. For instance, there are discussions of the saint complex in the Maghrib, especially Morocco, that mostly revolve around the theme of "maraboutism"; there are books on Sufism (often rather carelessly called "Islamic mysticism") that in many cases treat the subject in a past-time context and in terms of mystical abstractions that would not seem to touch the daily life of most people; there are discussions of the dervish sects that flourished in the latter part of the Ottoman Empire but seem to have declined since then; and there are discussions of the Shia concept of the Imams, with emphasis on Iran.

Recent thinking on the subject seems to be moving toward the idea that these seemingly disparate phenomena are actually related, and in fact are aspects of each other. Far from being removed from everyday life, they are the heart of many, if not most, Muslims' religious expression. This is a controversial subject because the ulama—who are canon lawyers rather than priests—have generally opposed the saint complex, and its many manifestations, on the grounds that it is unorthodox, if not heretical. Many of the modern Middle Eastern governments, too, oppose the saint complex. One reason for this is that the ecstatic performances characteristically include extravagant behavior (going into trance, flagellation, and head slashing, for example), and this is considered embarrassing or disgraceful behavior for citizens of "modern" nations.

As has already been mentioned, the saints are believed to be imbued with baraka, or "blessing." Their tombs are imbued with it, and their lineal descendants may inherit it. The ongoing leadership of the saints' brotherhoods is typically recruited from these people. In the case of the Shia Imams, descent from the Prophet reinforces the baraka principle, and in Morocco those saints who are accepted as being shorfa (descendants of the Prophet) bring a conviction of the immediacy of the Prophet's spirit to present-day believers (Geertz 1971, pp. 50–51). Although not all saints are believed to be descendants of Muhammad, the concept of descent from a holy person is an important element in the maintenance of the saints' brotherhoods. Not only are there thousands of saints' tombs where one can surround oneself with baraka, but the saints' brotherhoods also maintain lodges—zawiyas—that are not necessarily tombs but are places where the brothers can meet for spiritual communion. These are very numerous. For example, in Cairo there are 120 zawiyas of the Hamidiya Shadhiliya Brotherhood alone. This was founded in the twentieth century by a modern saint, Salama ibn Hassan Salama (1867–1939), and is now headed by his son (Gilsenan 1973, p. 57). In other words, the brotherhoods provide many localized opportunities for face-to-face interaction and support. The zawiya is a "true nook," as Geertz puts it (1971, p. 52).

The saint complex is present not just in Morocco and Iran but virtually everywhere in the Middle East except for Saudi Arabia, where the Wahhabi sectarian establishment has suppressed it. It enables the ordinary Muslim to get, and repeatedly renew, emotional reinforcement through exposure to baraka and to get emotional release by means of spiritual and physical exercises such as the dhikr (or "remembrance") and other ceremonial performances that induce trance. The rationale behind both types of activity is that they constitute immediate communion with God, either directly or through the mediation of the saint. Many observers feel that the great tradition of Islam is deficient in its provision of this kind of emotional and spiritual satisfaction.

In Chapter Four I described a pilgrim to a Sunni saint's shrine in Baghdad and the manner in which he made contact with baraka. The same "washing" ritual has been described in Shia shrines as well as at the visitation (ziyara) to the shrine of Shaykh Salama in Egypt (Gilsenan 1973, p. 48). However, Geertz thinks that to conceptualize baraka merely as a kind of "spiritual electricity" is to miss the significance and impact that these ziyaras have on the faithful. He suggests that baraka encompasses a whole range of related ideas such as material prosperity, physical well-being, bodily satisfaction, completion, good luck, and abundance, as well as magical power (Geertz 1971, p. 44). It is a sense of all this that the pilgrim seeks to reinforce at the same time that he or she may appeal to the saint for help in, or release from, personal problems.

Anyone may make a ziyara to a saint's shrine. There are, as I have said, thousands of shrines in the Middle East, and millions of people visit them. There are special occasions, too, when extraordinary numbers of people participate at one time. The most widespread type of such occasion is the saint's birthday. The Shias celebrate the Imams' birthdays, that of the Twelfth Imam being an especially happy celebration. In Egypt, the most conspicuous rituals are associated with the birthdays of saints, and they include banner-carrying processions going through the streets as well as shrine visits. For instance, in 1964 the mulid (birthday) of Shaykh Ahmad el-Bedawi attracted one million participants to the town of Tanta in the Nile Delta area (Gilsenan 1973, p. 48). There can be a strong carnival atmosphere at these affairs combined with the religious concern of many of the participants. In addition to Gilsenan's point on this, Fuller comments on the county-fair atmosphere of religious feast days in the central valley of Lebanon, where Christians and Muslims may attend each other's celebrations (Fuller 1961, p. 83).

The dhikr, or remembrance (of God), is a spiritual exercise that, like yoga, requires practice and discipline. It is the core members of the various brotherhoods who perform dhikrs. Gilsenan gives a close description of the modern dhikr of the Hamidiya Shadhiliya that is rather restrained and decorous by comparison with some others. The brothers, seated in carefully arranged rows, begin with rhythmical, repetitive recitations of words like "Allah," and "Hu." Emotional excesses build but are gently restrained by the leaders. However, in other orders, various forms of emotional abandon are reached and trance states are achieved (Gilsenan 1973, Chapter 6).

The form of dhikr that is probably most famous outside of the Middle East is the whirling exercise of the Mawlawi Brotherhood, which was very strong in the days of the Ottoman Empire. Julian Huxley's description of this dhikr, as performed at the Mawlawi tikkiyah, or lodge, in Tripoli, Lebanon, in 1948, dispels all of the sideshow-freak atmosphere that has been associated with it in the West (Huxley 1954, pp. 89–91). The emphasis is on the profound serenity of the men as they whirl. It is clear that this kind of activity has been in great decline since the nineteenth century, but the reasons are not really apparent. "Secularization" is hardly an answer. There is no evidence that the emotional needs met by these rituals are no longer felt. Speaking about the decline of Sufi orders generally, Gilsenan suggests that it may in part be due to the fact that the shaykhs of the orders have become less able to act as mediators between the poor people and the various new governments than their predecessors were (Gilsenan 1973, pp. 45–46). This is a sectarian consideration more than it is a religious one. However, if some orders are declining, others are growing. The saint complex is not moribund in the Middle East.

To a considerable extent the saint complex can be regarded as "parochialization" of certain aspects of the great tradition. Many saints are regarded as extensions of Muhammad, and the dhikr itself is justified on the grounds that "remembrance" of God is enjoined in the Quran. Though usually rejected by the ulama, the devotees of the little tradition do not, in turn, reject the religious great tradition. The saint complex tends to be regarded by them as supplementary to, not a substitution for, the expectations of the great tradition.

Another aspect of the religious little tradition, exorcism, is perhaps less closely tied, in theory, with the great tradition. I have already mentioned this exorcistic aspect in connection with some of the activities of the Hamadsha in Morocco. There also are exorcistic activities that have no connection with saints' brotherhoods or, for that matter, with Islam, notably the zar "cult" of the Nile area. The zar is a spirit that possesses women. Barclay has described the several kinds that are believed to possess women living in the environs of Khartoum (Barclay 1964, pp. 201–202). The depressed or frustrated woman who wishes a zar ceremony to be performed for her benefit engages the services of a shaykha (female shaykh). The shaykha is herself possessed, and she is able to diagnose the specific problem. The patient dances in the ceremony, speaking in the voice of the zar. Barclay suggests that there is a strong element in this ceremony of seeking to wrest favors from husbands, and he also relates it to the inferior position of women (Barclay 1964, p. 205). Kennedy, moreover, has interpreted the zar ceremony as a form of last-resort psychotherapy used after other religious rituals have failed (Kennedy 1967), and this is certainly evident in Elizabeth Fernea's rather touching description of a zar ceremony in Cairo (1970, pp. 11–15). In this case the celebrant was a man, a shaykh, and in the process of inducing the patient to release her feelings he did a whirling dance apparently similar to that described for the Mawlawis, though Fernea does not make this connection.

Why should the zar be limited to the Nile area? Why do not zarlike ceremonies occur in other parts of the Middle East? Perhaps they do but have not been adequately identified, observed, or described. In any case, the zar's possible origin in Ethiopia might explain why its specific forms have been diffused down the Nile, and the depression of women whose husbands are long absent in downstream cities (a frequent occurrence in the Nile area) may be particularly acute there. Is there some connection between the zar ceremony and female genital excision? No one, as far as I know, has explored this possibility with any thoroughness.

THE SECTARIAN LITTLE TRADITION

Many of the major Sufi orders, from which many of the saints' brotherhoods are derived, originated during the Abbasid Caliphate.

For example, the Qadiriyya Order originated in Baghdad toward the end of the Abbasid period. Its founding saint's tomb (previously described) is located there, and it has spread widely over the Middle East, with zawiyas in many places. Trimingham (1971) is a detailed source on the origins and relationships among these orders, the generic term for which is tariqa, meaning "way" or "path." But like all other social structures in the Middle East, the orders or brotherhoods have their vicissitudes. While some have been in existence for many centuries, others have declined into oblivion, and new ones have come into being and proliferated.

Gilsenan, who has studied a new Egyptian order that has come into being at the same time that others are declining, thinks that an essential for sectarian survival is the maintenance of the charisma of the original saint. His baraka must continue to be believed to be strong in the person of the saint's successors as heads, or shaykhs, of the order. These may themselves be regarded as living saints, and new brotherhoods can and do evolve through time, derived from newer saints. Gellner, in commenting on the "Malthusian" proliferation of saints in Morocco, emphasizes the structural—what I would call sectarian—rather than the religious elements in the process (Gellner 1969, pp. 140–141).

Established as a going concern, a brotherhood has a definite social structure, two instances of which are described in detail in the literature. One of these is the Ihansalen of Morocco, derived from a saint who was born in the fourteenth century (Gellner 1969). The other is the Hamidiya Shadhiliya of Egypt, derived from a saint who died in 1939 (Gilsenan 1973).

The Ihansalen are a Berber-speaking tribal group. They are organized on the common-ancestral, segmentary principles that were discussed in Chapters Two and Three. They are special, however, in that descent from a saint, continuation of the saint's baraka, and maintenance of the lodges (zawiyas) of the brotherhood are incorporated into the tribal structure. Segmentation within the tribe has led to differentiation between the people who belong to saintly lineages (singular: agurram; plural: igurramen) and the more numerous lay members. The igurramen are in rivalry with each other in regard to which lineage can produce the "most effective saints" as time passes. Gellner (1969, Chapter 7) deals in great detail with these matters in regard to the main lodge of the Ihansalen. In this case sectarian structure is a variant of kinship-regional social structure.

The Hamidiya Shadhiliya consist of Arabic-speaking Egyptians, many of them urban, and their founding saint has been dead for only three decades. They are different from the Ihansalen in many ways, yet they have important elements in common. They, too, are baraka brokers, and they, too, maintain lodges. The tariqa is headed by the shaykh who is a direct descendant (son) of the saint. The shaykh in his person provides the source of the healing that membership in the order facilitates. However, on a day-to-day basis, the guidance (murshid) of the shaykh is mediated through the khulafa (singular: khalifa) of the lodges. In this context "khalifa" connotes a second level administrator rather than a "successor" (as in the instance of the caliphs who followed Muhammad). There is also a central office of the tariqa headed by a wakil, or deputy shaykh.

In this new tariqa, efforts are being made to *avoid* letting inheritance become the means of succession to these offices. Award for achievement is encouraged instead (Gilsenan 1973, pp. 83ff.). This is, presumably, one of the ways in which the Hamidiya Shadhiliya order is adapting itself to new values and expectations among the Egyptian population, a reason for its success, while other orders—unable to adapt themselves to new needs—are declining. The Hamidiya Shadhiliya order provides status for status-less working-class people, but it also accommodates some members of the middle class (p. 144). It also provides a feeling of fraternity and ultimate worth (p. 150). How can there cease to be needs for such provisions, reinforced or symbolized by baraka, as long as peril-and-refuge is a major concern of life?

Berger says that in 1964 he was given the names of sixty-four functioning Sufi orders in Egypt (Berger 1970, p. 67). They were organized into the Supreme Sufi Council, whose head is appointed by the president of the Republic. Berger emphasizes the very broad social needs that the activities of the orders seek to satisfy—such as spontaneity, warmth, and intimacy—and he suggests that certain modern efforts to provide such things by a government that does not allow dissent may contribute to the continuing need for them (1970, pp. 75–76). He notes, as does Gilsenan, that the orders do not seem to be concerned with elevating the socioeconomic conditions of their members. This could make them lose their appeal among some elements of the population. Yet, since self-denial is a major theme of Sufism, and the involuntary self-denial of the poor may therefore be interpreted as being nobler than social striving, the Sufi orders may continue to have appeal to many people as social organizations of the poor per se. This, in any case, is what Berger seems to be suggesting (1970, p. 89).

THE SECTARIAN GREAT TRADITION

The point of much of the preceding discussion is that the sectarian great tradition constitutes only a part of the whole social structure of Islam, just as the religious great tradition constitutes only a part of the religious whole of Islam.

The people who are at the heart of the sectarian great tradition are the present-day successors of the original Islamic theocracy.

Some have argued that there never was a theocracy except in theory, at least after A.D. 632, inasmuch as there was always tension and rivalry between the sectarian and secular establishments. Nevertheless, sharia law covered a wide variety of criminal and civil issues until quite recently. It was administered by specialized functionaries who were trained and validated by the ulama, if, indeed, they were not themselves members of the ulama.

As has been mentioned already, sharia law has been abrogated in some Middle Eastern countries, while in others it has been reduced in scope essentially to personal-status and family-relations issues. This has, of course, reduced the power and influence of the ulama. While in some countries some members of the ulama are believed to be leaders in resistance to the secular powers, their influence in many cases only extends to religious issues. For example, consider the question of whether there are any circumstances under which abortion may be considered not to conflict with Islamic religious beliefs. In recent years various fatwas (declarations of religious judgment and interpretation) have been issued on this and similar questions (see Schieffelin 1967). They are generally issued by a mufti, the officer of a particular ulama who is authorized by his peers to carry out this responsibility.

Little has been published by behavioral scientists on the internal workings of present-day ulamas. This is a major gap in available knowledge of the social organization of the Middle East. As mentioned before, ulamas are essentially municipal in identity. Major cities have ulamas, and the ulama of a supremely major city like Cairo is likely to have national, if not international, influence. However, the sectarian structure is even more decentralized than that of the Eastern Orthodox Christian Church, which at least has national patriarchates in Eastern Europe and what amounts to an international, though not all-inclusive, patriarchate in the Middle East.

Members of the ulama are trained in Islamic theology and law. That much is clear, but beyond it, the processes of selection by which they become recognized as members of this board of doctors of theology and jurisprudence have not been described in detail by social scientists in any specific instance that I know of. Similarly unclearly understood are the processes by which muftis, qadis, heads of the awqaf administration, and other functionaries are appointed, whether by their peers or others. Where the judicial system and awqaf properties have been placed under national administration, qadis and awqaf administrators have become subject to civil service regulations, and the new legal codes of the countries concerned probably give more details. However, the fact remains that involved in all this are networks of communication and patterns of decision making that remain closed and unknown to outsiders. Being unknown, their significance has probably been understated and underestimated. Of special interest are the awqaf endowments, investments, and disbursements. These are very large and involve bureaucracies, not just specialists among the ulama. Some observers think that the awqaf organization, as it operates in various municipal and government ministerial surroundings, is actually the core of each of the many municipal and regional organizations that, collectively, constitute the decentralized Islamic sectarian establishment.

The ulama are selected from among a larger aggregation of religiously trained persons who usually wear distinctive dress and have scriptural training so that they can at least recite passages from the Quran and say prayers appropriate to various occasions, including life crises. These clerics are not priests. That is to say, no ritual act is performed exclusively by them that is believed to be required or essential for the salvation of individuals' souls. Their training and competence vary widely, and characteristics of personality seem to be important in the process of gaining prominence. Prominence—in terms of establishing a following among local people—is a factor in becoming accepted as a member of the ulama, or becoming, in Iranian Shia terms, a mujtahed or an ayatollah.

The ordinary clerics are known by various titles. Those most commonly used are shaykh (Arabic), hoja (Turkish), and mullah or akhund (among Persian-speaking Shias). Shaykh is basically a respectful-reference term, and it has several specific denotations, only one of which is cleric as discussed here. Head of a kinship group is another very common, and quite different, usage of the word.

Among these clerics there are various specialists, and Berger's listing of them, in connection with modern Egypt, is a useful reference on the subject. Among the Sunnis the chief officer of a mosque is called an imam, and he is the leader of the congregational prayers in the mosque. Among the Persian-speaking Shias, this officer is called a peesh-namoz ("he who stands in front of the prayer"), for the Shias reserve the word Imam for their twelve most important saints, as discussed earlier. The khatib, who delivers the Friday sermon, and the waiz (pronounced "vaez" in Persian), who delivers moral lessons in the mosque in the early evenings on weekdays, are other specialists. However, Berger points out that in small mosques the same individual may serve as imam, khatib, and waiz. The muezzin is the public prayer caller, far more frequently heard than seen. Large mosques in Egypt, and doubtlessly elsewhere, have an overseer—assisted by at least one servant—who is responsible for the upkeep of the building. Berger says that most mosques in Egypt have at least three of these various officials (Berger 1970, p. 10).

Other specialists who are active outside of mosques include the qari—the "reciter of the Recited" (the Quran)—who must know the Quran by heart and have a good voice, and the many clerics who serve as teachers of the scriptures. The word "mullah," in fact, denotes a teacher.

Mosques may be privately owned, or they may be administered by the waqf organization, but not many details of these arrangements are publicly known. In 1962 there were about 14,000 privately owned mosques in Egypt and about 3,000 government-administered ones that had previously been under waqf control. At that time there was approximately one mosque for every 700 Muslim males in Egypt. There were relatively fewer mosques per capita in the larger cities than elsewhere, but the largest and most prestigious mosques are generally concentrated in the largest cities (Berger 1970, pp. 18–21). Most of the officials serving in Egyptian mosques are unpaid volunteers (p. 40). This fact, derived from government data, raises further interesting questions about the practicalities of the sectarian structure of Islam. More study is needed in order to answer these questions.

Berger (p. 13) asserts that mosques do not have regular congregations, but he also says that worshippers do tend to go to a particular mosque on the basis of its nearness to home or place of work. Does this not imply that there is a core of "regulars" at each mosque? What Berger probably means is that people are not formally registered at a certain mosque in the same way that many Christians are at a particular parish church. This subject was mentioned in Chapter Four in connection with Paul English's suggestion that mosques in Herat apparently do serve a parish function. There seems to be confusion between "parish" in the sense of an administrative unit and the idea of the mosque serving as the location for organized activities, such as those of the Iranian heyats and the Egyptian saints' birthday groups. One thing is clear beyond question: Mosques differ greatly in size. A few are very large and famous in their own right, but many others are small, humble structures, often lacking minarets and other supposedly standard ornamentation. The nature of the social relations of the faithful in such different types of mosques probably varies greatly, but we do not know anything of substance about this. While the literature on the types of interpretative decision that are made by the Shia ulamas and the ulamas of the four Sunni schools of canon jurisprudence is vast and highly technical, there is virtually no literature on the subject of who goes to which mosque, how regularly, for what specific purposes, and in interaction with what other individuals. There are thousands of references to, and discussions of, the procedural principles by which ulamas make judgments on moral and theological issues, one of these being "consensus" (ijma) and another being "analogy" (qiyas) with events and circumstances in the life of the Prophet. These are important in the inner workings of the sectarian great tradition, but they are logical principles used by specialists. They are not social relationships, and their connection with everyday sectarian and religious behavior is undocumented, as far as I know. Much remains to be learned and understood about all these everyday types of behavior.

CONCLUSION

It seems to me that permeating the mass media of the West are some assumptions about Islam that represent seriously distorted views. Here are some of the more common ones: Islam is a cold, formalistic religion; it has no priests or ministers to provide the comforts of sacramental rituals; its prayers are merely rote-memorized formulas that are impervious to personal involvement and are recited in a rigidly prescribed calisthenic fashion. What emotional support can such a religion give? What sort of emotions is it likely to generate in its followers? For many, one answer seems to be clear: The chief emotion of Islam is fanaticism. The fanatic image includes vignettes like hordes of pilgrims swarming to Mecca, mass prayers performed like military drills, and an implacable medievalism that amputates the hands of thieves and enlists eager recruits for "holy war" against infidels and any other targets decreed by the leadership. Isn't such a religion fundamentally defective, and aren't its followers ripe for conversion to emotionally more satisfying religions like Christianity or secular faiths like Communism? Isn't Islam obviously a block to liberal modernization? If it should become armed with modern technology, would it not be a menace to the non-Muslim world?

I reject these assumptions and those that are implied in the questions. This entire chapter consists of an account of Islam that I believe to be more realistic, more humane, and certainly more complicated. The distorted, popularized images focus on the ulama and a few of the great tradition elements, exaggerating their negative potentials. They totally disregard the little tradition, whose saint complex abundantly facilitates emotional discharge and provides many supportive communal activities for the faithful. Moreover, hardly ever mentioned in journalistic impressions of Islam is the serenity of mosques, where one is free not only to pray but also to meditate, study, visit with one's friends, and even sleep. The mosque, with its large, uncluttered, and sheltered spaces, is a marvelous adaptation to the needs of people living at high densities and often in a state of acute social tension.

As for medieval fanaticism, it is true that the Quran prescribes the amputation of hands as a punishment for thievery, but this continues to be practiced only where the most extreme fundamentalist interpretations hold sway. The vast majority of Muslims and

Muslim countries now reject it, just as the vast majority of Christians and Jews now reject the eye-for-an-eye injunctions of the Old Testament. "Holy war" (jihad) *is* an Islamic concept, and it has been invoked at various times and in various places. However, it is of little concern or interest to most Muslims in their everyday lives. They are not in a constant state of eager readiness for it, and this is why it was not mentioned previously in this chapter.

Islam and the hypothesized peril-and-refuge mentality exist together. Islamic sectarianism has certainly contributed to the perils of life, but Islamic religion continually provides refuge from those perils. It is a viable and adaptable system of belief that has persisted, grown, and spread to many different cultures. As is the case with all religions that have fixed scriptures, some of its tenets have been used to rationalize resistance to the careful consideration of new ideas and to the acceptance of new realities. There are Middle Eastern modernists who have rejected Islam for this reason. Possibly, the Middle East will eventually become largely secularized and de-Islamicized, but there are signs to the contrary; signs that in various ways it is being adapted to new conditions, remaining a need-fulfilling religion in the process. Uniform generalizations are likely to be incorrect, however, for Islam's sectarian structure is decentralized at the level of individual cities, and the cities of the Middle East are subject to different regional and national influences. Consequently, one must suspend judgment and refrain from prediction when faced with such facts as the following: (1) The Turkish government, which in the 1920s and 1930s attempted a radical secularization program, is now accommodating to, and actually using, the persistently religious reactions and needs of its people (Magnarella 1974, p. 175); (2) the Saudi Arabian government is, in 1975, planning a multibillion-dollar modernization program without, apparently, considering any modifications in Wahhabi conservatism. Turkey's concerted modernization efforts did not de-Islamicize its people, but there has been an accommodation between the religious and secular spheres of life. Generally similar accommodations can be expected in other countries and regions of the Middle East, but detailed predictions are beyond the vision of this anthropological perspective.

REFERENCES

Abd al-Ati, Hammudah. *Islam in Focus: A Muslim's Interpretation of the Fundamental Principles of Islam.* Edmonton, Alberta: Canadian Islamic Centre, 1963.

Alberts, Robert C. *Social Structure and Culture Change in an Iranian Village.* Ph.D. dissertation, University of Wisconsin, 1963.

Ammar, Hamed. *Growing Up in an Egyptian Village.* London: Routledge & Kegan Paul, 1954.

Barclay, Harold B. *Buurri al Lamaab: A Suburban Village in the Sudan.* Ithaca, N.Y.: Cornell University Press, 1964.

Berger, Morroe. *Islam in Egypt Today: Social and Political Aspects of Popular Religion.* Cambridge: at the University Press, 1970.

Berque, Jacques. *Structures sociales du Haut-Atlas.* Paris: Presses Universitaires de France, 1955.

Callender, Charles, and Fadwa el-Guindi. *Life Crisis Rituals among the Kenuz.* Cleveland: Case Western Reserve Studies in Anthropology, no. 3, 1971.

Coon, Carleton S. *Caravan: The Story of the Middle East.* Rev. ed. New York: Holt, 1958.

Crapanzano, Vincent. *The Hamadsha: A Study in Moroccan Ethnopsychiatry.* Berkeley: University of California Press, 1973.

Evans-Pritchard, E. E. *The Sanusi of Cyrenaica.* Oxford: at the University Press, 1949.

Fernea, Elizabeth W. *A View of the Nile.* Garden City, N.Y.: Doubleday, 1970.

Fernea, Robert A., and Elizabeth W. Fernea. "Variation in Religious Observance among Islamic Women." In *Scholars, Saints, and Sufis: Muslim Institutions in the Middle East Since 1500,* edited by Nikki R. Keddie, pp. 385–401. Berkeley: University of California Press, 1972.

Fischer, Michael M. J. *Zoroastrian Iran Between Myth and Praxis.* Ph.D. dissertation, University of Chicago, 1973.

Fuller, Anne. *Buarij: Portrait of a Lebanese Muslim Village.* Cambridge, Mass.: Harvard Middle Eastern Monographs, no. 6, 1961.

Geertz, Clifford. *Islam Observed: Religious Development in Morocco and Indonesia.* Chicago: University of Chicago Press, 1968. Phoenix Edition, 1971.

Gellner, Ernest. *Saints of the Atlas.* Chicago: University of Chicago Press, 1969.

Gibb, H.A.R., and Harold Bowen. *Islamic Society and the West.* Vol. I, Part 2. New York: Oxford University Press, 1957.

Gilsenan, Michael. *Saint and Sufi in Modern Egypt: An Essay in the Sociology of Religion.* Oxford: at the Clarendon Press, 1973.

Granqvist, Hilma. *Birth and Childhood Among the Arabs: Studies in a Muhammadan Village in Palestine.* Helsingfors, Finland: Söderström & Co., 1947.

Gulick, John. "The Religious Structure of Lebanese Culture." *Internationales Jahrbuch für Religionssoziologie* 1(1965): 151–187.

Huxley, Julian. *From an Antique Land.* New York: Crown, 1954.

el-Kayyali, Haseeb. "Dearly Beloved Brethren!" In *Arabic Writing Today: The Short Story,* edited by Mahmoud Manzalaoui, pp. 212–218. Cairo:

American Research Center in Egypt, 1968 (also published by University of California Press, 1970).

Kennedy, John G. "Nubian Zar Ceremonies as Psychotherapy." *Human Organization* 26(1967): 185–194.

Lane, E. W. *The Manners and Customs of the Modern Egyptians.* New York: Dutton, 1908 (originally published in 1836).

Libassi, Paul T. "Sacred Remains: Is Digging a Desecration in Old Jerusalem?" *The Sciences* 14, no. 3 (1974): 6–12.

Loeb, Laurence D. *The Jews of Southwest Iran: A Study of Cultural Persistence.* Ph.D. dissertation, Columbia University, 1970.

Magnarella, Paul J. *Tradition and Change in a Turkish Town.* New York: Wiley, 1974.

Makal, Mahmut. *A Village in Anatolia.* London: Vallentine, Mitchell & Co., 1954.

Makarem, Sami Nasib. *The Druze Faith.* Delmar, N.Y.: Caravan, 1974.

Mansur, Fatma. *Bodrum: A Town in the Aegean.* Leiden, Netherlands: E. J. Brill, 1972.

Marriott, McKim. "Little Communities in an Indigenous Civilization." In *Village India: Studies in the Little Community,* edited by McKim Marriott, pp. 171–222. American Anthropological Association, Memoir no. 83, 1955.

Naim, C. Mohammed. "Arabic Orthography and some Non-Semitic Languages." In *Islam and its Cultural Divergence,* edited by Girdhari L. Tikku, pp. 113–144. Urbana: University of Illinois Press, 1971.

Patai, Raphael. *The Republic of Lebanon.* New Haven, Conn.: Human Relations Area Files, Subcontractor's Monograph, 1956.

Rubin, Morton. *The Walls of Acre: Intergroup Relations and Urban Development in Israel.* New York: Holt, Rinehart and Winston, 1974.

Schieffelin, Olivia, ed. *Muslim Attitudes Toward Family Planning.* New York: Population Council, 1967.

Schimmel, Annemarie. *Islamic Calligraphy.* Leiden, Netherlands: E. J. Brill, 1970.

Trimingham, J. Spencer. *The Sufi Orders in Islam.* London: Oxford University Press, 1971.

Welch, Stuart C. *A King's Book of Kings: The Shah-Nameh of Shah Tahmasp.* New York: Metropolitan Museum of Art, 1972.

ANNOTATED BIBLIOGRAPHY

Alberts, Robert C. *Social Structure and Culture Change in an Iranian Village.* Ph.D. dissertation, University of Wisconsin, 1963.

This is one of the most detailed first-hand village studies in the Middle Eastern literature. Thanks to University Microfilms it is reasonably accessible. It is 1,110 typescript pages long, not counting the 44-page bibliography. Davarabad is a new village, an outgrowth of a demonstration farm established in 1934, and in other ways it is a "special" case. While one must be careful about automatic generalizations from Alberts' data, his minute observations are immensely valuable. This is especially so because he is highly aware of stereotypes and shams, as in religious and sectarian behavior, and he makes this awareness explicit.

Barclay, Harold B. *Buurri al Lamaab: A Suburban Village in the Sudan.* Ithaca, N.Y.: Cornell University Press, 1964.

Barclay is especially interested in religion, and much of this book —though it is also a "community study"—is devoted to detailed descriptions and discussions of religious behavior.

Crapanzano, Vincent. *The Hamadsha: A Study in Moroccan Ethnopsychiatry.* Berkeley: University of California Press, 1973.

Very valuable both as a study of modern urban life and as an analysis of religious behavior. This is one of the very few sources on the actual performances of a tariqa based on first-hand observation.

Dermenghem, Emile. *Le culte des saints dans l'Islam maghrebin.* Paris: Gallimard, 1954.

A vivid portrayal of the feeling of baraka in the saint complex. The book contains specific descriptions and is illustrated.

Donaldson, Bess Allen. *The Wild Rue: A Study of Muhammadan Magic and Folklore in Iran.* New York: Arno Press, 1973.

This book, first published in 1938, belongs to a genre that is now viewed with some contempt by many anthropologists as being merely a collection of curiosities. It is, notwithstanding, a very detailed source book on the particulars of the religious little tradition in Iran, many of the details being similar to those found elsewhere.

Fischer, Michael M. J. *Zoroastrian Iran between Myth and Praxis.* Ph.D. dissertation, University of Chicago, 1973.

Based on field work done primarily in the city of Yazd in 1970–1971, this study combines detailed descriptions of behavior with sophisticated analysis. Despite the title, much of the work is concerned with the religious and sectarian integration of Islam with Iranian national culture, and one chapter discusses the Zoroastrians, Muslims, Bahais, and Jews as they live and worship simultaneously in the city of Yazd.

Geertz, Clifford. *Islam Observed: Religious Development in Morocco and Indonesia.* Chicago: University of Chicago Press, 1968. Phoenix Edition, 1971.

Based on extensive field experience in both countries, this book is particularly insightful in regard to the little tradition and what is "Middle Eastern" in Islam (exemplified by Morocco) in contrast to the many non-Middle Eastern characteristics of the Muslim Indonesians.

Gellner, Ernest. *Saints of the Atlas.* Chicago: University of Chicago Press,
1969.

A very useful complement to Dermenghem and Crapanzano, this
book emphasizes the social structure and ecology of a brotherhood in
a very detailed and specific manner.

Gibb, H.A.R. *Modern Trends in Islam.* Chicago: University of Chicago
Press, 1947.

A highly authoritative reference by one of the modern masters of
Islamic history.

Gilsenan, Michael. *Saint and Sufi in Modern Egypt: An Essay in the
Sociology of Religion.* Oxford: at the Clarendon Press, 1973.

In many ways this book is an Egyptian counterpart to the Moroccan
studies of Crapanzano, Gellner, and others. What really goes on in a
brotherhood? What is the significance of that behavior for its participants? How is a brotherhood actually organized? This, like the others,
is an excellent source on these subjects.

Granqvist, Hilma. *Birth and Childhood Among the Arabs: Studies in a
Muhammadan Village in Palestine.* Helsingfors, Finland: Söderström
& Co., 1947.

This is one of the four monographs (one consisting of two volumes)
that were published by Granqvist on the field work that she did in
Artas, a Muslim village near Bethlehem, between 1925 and 1931.
(Exact citations for the others will be found on p. 148 of Sweet's *The
Central Middle East* cited at the end of Chapter Three). Granqvist was
especially interested in women, children, and religion, and the religion she described was primarily the little tradition in a particular
village. Her monographs are examples of a genre that was popular in
the late nineteenth and early twentieth centuries: the search for Bibli-
cal parallels or survivals in the customs of the modern Palestinians.
However, whatever her biases may have been, she was meticulous in
her observations, and her work is of great and enduring value.

Grunebaum, Gustave E. von. *Modern Islam: The Search for Cultural
Identity.* Berkeley: University of California Press, 1962.

In recognition of the enormous scholarship that has been devoted to
Islam, almost entirely not by anthropologists, this book is included in
this bibliography. The author, a much respected and beloved scholar
who died in 1972, was a historian who was acutely sensitive to the
realities of present-day life in the Middle East. That sensitivity is
quite apparent in this book.

Keddie, Nikki R., ed. *Scholars, Saints, and Sufis: Muslim Institutions in
the Middle East Since 1500.* Berkeley: University of California Press,
1972.

The first part of this collection of papers emphasizes aspects of the
recent history of ulamas in various countries. The second part emphasizes the little tradition and includes papers by Gellner, Crapanzano, Thaiss, and the Ferneas.

202   Lane, Edward W. *The Manners and Customs of the Modern Egyptians.*
New York: Dutton, Everyman's Library No. 315, 1908.

The latest printing of this title was in 1944, in a reduced format but
retaining many of the engravings done by Lane himself. Originally
published in 1836, when Lane had lived in Egypt for about eleven
years, this is probably the best description of everyday life, including
religious behavior, in the early part of the Machine-Age Islamic
period. Despite its upper-class and Cairene biases, it is essential reading for anyone who wants specific perspectives on the cultural
changes and continuities of the past 150 years.

Roper, Joyce. *The Women of Nar.* London: Faber & Faber, 1974.

An account of the author's sojourn in Nar, a small town in central
Turkey. The descriptions are vivid, detailed, and sensitive, with emphasis on human relationships. Considerable attention is paid to the
women's participation in, and reactions to, a number of the religious
phenomena discussed in this chapter. Animal sacrifice and boys' circumcision are described. Roper was particularly distressed by the
latter and by what she felt to be the old peoples' sadistic enjoyment of
the occasion.

Smith, W. Cantwell. *Islam in Modern History.* Princeton, N.J.: Princeton
University Press, 1957.

A frequently cited source.

Thaiss, Gustav E. *Religious Symbolism and Social Change: The Drama of
Husain.* Ph.D. dissertation, Washington University, 1973.

In many respects this is an Iranian counterpart to the already noted
Moroccan and Egyptian monographs on modern religious behavior, an
urban counterpart to Alberts' Iranian village study, and a big-city
counterpart to Fischer's small-city study in Iran. It concentrates on
the Shia concepts of Imam and martyrdom and the significance of
these in the everyday religious behavior of bazaar merchants in
Tehran.

Westermarck, Edward. *Pagan Survivals in Mohammadan Civilisation.*
Amsterdam, Netherlands: Philo Press, 1973.

Originally published in 1933, this book does for the religious little
tradition of Morocco very much what Donaldson does for that of Iran.
The book is the target of the same type of criticism, and it is valuable
and interesting for the same reasons that Donaldson is.

SEVEN

THE ESSENTIAL SELF

SEX AND GENDER

Every individual is either female or male as determined by her or his genetic structure. Every individual is also a personality, a complex of habitual behavior and thinking. A very strongly held view in both the West and the Middle East is that individuals' basic characteristics of personality are determined by their sex, that female and male are opposites, and that therefore typical men's and women's personalities are naturally opposites in all important respects. This view implies that many attitudes and activities associated with one sex are automatically incompatible with the nature of the other.

The rigidity of these beliefs is of concern to those who perceive the severe constraints that they impose on individuals of both sexes, especially when they must adapt to massive changes in cultural expectations. Yet anthropologists have shown that, while rigid definitions of what is appropriate behavior and attitude for each sex are typically found within particular cultures, comparisons of different cultures show that behavior considered natural for one sex in one culture may be considered natural for the other sex in another culture (Friedl 1975, pp. 1–3). Clearly, but contrary to conventional wisdom, sex alone is not the determinant in such matters. Furthermore, recent psychological studies raise very serious doubts in regard to the traditional assumptions that most of the personality traits in question are determined by the biology of sex and sex differences. A reviewer of two of these studies says, "To a great extent it seems, there is nothing either male or female but thinking makes it so" (Edmiston 1975, p. 3).

Edmiston is not referring to sex—the biological mechanics and structures of reproduction—but to individual selves as wholes. In order to help disentangle the strictly sexual aspects of the individual from all the rest of her or his personal makeup that may be associated in some way with sex, the latter is increasingly being referred to in the literature as *gender.* The word is borrowed from the study of grammar. In many languages (for example, Arabic and French) all nouns are categorized as belonging to either the feminine or the masculine gender. In other languages (for example, English and Persian) this is not the case. In some instances the correspondences between grammatical gender and the sex of the object seem obvious, and it might be assumed that the gender identification "naturally" follows from the sex. For example, the French word for mother is feminine. That the gender system is not necessarily sex-determined is, however, easily shown by the fact that masculine and feminine genders are frequently applied to nouns whose objects have no sex at all. Sometimes these applications actually seem to *defy* "nature," as in the case of the masculine gender of the French word for milk.

Though gender is, to be sure, linked in part to sex, it is elaborated far beyond what is clearly sexual in nature. Furthermore, sociocultural gender systems often accentuate or exaggerate, even polarize, peoples' conceptions of sexual characteristics and differences. What this amounts to is the taking of enormous liberties with sexual characteristics and differences as actually given by nature. Viewed another way, these differences can be seen as complementary, rather than opposed, and relative or overlapping, rather than mutually exclusive. Nevertheless, many people confuse gender definitions with sexual characteristics and are seriously handicapped in seeing the difference between sex and gender because of the powerful emotional vested interests that they apparently have in the idea of absolute, all-inclusive female-male opposites.

Gender definitions and expectations are patterns of culture. Cultural patterns are subject to change, and when some of them change, others usually adapt and modify themselves in reaction. Given the many other cultural changes in the Middle East, changes in gender definitions and expectations should therefore not be surprising, nor should heated controversy over what directions those changes should take be surprising.

That the traditional gender patterns of Middle Eastern culture will not and cannot change because they are determined by nature is a position taken by various people, both Middle Easterners and outsiders. There are others, however, who question this position, especially when it seems to be used as a self-interested rationalization for the maintenance of the status quo.

The Middle East is certainly not the only area of the world in which gender definitions and expectations (culturally learned but susceptible to conscious change) are confused by most people with the characteristics of sex (biologically determined and relatively unchangeable). However, Western observers of the Middle East have viewed it through the filter of the gender definitions of their own cultures, and their interpretations of their observations may sometimes be projections of the sex-gender-expectation problem in their own cultures. These probable ethnocentric biases are intensified by the very strong emotions (for example, fears about precarious self-esteem) that are often involved. This caution should be borne in mind when we consider the data and conclusions of the various observers.

As has been mentioned before, the Islamic and Christian traditions differ in that the former lacks the two antisexual themes that are generally acknowledged to be part of the latter: the Christian veneration of celibacy and the association of sexual pleasure with sin. Nevertheless, there are Middle Eastern sexual strictures. Basic modesty (shame associated with exposure of the genitalia) is reported to be inculcated early in life. Nudity in general is not condoned, nor is it idealized as it is among some elements in Western culture. In fact, it is discouraged. At childbirth the mother is attended by women only. After death, corpses are washed by persons of the same sex as the deceased. In adaptation to modern cultural change there are serious controversies on such subjects as abbreviated bathing suits (Should women, in particular, go to public bathing beaches at all?); on the censorship of explicit Western movies, magazines, and books; and on the intimate examination of women by men physicians.

A certain prudishness does seem to be involved, but so also are concepts of decorum and dignity. Sexual shame is not the only factor. This point was highlighted some years ago when the new socialist government of Egypt decreed that belly dancers (whose breasts, buttocks, and genitalia are always completely and carefully clothed) also cover their middles with gauzy material. Widely regarded either as a bureaucratic aberration or a response to Soviet Russian influences, the edict did not ban the belly dance itself. In other words, this dance, which has been interpreted as being an expression of Middle Eastern *acceptance* of sexuality free of Western voyeurism (Berger 1961, p. 26), was left intact. Other types of behavior that seem to reflect acceptance, rather than denial, of the physical aspects of sex are the public circumcision ceremony for boys and the display of the new bride's hymenal blood after the consummation of the marriage. The fact that genital discharges are ritually polluting may seem to run counter to the idea of acceptance of sexuality, but it must be remembered that *all* bodily discharges are defined as ritually polluting.

The great concern about the virginity of new brides is easily misunderstood by Westerners, who see it in the light of their own traditions in which nonsexuality is regarded as virtuous per se. The distinction between sex and gender is helpful in clarifying this misunderstanding. Middle Eastern behavior and feelings in this matter appear to be far more concerned with gender than they are with sex. Premarital virginity is a sign of the successful seclusion of females by their male relatives. This is connected with the code of kin-group honor, which is, in turn, linked with the peril-and-refuge mentality. The bride's premarital nonsexuality, as such, seems to be of secondary concern. Indeed, her wedding is accompanied by ceremonial recognitions of sexuality, and as soon as possible after she is married, her own sexuality is celebrated in a manner that seems highly indecorous to many Westerners.

Two other possible indicators of acceptance of physiological functions not unrelated to sex are men urinating in open, public places and women suckling their babies in public. This is not random or aberrant behavior. The men turn away from where other people are so that the penis is not exposed to casual view, and the women do not uncover their breasts to an unnecessary degree. Certain rules of decorum are observed, but there is no concealment of the fact that bodily functions are being performed.

These patterns of public behavior have a strong sensory impact on middle-class Western observers. So, to, does another pattern of public behavior: two adult males walking along hand-in-hand or with fingers entwined. The common Western reaction to this practice (which actually occurs all across southern Asia) is to assume that the two men must have a homosexual relationship and that homosexuality must be more openly approved, or less disapproved, in the Middle East than in the West. Actually, this custom is primarily an expression of warm friendship and is not necessarily an indication of homosexuality. The truth is that homosexuality is not generally or openly approved in the Middle East. However, there is a widespread, essentially underground, Western stereotype that it is and that male homosexuality is very common. Dramatic instances, such as the experiences that T. E. Lawrence made famous, probably have fed the stereotype. Its plausibility has been asserted on the grounds of excessive heterosexual deprivation due to the social segregation of the sexes. Plausible or not, there has not been, to my knowledge at least, any convincing substantiation (or refutation, either) of the hypothesis that male homosexuality is significantly more frequent in the Middle East than it is in other areas. There is no question about the existence of male (and female) homosexuality in the Middle East. That is not the issue. The issue has to do with homosexuality's reputed high frequency and acceptability. In any case, if studies were to demonstrate that homosexuality is significantly more common in the Middle East (as many people would predict), then there would be the problem of how to account for two general behavioral tendencies that have in fact been reliably established: high fertility rates and relative infrequency of unmarried and never-married adults. One explanation could be that significantly large numbers of people have bisexual capabilities, but no evidence for this exists at present.

The discovery of verifiable facts in regard to Middle Eastern norms of sexuality is considerably impeded by the conventional reticence of Middle Easterners on the subject. This is similar to the "Victorian" reticences of the West that have substantially been modified only among some Westerners and only during the past two to three decades. It has been largely within the confines of their own inhibitions that a few Western observers have suggested that when groups of men and groups of women gather separately, there is much bawdy and ribald talk. The suggestions seem to be based on rumors, however. The conventional reticence may well extend to situations where an outsider (such as a foreign observer) is present, even when he or she is of the same sex as the members of the group. Reportedly, men's ribaldry is limited by care not to make any explicit or implied references to the wives or close female relatives of the men involved. There have been reports that among women, however, references to the sexual behavior of husbands, brothers-in-law, and others, are made. It would seem that there is far more activity in this aspect of life than has been reliably described. The little that has been hinted at suggests that while sexuality per se is explicitly accepted, it is circumscribed by the social segregation of males and females.

The social segregation of males and females is one major aspect of Middle Eastern life that is so well documented, at least in its superficial manifestations, that there is no need to describe or discuss those manifestations in detail (for source materials see Gulick and Gulick 1974). A brief listing of them should suffice. Women are expected to get married at an early age, to become the mothers of numerous children, and to devote their lives to caring for their homes and children. Even within their own homes (whether house or tent) they should be secluded from male visitors who are the guests of their husbands. While peasant women frequently help in doing the chores of farming and gardening, they do so under the supervision of their husbands and male relatives. This is not felt to be work outside of the home any more than are women's cottage industries such as carpet weaving and dressmaking. Nondomestic occupations and responsibilities are the domain of the men. When women venture forth into public nondomestic places where they will encounter strangers (such as in towns and cities, but less frequently in small communities), they continue to be segregated by observing the decorum of minimal interaction with strangers and by wearing enveloping gowns or veils, or both. Middle Eastern women frequently go out to do the household shopping, but many husbands prefer to do this instead, if possible. In considerable contrast to Southeast Asia, Africa, and even Latin America, very few shopkeepers and vendors are women.

The foregoing discussion is a precis of some of the highlights of the traditional pattern of female-male social segregation in terms of its external manifestations. I think that it also represents fairly well the complex of values and expectations that most Middle Eastern men and women are aware of, regardless of how they, individually, may feel about those expectations and regardless of how much their own observable behavior may diverge from them or even conflict with them. Divergent behavior (for example, women going about in public without gowns or veils) is certainly present, and it is conspicuous, especially in certain parts of many cities. Moreover, statistics provided by Middle Eastern governments—such as data showing the increasing numbers and proportions of girls and women in primary, secondary, and vocational schools, and in universities and even professional schools—further emphasize the substantial extent of divergence from the traditional norms. Eventually, these divergences may indeed become the new norms. At present, however, they are felt by many Middle Eastern people to be uncomfortable deviations, and even those who have adopted them as part of their life style are likely to be defensive about them.

In the city of Isfahan, Iran, in 1970–1971, most females (starting before the age of puberty) wore the chador in public. This is a one-piece, semicircular cloth that envelops the wearer from head to heels and can be drawn across the face if need be. The wearer is fully clothed underneath; it is an outer covering. Many women students at the University of Isfahan came to campus wearing the chador, but they took it off after entering the gate, revealing themselves to be clad in a variety of costumes, from knee-length dresses, to slacks, to miniskirts. Some of the university students were among the minority of women in the city who did not ordinarily wear the chador in the streets either, and among some of these there were reports of having been spat upon by little girls wearing chadors. Exactly what motivated this grossly hostile behavior (presumably suppressed in, but stimulated by, the little girls' elders) is not clear, but it is a reasonable guess that it was fear generated by threat to deeply engrained identity- and security-reinforcement patterns. The expressed notion that such behavior would be unthinkable or impossible in larger or more cosmopolitan cities like Casablanca, Beirut, Tehran, or Shiraz, would not, I believe, prevent Middle Eastern women who do not wear gowns or veils in public from being careful and feeling on the defensive in the sections of those cities where gowned and veiled women do predominate.

Women working in nondomestic occupations is another divergence from the norms of female-male segregation. Indeed, there are women physicians and a few women in administrative positions; there are women nurses, typists, and schoolteachers; there are women in some countries' military systems, such as those in the Health and Literacy Corps of the Iranian army; there are women factory workers; and there are women in domestic service. Some of these women are startlingly conspicuous, especially when they are seen together with veiled women. However, despite the fact that they are conspicuous, and frequently made more so by publicity in the mass media, they are statistically unusual. Available information shows that no more, and often less, than 10 percent of the labor force in Middle Eastern countries consists of women. This is far less than in Europe or North America, and less even than in Latin America, where ideas similar to Middle Eastern ones about gender definitions are norms. The reason for the differences is the continuing importance of female-male segregation as a principle in the Middle East (Youssef 1974). Of course, it must be remembered that all those women who are not employed outside their homes are not necessarily inured to, and accepting of, the traditional segregation and seclusion ethos. Fox's study of the differences in attitude and orientation among home-bound women in Ankara (1973), mentioned in Chapter Four, demonstrates this very forcibly. Female-male segregation involves (essentially, if not always in literal fact) the seclusion of women in their homes. The privacy of the home is highly valued and carefully protected, and, as I have mentioned, domestic architectural styles definitely reflect these concerns.

Female-male segregation, as a complex of expectations and patterns of actual behavior, rests on concepts of gender definition, and these are important elements in the hypothesized peril-and-refuge mentality. Bearing this in mind, let us consider one particular system of gender definitions in the literature that is readily accessible for more detailed study. This is Bourdieu's presentation of the fundamental postulates of the sentiments of honor among the Kabyles (Bourdieu 1966). The Kabyles are Berber-speaking, generally tribally organized, mountain and village dwellers in Algeria. While various details in the analysis may be peculiar to them, and while different words for some of the same key concepts are used elsewhere in the Middle East, this is but one specific example of a system of concepts that is common to the Middle East as a whole. Bourdieu (1966, p. 222) presents the Kabyles' concepts in the form of a dualistic model, as shown in Figure 2.

The obvious dualities and polar oppositions shown in Figure 2 imply maximum differentiation of the two genders. Hurma, haram, and nif are variously defined as respectability and honor. Hurma or haram can be lost (by *women's* misconduct), and men are vulnerable to such loss. Nif must be defended and asserted publicly to protect hurma and haram (Bourdieu 1966, pp. 218–219). These concepts—and the behavior associated with them—appear to be very similar to, if not identical with, the sharaf of the men and the ird of the women among pastoralists in Egypt (Abou-Zeid 1966, pp.

HURMA-HARAM SACRED OF THE LEFT HAND	NIF SACRED OF THE RIGHT HAND
Feminine, femininity.	Masculine, virility.
Woman, the possessor of harmful and impure powers.	Man, the possessor of beneficent, fertilizing and protecting powers.
Left, twisted. Vulnerability, nakedness.	Right, straight. Protection, enclosure, clothing.
INSIDE	OUTSIDE
The preserve of women: house, garden.	The preserve of men: assembly, mosque, fields, marketplace.
Enclosed and secret world of the intimate life: food, sexuality.	Open world of public life, of social and political activities. Exchanges.
Magic	Religion
DAMP, WATER, etc.	DRY, FIRE, etc.

Figure 2.   Gender Polarities of the Kabyles.

Source: Reprinted from "The Sentiment of Honour in Kabyle Society" by Pierre Bourdieu, in *Honour and Shame*, edited by J. G. Peristiany, by permission of The University of Chicago Press and J. G. Peristiany. © 1966 by Pierre Bourdieu.

256–257). Moreover, these same terms are used very widely in other parts of the Middle East, together with namus, which is used by Turks and Iranians in very much the same sense as ird.

Gender expectations are that the male protects the female by secluding her, but that the female is also dangerous to the male; he is vulnerable to her misconduct, especially sexual misconduct, and because of his vulnerability, his impulses to seclude her are intensified. Apart from the psychoanalytic interpretations that these phenomena invite, two considerations are important to note. One is simply a reminder of Papanek's idea that the seclusion of females is a behavioral complex that has evolved over centuries of living in a perilous and uncontrollable social environment, a system of controls asserted in an otherwise uncontrollable reality (see Chapter Two).

The other consideration has to do with dominance and submission. Many discussions of this whole aspect of Middle Eastern culture attempt to reduce it to male dominance and female submission. The evidence adduced includes many details of public behavior (husband walking ahead of wife, men being served first at meals, and so on), not to mention husbands' unilateral right to uncontested divorce (now widely illegal) and to having as many as four wives at the same time (now generally illegal or greatly circumscribed), as well as the famous "right" or "duty" to chastise or kill sexually errant female relatives. Male dominance also seems to be clearly indicated by the prevailing system of patrilineal inheritance and affiliation and by men's monopoly on positions of authority and public behavior generally.

That the dominance-submission theme has perhaps been exaggerated, however, is suggested by certain types of information that have long been known but have heretofore either been disregarded or differently interpreted. First is the concept—or feeling —that women are (or female sexuality is) dangerous to men. Whatever the best explanation for this may be, it certainly should raise doubts about there being complete male dominance. Second, certain female saints are important. Fatima, daughter of Muhammad, is the acknowledged ancestress of all his later descendants. Among the latter was the sister of the Eighth Imam (Ali ar-Reza), whose shrine at Qom, Iran, is the second most important shrine in the country; and Sayyida Zaynab, sister of the martyred Husayn, who is buried in Cairo. Her tomb is a major shrine that gives its name to one of the quarters of the city, and her spirit has been evoked in two short stories by Yahya Haqqi, "The Saint's Lamp" (1973) and "Mother of the Destitute" (1967). There are many less famous female saints, including some, like Lalla Aziza of the Seksawa in Morocco (Berque 1955, pp. 281–298), who are predominant in certain regions of the countryside. Third, and possibly most important, there are various indications that women not only may achieve dominant roles in their secluded, domestic milieu, but also—within that milieu—may consciously and effectively involve themselves in the "public" activities of their husbands and male relatives. Their role as mediators between kin groups, for example, can have very important public implications. In such roles women may become powerful persons, even though they appear to be in submission to male-enforced seclusion. This whole matter is thoroughly set forth, and extensively documented, in an article by Cynthia Nelson (1974). Nelson emphasizes that the general neglect of this dimension of Middle Eastern life is in part due to the biases and limitations in access to women on the part of the male scholars who have done most of the relevant field research. Doubtless there is truth in this, but not all the female scholars who have worked there have done as much as they might have with the issue, either.

A difficulty faced by both female and male researchers is the privacy of the domestic scene, a privacy in which both female and male Middle Easterners have a stake, if our hypothesis about the peril-and-refuge mentality is valid. Thus, although there is a large literature on kinship, marriage, and family structure, there is very little on internal intimacies and deeply felt emotions in regard to gender definitions and gender roles. Furthermore, there is absolute contradiction in the available literature on how women feel about the basic system of female-male segregation. For example, a conclusion that could be drawn from the observations assembled and discussed by Nelson (1974) is that those women who do become powerful persons within that system may be quite content with it the way it is. This is certainly Hansen's impression of the situation as she observed it among some Kurdish women in Iraq (Hansen 1960, pp. 56, 178–179). And among the women in a Christian Lebanese village, des Villettes felt that there was general contentment with their domestic seclusion (des Villettes 1964, p. 128). On the contrary, however, Germaine Tillion (1966, pp. 21–22) perceives the lot of women in the Middle East (and around the Mediterranean) to have been one of degradation since pre-Christian and pre-Islamic times, and Fadéla M'rabet's two books in one (1969) are a long cry of outrage at what she considers to be the continued oppression of women in Algeria. Of course, we must not lose sight of the fact that we are trying to generalize about millions of women whose situations, both within the traditional system and diverging from it, vary greatly. It is safe to assume that there are different women with feelings that are contradictory, including women who may have to cope with contradictory feelings within themselves.

Ultimately, consideration of the interaction of gender roles leads to consideration of the relationships between husbands and wives. Characteristically, very little is publicly known or said about these relationships, though, of course, most Middle Eastern adults know much about them privately. Vieille (1967, p. 119) expresses a commonly made assumption—that he may have drawn only from external appearances—that Iranian village husbands and wives do not communicate with each other about such intimate and important matters as whether or not to limit their fertility by means of contraception. However, a study of a sample of working-class husbands and wives in the city of Isfahan indicated that there very definitely was communication between those husbands and wives, at any rate, on this subject (Gulick and Gulick 1974), whatever else they may not have communicated about. In a Turkish town it has been found that husband-wife communication seems to have increased as a result of certain modern changes (Magnarella 1972). This implies, of course, that there was less communication under previous, more traditional, conditions. These are only very small and fragmentary probes into a subject that is of universal importance.

Middle Eastern expressions directly concerning these matters are rare, and this should not be surprising if it is generally true, as Bourdieu says it is among the Kabyles, that "the principal imperative is to conceal the whole domain of intimacy" (Bourdieu 1966, p. 223). However, there are three modern Middle Eastern short stories, originally written in Arabic, that are compelling, no matter how much one must keep aware of the fiction writers' prerogative to project into their work their own, possibly highly idiosyncratic, views.

Consider the idea that female sexuality is felt to be dangerous, especially to males (Bourdieu 1966, p. 221; Schneider 1971). There are possible hints of this in Youssef Idris's "Peace with Honor," set in rural Egypt (Idris 1968). Fatma is the local beauty, a sensational woman admired and loved by one and all, but she is neither married nor engaged. Why? Idris suggests that no man would be rash enough to marry her, for his enjoyment of her beauty would be outweighed by the extra anxieties of protecting her. The danger, however, is unspecified. One can guess that it could be the threat that she would pose for her husband in being such a temptation to other men, or it could be the jealousy of other women, such as her sister-in-law who claims she deliberately shakes her breasts as she walks. Or could it be subliminal fear of her apparently abundant sexuality? In any event, Fatma unmarried is a continual source of anxiety to her brother, Farag, with whom she lives and who is responsible for her. One day, Gharib, a long-time silent admirer, startles Fatma with a greeting, hoping for one in return, but both become terrified; she starts screaming, and he runs away. Everyone assumes she has been raped, and finally she is examined by Umm George, a Coptic Christian woman who is more educated and citified than the others and is also Fatma's friend. To everyone's joy and relief, Fatma is found still to be a virgin, but Farag gives her a beating anyway—though showing evident restraint—in order to "answer . . . suspicions" and "silence rumors." He adamantly refuses to let Gharib marry her, and Fatma eventually resumes her old naive-provocative ways, but with a subtle air of lost innocence. Some of the ingredients of "dangerous female sexuality" can be read into this story, but its major impact lies in its many nuances of dialogue, commentary, and incident that soften the extreme harshness and rigidity of the Middle Eastern stereotypes of sex and gender.

While many of the troubles of Fatma, Farag, and Gharib could have been observed by an outsider, the characters in Yusuf Sharouni's "The Man and the Farm" (1967) and Laila Baalabaki's "A Spaceship of Tenderness to the Moon" (1967) express the intimate concerns of husbands and wives in a way that could not be directly observed by an outsider and would not very likely be revealed to an outsider, either. In Sharouni's story, Munira, wife of Badawi Effendi, finally goes into labor with her first child, after seven years of marriage. Badawi and Munira have had a mutually satisfying sexual relationship, and, pressured by their mothers' and their own anxieties, have considered or tried all sorts of remedies for their inability to conceive a child. Contrary to stereotypes, neither has blamed the other for their problem, and Badawi has rejected the option of unilateral divorce. Recently, Munira, on the advice of acquaintances, has resorted to magic and thereafter has become pregnant.

The protagonists of Baalabaki's story have a different problem: She does not want to have children, and the story describes one of their quarrels on the subject. Baalabaki is famous in the Middle East for her avant-garde views, and the private thoughts of the wife in her story may (or may not) be highly unusual for a Middle Eastern woman. Yet there is evidence that many Middle Eastern women would have preferred, if they had had a real choice, to bear fewer children than they actually did. Fulfillment of that preference would have involved decisions not to bear those children, and in the future many more Middle Eastern women may be acting on thoughts and feelings like those of Baalabaki's heroine.

In both stories the characters have their private thoughts, not shared with their spouses, yet they are also very much in affectionate communication with one another. Though fictional in form, these expressions of behavior and feeling come from within Middle Eastern experience and are in obvious contrast to the many outsiders' suppositions about husband-wife relationships—suppositions that seem to have been based only on inferences drawn from the reserved demeanor of husbands and wives in public.

My purpose in discussing these three short stories is to emphasize the sense of humanity that they infuse into this subject—a sense that is too often missing in the literature. It is not my purpose, however, to promote any revisionist hypothesis to the effect that Middle Eastern marriages are idyllic in terms of certain Western ideals of romantic companionability. On the contrary, I have hypothesized that female-male relationships (including marriage) are central in the peril-and-refuge mentality, and I think that this position is supported by recent studies that take changing styles and situations, as well as traditional norms, into account. For example, Dodd (1973) believes that al-ird (the honor that is vulnerable to female misconduct) continues to be an important value even in "modernized" contexts. If he is correct, al-ird will continue to exercise influence on gender definitions and expectations unless and until (in my view) the peril-and-refuge mentality is significantly modified. Amal Vinogradov, an anthropologist who is also a Middle Easterner, thinks that in present-day Morocco the husband-wife relationship is "uneasy . . . and marked by a mutual lack of trust, by anxiety, and by a large measure of hostility" (Vinogradov 1974, p. 198). She believes that while French colonialism certainly aggravated these conditions, it did not originate them. Vanessa Maher makes the same point in the course of her extensive study of Moroccan women's social structure and economic concerns. She says, "Only after a long testing process . . . and the birth of children, do husband and wife acquire any confidence, and it is tenuous at that, in the loyalty of the other. The antagonism of husband's and wife's interests is taken for granted ... The marital scene ... is generally riddled with half-truths and deceit, until the couple either divorce or with the passage of years ... become more or less ... mutually trusting" (Maher 1974, pp. 154, 157).

KINSHIP

Kinship is such an important dimension of Middle Eastern life that it has already been discussed in this book in several different connections. In Chapter Two the idea of patrilineal descent from a common ancestor as a metaphor of alliance was included in the mentality of peril and refuge. Tribal, lineage, and family alliances and segmentations, as well as the gender definitions of members of the nuclear family, were also considered in terms of peril and refuge.

In Chapter Three the macrocosmic level of kinship was considered in connection with regional kinship structures (tribally organized pastoralists and villagers) and local-community kinship structures (chiefly, non-tribally organized villages). The point was made that the existence of macrocosmic kinship structures is not necessarily incompatible with urban life. In Chapter Four urban domestic social organization (household composition and structure) was discussed, with emphasis on its variety. While the nuclear family is statistically the most frequent type of household in cities (and in villages and among pastoral nomads), patterns of kinship alliance and dependence beyond the household itself are very important. These more extended kinship ties predictably include the individual's grandparents, her or his parents' siblings and their children (that is, first cousins), or selected members within this circle of what is sometimes called the bilateral kindred. Beyond the bilateral kindred, however, the individual's kinship ties (expectations of alliance and mutual support and recognition of common descent) vary greatly. It is presumed that all Middle Easterners are aware of and understand the metaphor of descent from a common ancestor, with its tribes and lineages, but it seems evident that many Middle Eastern individuals do not actively participate in the larger groups that are based on this concept. Pragmatic concerns, such as evaluating the trade-offs between the burdens and the rewards of widely extended kinship ties, seem to be important. Also important, in fact essential, are the effects of ambitious individuals who assume leadership roles using the metaphor of common descent from an ancestor as the legitimization of political alliance. These circumstances are different for different individuals at any given time, and they can change through time for any given aggregation of descendants of a particular ancestor. This variety and changeability can be seen as perilous, but it can also be seen as flexible and adaptable. It is, indeed, both, and so it is at the heart of the peril-and-refuge theme for most individuals. Change due to the segmentation or division of lineages or tribes has been amply documented and illustrated in many of the books cited and annotated in earlier chapters. Less frequently reported is the recombining of common descent groups, which is consistent with precisely the same metaphor. This recombining does occur, however, as has been observed recently among the Ghilzai Pashtun of Afghanistan (Anderson 1975, pp. 588–589). The same principles are also being used in suburban Beirut, where putative genealogical links are manipulated in the formation of the new family associations that are among the many adaptations to a rapidly changing cultural scene (Khuri 1975, pp. 227–229).

The earlier part of this chapter dealt with yet another aspect of kinship: the relationships between female and male individuals. Central in this is the conventional, traditional understanding that close female-male relationships should be confined to life in the domestic household. Extending the view outward from this domestic core, recent studies (in some contrast to earlier ones) suggest that the Middle Eastern individual encounters, or finds herself or himself involved in, a variable system of networks. Older studies tended to present a view of the individual as a member of a rigidly defined patrilineal group, involving fixed inheritance rights, absolute responsibilities in regard to liabilities in the case of feuds and other disputes, transfer of females out of their natal lineages upon marriage (except, of course, in cases of patrilateral parallel cousin marriage), and corresponding disregard of ties of kinship through females. More recent modifying interpretations have involved new thinking about some of the information that has been available all along, such as the segmentation of lineages, which can be looked upon as a means whereby people can opt out of a kinship situation that has ceased to be sufficiently advantageous to warrant the cost of maintaining a wide range of obligations. Segmentation does not eliminate kinship obligations, but it does reduce the number of kinsmen with whom the individual has these obligations.

In many cultures of the world where membership in kinship groups is determined by unilineal descent from a common ancestor, the individual's immersion in that group is symbolized by names and/or by the terminology used to designate kinsmen. In many cases the names or the kinship terms, or both, code the individual as being one member of large, constant classes of individuals, such as descent lines several generations in depth. This is true in the Middle East only to a very limited extent.

In regard to naming, let us consider the hypothetical genealogy shown in Figure 3. In this diagram eight consecutive generations are partially indicated. Only the descendants of Musa ibn Abdul-

Hamid (Musa, son of Abdul-Hamid) are extensively shown, but let us assume that his brothers and his first cousins, who are named in generation III, had descendants also. Except for Aziza bint (daughter of) Mahmud and Mahbubah bint Karim, only males are shown. This is for convenience, but it happens to conform to the usual Middle Eastern practice in constructing genealogies. Notice that no son is named directly after his father; the "Junior" pattern so frequent among Americans is absent. However, every person's second name is his or her father's name. The Arabic words for son and daughter (ibn and bint), and their equivalents in other Middle Eastern languages, are often omitted, and so the two persons noted in generation VII are very frequently called, simply, Nur al-Din Karim and Mahbubah Karim. Karim is not their "family name" in the Western sense of the term. It is specifically their father's name. The father and his brother are, in turn, known as Karim Muhammad and Habib Muhammad. These may well be the only formal names that these people have. After she marries, Mahbubah Karim will continue to be called that until Hassan is born, and then she will be called Umm Hassan (Hassan's Mother). This naming system emphasizes immediate ancestry, as does the system of kinship terminology, but it does not automatically or readily lump together individuals in different generations as members of large groups of descendants.

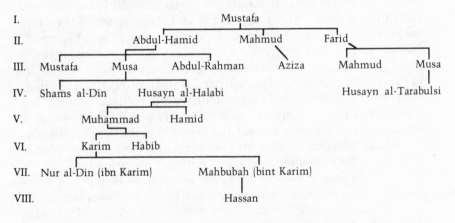

Figure 3. Hypothetical Genealogical Chart.

Approximations of Western-style family names are possible in Middle Eastern usage. Especially where tribal structures are in operation, the name (or a nickname or a title) of the person considered to be the common ancestor will usually be the basis of the tribal name. Thus, Nur al-Din Karim and Mahbubah Karim may also be surnamed Mustafa (after the original ancestor) or referred to as members of the Al Mustafa, Awlad Mustafa, or Bani Mustafa ("descendants," "offspring," or "sons" of Mustafa). However, if the descendants of Mustafa have not, after seven generations, already segmented into different lineages, they presumably soon will, and the surnames (if any) will reflect this. For instance, the descendants of Aziza bint Mahmud may use *her* name to distinguish themselves from other descendants of Mustafa, if it is more advantageous to retain that identity than that of her husband. This divergence from the usual patriliny (and such divergences do occur) could be due to various circumstances. Perhaps, for instance, Aziza's father was wealthy, and, as an only child, she inherited considerable property in her own right. To call her descendants after her father, however, might have confused them with the descendents of Mahmud ibn Farid, who are poor and inclined to make claims on their wealthy kinsmen. Such claims can be blunted by the segmentation of the descendants of Aziza from those of Farid, and the names will reflect this segmentation.

A variant on this theme is represented by the nicknames of the two Husayns in generation IV. Since their fathers were both named Musa, their own names are identical. How can these two men named Husayn Musa be distinguished from each other? A typical method is to nickname them differently, calling one "large" and the other "small," for instance, or giving them different occupational names, or—as in this case—giving them different city names. One Husayn Musa migrated to Tripoli (Tarablus) and thereafter became known as Husayn al-Tarabulsi, while the other migrated to Aleppo (Halab) and became known as Husayn al-Halabi. In response to certain needs, such as the enhancement of prestige or increasing Western-style pressures, the descendents of these men may adopt Tarabulsi and Halabi, respectively, as their surnames. The principle is consistent with patrilineal descent, but the form is more suggestive of Western-style surnames, owing to the fact that the names are not the personal names of individuals.

Many Western-style pressures are being felt in the Middle East, and they include changing customs in regard to family names. The late president of Egypt is commonly referred to as President Nasser, as if Nasser were a Western-style surname. It is not. His name actually was Gamal Abdul-Nasr, Abdul-Nasr being his father's name, used in exactly the manner just discussed. Given the enormous prestige in this instance, Nasser may become the "family name" of his descendants, just as it already has in popular thinking.

In Iran, each person now has a family name irrespective of her or his father's own name. This was imposed by edict in the reign of the present Shah's father. To set an example, he adopted Pahlavi as his family name, this word being associated with some of the glories of the pre-Islamic culture of Iran. Places, occupations, descent from certain persons, or personal attributes are often the bases of other modern Iranian family names. Other Middle Eastern countries are in the process of making Western-style family names legal and standard, but I am aware of only one reference to the effects of these changes. This is Magnarella's brief comment. He says that in Turkey the stipulations of the 1934 law made it improbable for many people to register their non-Turkish lineage or tribal names as family names. Hence these were lost. Furthermore, the law limited the number of households in any one community who could choose the same family name, and this meant that many people could not register their old lineage names even if they were Turkish. The results have been to make the recognition of extensive kinship ties much more difficult. This has been compounded by the fact that many unrelated people have chosen the same surname (Magnarella 1974, p. 86).

On the whole, Middle Eastern naming patterns, while accommodating to the metaphor of common descent, allow for varied forms, resulting in considerable inconsistency. Yet this inconsistency in itself reflects the different degrees of involvement of different people in extensive kinship groups. In other words, the naming system is adaptible to the varying expressions of extensive kinship involvement and is, indeed, a function of it.

The same can be said of the various Middle Eastern kinship terminologies. They differ from each other just as the various languages do. For example, the Persian equivalents of abu, umm, ibn, and bint are pedar, madar, pesar, and dokhtar. However, though the words differ, the basic pattern of the terminological system is the same in all the major Middle Eastern languages. Consider, for example, yourself as being the referent person ("ego") among relatives. In addition to there being distinctive terms for your father and mother, there are distinctive terms for your father's brother and for your mother's brother. Instead of saying "uncle" for both of them, you automatically use different terms for each of them. The same is true for your father's sister and your mother's sister. The spouses of these four types of parents' sibling, rather than being called "aunt" or "uncle"—further weakening the specificity of those words—are also referred to in various distinctive ways, one of which is to group together with one term the wives of brothers. The children of your parents' siblings are called son or daughter of "father's brother," or "mother's sister," and so on, rather than all being referred to as "cousin" regardless of which parent's sibling is their parent. The system of kinship terminology thus automatically sets apart from one another five mini-descent-groups: one's own parentage and those of four possible sets of first cousins. Members of only one of those sets are automatically members of one's own lineage (for example, father's brother's daughter and son), although some of the others may be so as the result of cousin marriages in previous generations.

In any case, the system combines precision on gender and descent (key concepts in the principle of common ancestry and segmentation), but it does not unequivocally lump together large groups of relatives as being members of lineages (as some kinship terminologies in the world do). It does appear to be true, however, that beyond the bilateral kindred, the same terms that have been mentioned may also be used for more distant relatives, so that the terms themselves can no longer, in such cases, be taken literally. There is an area of ambiguity in this regard that needs more study, and there is some new information on instances of adaptations of the system to fit actually felt sentiments. An instructive example is provided by Keyser: A Turkish man habitually addressed and referred to his mother's father's brother not as "mother's brother" (the usual matrilateral extension) but as "father's brother," because this expressed the true quality of this important relationship as it had developed during his life (Keyser 1974, p. 303). It is by rationalizations such as this, as well as those mentioned in Chapter Two, that genealogies are adjusted to on-going realities, making them nearly worthless for studies of genetics but highly significant as metaphors of perceived reality.

The uses of kinship terminologies in the Middle East are actually far more complex than has been indicated here, and the subject—a specialty of anthropology—is being refined by increasingly technical analyses, such as those of Casson (1973 and 1975) and Brown and Sowayan (1974).

The interests of kinship networks are expressed in marriage choices, and marriage and procreation continually renew those networks or initiate new ones. The Middle East is famous for the fact that the marriage of patrilateral parallel cousins (son and daughter of brothers) is generally preferred, except among Christians and some Turkish Muslims (Magnarella 1974, pp. 87–90). Given the patrilineal descent emphasis, this is a marriage choice that is endogamous within the lineage, and some of the literature has treated it as if it were a strange exception to the preference for marriage choices *outside* of the lineage that is indeed typical of many cultures with unilineal descent groups. This view has increasingly been challenged. In the first place, it is only a conventionally reiterated preference. In most of the cases where it has been studied, it is not involved in the majority of marriages recorded, and when it is involved, the spouses are often not as closely related as first cousin. In the second place, the stated preference for endogamy is consistent with the preference for endogamy in general that I have previously referred to and linked with the peril-and-refuge mentality. Hilal (1970) and Keyser (1974) are very insightful on this subject. Hilal associates the conventional preference with a resolution of two conflicting male-gender roles (protector and exploiter of women), and Keyser associates it with, among other things, the general fact that when a Middle Eastern woman marries, she does not cease to be a member of her natal kin group. Instead, she acquires a second kin group membership if she marries outside her own lineage, and this may or may not be advantageous. Recent research in Isfahan, Iran, reveals ambivalent feelings among parents (about 40 percent of whom were married to cousins of some sort, both matrilateral and patrilateral) in regard to their children's marrying close relatives. One feeling is that it is better to marry a relative because the spouse and his or her family are known and already tied by obligations, and therefore the marriage is a low-risk venture. A contrary feeling that is frequently expressed is that when the husband and wife are related, they are more likely to be interfered with, and their quarrels are more likely to ramify and intensify. This ambivalence epitomizes the peril-and-refuge mentality. One of the most detailed descriptions of husband-wife quarrels and the involvement of other people in them is Granqvist's extended account of the aggrieved wife's condition of estrangement as observed in the Arab village of Artas (Granqvist 1935, p. 218).

An important factor that is becoming increasingly apparent is that, although Islamic law does emphasize patrilineal rights and expectations, a person's relatives through his or her mother may be important and influential people, either in their own right or because they are also simultaneously related through the father because of previous cousin marriages. In connection with this, the mother herself may also be a formidable person, a woman who is, as the Iranians put it, a khanom-e bozorg (a "big lady"). Once again, while the emphasis on parentage and descent is very important, the alliances and expectations based on the descent principle are flexible, adaptable, and changeable. Mothers and mother's relatives are not necessarily set apart from this system but are, on the contrary, frequently integrated into it.

PERSONALITY

That there are standard types of personality and that they are predictable in terms of national, ethnic, or other identities are two very widespread assumptions. Various social-scientific efforts have been made to establish verifiable personality profiles on this scale of generality. They often make fascinating reading, but all of them oversimplify an enormously complicated and problematic subject and should be regarded as exploratory studies. Some pertinent sources for the Middle East are Hamady (1960), Miner and DeVos (1960), Patai (1973), Beeman (1973), and Bateson, et al. (1973). Apart from the question of whether there is any Middle Eastern "national character," or a congeries of "national characters" for various Middle Eastern aggregates, there certainly are millions of individual Middle Eastern personalities.

Studies of personality formation in the Middle East emphasize the enculturation of the infant and small child primarily in the milieu of her or his immediate family. This is familiar ground to everyone with a serious interest in the subject, and some of the more important Middle Eastern studies will be commented on in the annotated bibliography of this chapter. Phenomena that recur in those studies published to date include (1) early and clear-cut differentiation between the two genders; (2) greater emphasis on negative than on positive reinforcement; (3) insistence on obedience to outward forms, emphasized by corporal punishment and threats; and (4) emphasis more on shame and less on guilt as a control emotion. These conclusions must be regarded as subject to review, reassessment, refinement, and outright revision.

One of the important aspects of Middle Eastern culture that has been neglected is adolescence and young adulthood. Influences on personality do not cease with childhood, although the psychoanalytic approach has tended to reinforce the idea that they do. For many females the transition from pubescent girlhood to adult wifely status has been early and abrupt. For males the equivalent transition has tended to be less abrupt and more attenuated. The female's becoming a responsible (but constricted) adult early in life and the male's being an irresponsible or confused adolescent for a longer period are two generalizations that have been suggested, and illustrated in the case of one Lebanese Muslim village (Williams 1968). Adolescent boys' gangs have been mentioned, too, as for example in Iraqi cities (al-Wardi 1965, pp. 324–325).

Most of the information on adolescence, meager as it is, is concerned with adolescents and young adults in the new, modern educational systems of various Middle Eastern countries. The impact (or lack of it) of the new institutions on the students' domestic culture that they bring from home is one concern, and dissonance or conflict is its theme (see Sack 1973; Klineberg 1973). The characteristics of "youth," particularly in connection with new cultural styles and the intergenerational conflicts that result, have been given some consideration (Arasteh 1969; Dodd 1968; Hudson 1959; Melikian 1973). It is certainly possible that many of the cultural patterns that have been presented in this book as continuities in tradition may be radically changed in the quite near future. This will come about if sufficient numbers of people who are presently adolescents and young adults become permanently divergent from traditional continuities in their normal behavior. However, it must also be remembered that many youths are conservative and conformist in orientation (see Kagitbasi 1973). Furthermore, insofar as changed norms are probably most likely to be generated among students in secondary schools and universities, we must bear in mind that only very small proportions of any of this educational subculture.

Expressiveness

The personalities of Middle Eastern people are expressed in all of the cultural patterns that have been considered in this book, and the most pervasive of these may be the hypothesized peril-and-refuge mentality. There are, in addition, some styles and codes of expressiveness that require some attention at this point.

The foreign visitor to any part of the Middle East immediately feels the impact of the expressive styles of the people. The contents and structures of the various languages are of course of central importance to this expressiveness, but these are subjects that are far beyond the scope of this book. Speaking is accompanied by body language that is highly visible to anyone, but whose sophisticated meanings and cues need extensive elucidation, as in Barakat (1973). Hall (1966, p. 147) has suggested the idea that Arabs may sense their egos (essential selves) to be inside their bodies rather than coterminous with their skins, as he claims is true of typical Westerners. If this hypothesis could be supported by further study, it might explain why many Middle Easterners seem to have reactions to crowding and touching (an important element in Middle Eastern body language) that seem to be different from those of many Westerners.

Music. The air is filled with it, especially in village and urban public places where radios, cinemas, and recordings are now firmly established aspects of Middle Eastern culture. The scale and the instrumental and vocal patterns are all distinct and different from Western modes. While Western popular and classical musical forms have their Middle Eastern devotees, the traditional Middle Eastern music, in pure and modified forms, remains immensely popular and highly characteristic of the living environment. It is itself differentiated into a variety of styles, some considered folksy, others vulgar and uncouth, and still others classical (Zonis 1973; Bishai 1973, pp. 113–133). The vocal patterns are related, in turn, to poetry. There is not only a poetic literary tradition, but much poetry is also committed to memory, quoted, played games with, and extensively recited by large numbers of people who do not otherwise have literary interests.

While the distinction between fine arts and crafts can be very subtle (see Wulff 1966), Middle Easterners' interest in their own traditional fine arts appears to be specialized and limited to only a few people. The old utilitarian crafts are indeed threatened with extinction because of inability to compete with mass-produced goods, and many splendid specimens of traditional architecture are being destroyed as the cities, in particular, grow. One effect of this

224   is to reinforce the impression that the Middle East is being over-whelmed by the material forms of the West and thereby being transformed into a copy of the West. However, there is a counter-impression that leaves little doubt that there remain in the Middle East cultural themes that are distinctive and special. This impression is conveyed by the modes of personal expressiveness that have just been mentioned, as well as the cultural and characterological themes that were discussed earlier in the chapter and in previous chapters of the book.

REFERENCES

Abou-Zeid, A.M. "Honour and Shame among the Bedouin of Egypt." In *Honour and Shame*, edited by J. G. Peristiany, pp. 245–259. Chicago: University of Chicago Press, 1966.

Anderson, Jon. "Tribe and Community among the Ghilzai Pashtun, Preliminary Notes on Ethnographic Distribution and Variation in Eastern Afghanistan." *Anthropos* 70 (1975), pp. 575–601.

Arasteh, A. Reza. *Education and Social Awakening in Iran, 1850–1968.* Leiden, Netherlands: E. J. Brill, 1969.

Baalabaki, Laila. "A Spaceship of Tenderness to the Moon." In *Modern Arabic Short Stories*, edited and translated by Denys Johnson-Davies, pp. 130–136. London: Oxford University Press, 1967.

Barakat, Robert A. "Arabic Gestures." *Journal of Popular Culture* 6 (1973): 749–793.

Bateson, M. C., J. W. Clinton, J. B. M. Kassarjian, H. Safavi, and M. Soraya. "Safa-yi Batin: A Study of the Interrelations of a Set of Iranian Ideal Character Types." Paper submitted to Conference on Psychology and Near Eastern Studies, Princeton University, May 1973.

Beeman, William O. "Is There an Iranian National Character? A Sociolinguistic Approach." Paper prepared for Annual Meeting of Middle East Studies Association, Milwaukee, Wisc., November 7–12, 1973.

Berger, Morroe. "The Arab Danse du Ventre." *Dance Perspectives* 10 (1961): 4–49.

Berque, Jacques. *Structures Sociales du Haut-Atlas.* Paris: Presses Universitaires de France, 1955.

Bishai, Wilson B. *Humanities in the Arabic-Islamic World.* Dubuque, Iowa: Brown, 1973.

Bourdieu, Pierre. "The Sentiment of Honour in Kabyle Society." In *Honour and Shame*, edited by J. G. Peristiany, pp. 193–241. Chicago: University of Chicago Press, 1966.

Brown, Cecil H., and Saad Sowayan. "Descent and Alliance in an Endogamous Society: A Structural Analysis of Arab Kinship." Unpublished manuscript, Northeastern Illinois University, 1974.

Casson, Ronald W. "Paired Polarity Relations in the Formal Analysis of a Turkish Kinship Terminology." *Ethnology* 12 (1973): 275–297.

Casson, Ronald W. "The Semantics of Kin Term Usage." *American Ethnologist* 2 (1975): 229–238.

des Villettes, Jacqueline. *La vie des Femmes dans un village Maronite Libanais: Ain el Kharoubé.* Tunis: Imprimerie N. Bascone & S. Muscat, 1964.

Dodd, Peter C. "Youth and Women's Emancipation in the United Arab Republic." *The Middle East Journal* 22 (1968): 159–172.

Dodd, Peter C. "Family Honor and the Forces of Change in Arab Society." *International Journal of Middle East Studies* 4 (1973): 40–54.

Edmiston, Susan. Review of E. E. Maccoby and C. N. Jacklin, *Psychology of Sex Differences* and R. C. Friedman, R. M. Richart, and R. L. Vande Wiele, eds., *Sex Differences in Behavior.* New York Times Book Review, April 13, 1975, p. 3.

Fox, Greer L. "Some Determinants of Modernism among Women in Ankara, Turkey." *Journal of Marriage and the Family* 14 (1973): 92–123.

Friedl, Ernestine. *Women and Men: An Anthropologist's View.* New York: Holt, Rinehart and Winston, 1975.

Granqvist, Hilma. *Marriage Conditions in a Palestinian Village*, part 2. Helsingfors, Finland: Akademische Buchhandlung, 1935.

Gulick, John, and Margaret E. Gulick. *An Annotated Bibliography of Sources Concerned with Women in the Modern Muslim Middle East.* Program in Near Eastern Studies, Princeton University: Princeton Near East Paper, no. 17, 1974.

Hall, Edward T. *The Hidden Dimension.* Garden City, N.Y.: Doubleday, 1966.

Hamady, Sania. *Temperament and Character of the Arabs.* New York: Twayne, 1960.

Hansen, Henny Harald. *Daughters of Allah: Among Moslem Women in Kurdistan.* London: George Allen & Unwin, Ltd., 1960.

Haqqi, Yahya. "Mother of the Destitute." In *Modern Arabic Short Stories*, edited by Denys Johnson-Davies, pp. 97–105. London: Oxford University Press, 1967.

Haqqi, Yahya. *The Saint's Lamp and Other Stories.* Leiden, Netherlands: E. J. Brill, 1973.

Hilal, Jamil M. "Father's Brother's Daughter Marriage in Arab Communities: A Problem for Sociological Explanation." *Middle East Forum* 46, no. 4 (1970): 73–84.

Hudson, Bradford B., ed. "Cross-Cultural Studies in the Arab Middle East and United States: Studies of Young Adults." *The Journal of Social Issues* 15, no. 3 (1959): 1–76.

Idris, Youssef. "Peace with Honour." In *Arabic Writing Today: The Short Story*, edited by Mahmoud Manzalaoui, pp. 234–255. Cairo: American Research Center in Egypt, 1968.

Kagitbasi, Cigdem. "Psychological Aspects of Modernization in Turkey." *Journal of Cross-Cultural Psychology* 4 (1973): 157–174.

Keyser, James M. B. "The Middle Eastern Case: Is There a Marriage Rule?" *Ethnology* 13 (1974): 293–309.

Khuri, Fuad I. *From Village to Suburb: Order and Change in Greater Beirut.* Chicago: University of Chicago Press, 1975.

Klineberg, Stephen L. "Parents, Schools and Modernity: An Exploratory Investigation of Sex Differences in the Attitudinal Development of Tunisian Adolescents." *International Journal of Comparative Sociology* 14 (1973): 221–244.

Magnarella, Paul J. "Conjugal Role-Relationships in a Modernizing Turkish Town." *International Journal of Sociology and the Family* 2 (1972): 179–192.

Magnarella, Paul J. *Tradition and Change in a Turkish Town.* New York: Wiley, 1974.

Maher, Vanessa. *Women and Property in Morocco: Their Changing Relation to the Process of Social Stratification in the Middle Atlas.* Cambridge: at the University Press, 1974.

Melikian, Levon H. "The Modal Personality of Saudi College Students: A Study in National Character." Paper presented at Conference on Psychology and Near Eastern Studies, Princeton University, May 1973.

Miner, Horace M. and George De Vos. *Oasis and Casbah: Algerian Culture and Personality in Change.* Ann Arbor: Museum of Anthropology, University of Michigan, Anthropological Papers, no. 15, 1960.

M'rabet, Fadéla. *La femme algérienne suivi des algériennes.* Paris: François Maspero, 1969.

Nelson, Cynthia. "Public and Private Politics: Women in the Middle Eastern World." *American Ethnologist* 1 (1974): 551–563.

Patai, Raphael. *The Arab Mind.* New York: Scribner's, 1973.

Sack, Richard. "The Impact of Education on Individual Modernity in Tunisia." *International Journal of Comparative Sociology* 14 (1973): 245–272.

Schneider, Jane. "Of Vigilance and Virgins: Honor, Shame, and Access to Resources in Mediterranean Societies." *Ethnology* , 10 (1971): 1–24.

Sharouni, Yusuf. "The Man and the Farm." In *Modern Arabic Short Stories*, edited by Denys Johnson-Davies, pp. 56–66. London: Oxford University Press, 1967.

Tillion, Germaine. *Le harem et les cousins.* Paris: Editions du Seuil, 1966.

Vieille, Paul. "Birth and Death in an Islamic Society." *Diogenes* 57 (1967): 101–127.

Vinogradov, Amal. "French Colonialism as Reflected in the Male-Female Interaction in Morocco." *Transactions of the New York Academy of Sciences,* series 2, vol. 36, no. 2, pp. 192–199, 1974.

al-Wardi, Ali. *A Study in the Society of Iraq.* Baghdad: Al-Ani Press, 1965 (in Arabic). (German edition available through Kegan Paul: *Studie über die Irakische Gesellschaft,* 1972.)

Williams, Judith R. *The Youth of Haouch el Harimi, a Lebanese Village.* Cambridge, Mass.: Harvard Middle Eastern Monographs, vol. 20, 1968.

Wulff, Hans E. *The Traditional Crafts of Persia.* Cambridge, Mass.: M.I.T. Press, 1966.

Youssef, Nadia H. *Women and Work in Developing Societies.* University of California, Berkeley, Population Monograph Series, no. 15, 1974.

Zonis, Ella. *Classical Persian Music: an Introduction.* Cambridge, Mass.: Harvard University Press, 1973.

ANNOTATED BIBLIOGRAPHY

Bibliographies

In addition to Gulick & Gulick 1974, cited above, the following two works are important.

Gray, Audrey Ward. *Childhood, Children and Child Rearing in the Arab Middle East: A Selected and Annotated Bibliography.* Beirut: Ford Foundation, 1973.

Some overlap with Gulick and Gulick, but not enough to be repetitious.

Racy, John. *Psychiatry in the Arab East.* Copenhagen: Munksgaard, 1970.

The author is a psychiatrist of Lebanese origin. Part of this work is a short monograph on Middle Eastern psychiatry and psychiatric phenomena. The annotated bibliography includes not only clinical works but relevant behavioral science works as well.

Family and Islamic Law

Anderson, J. N. D. *Islamic Law in the Modern World.* New York: New York University Press, 1959.

A succinct monograph on sharia law, whose modern applications are increasingly restricted to family relations and personal status.

Coulson, N. J. *Succession in the Muslim Family.* Cambridge: at the University Press, 1971.

Detailed, technical analysis of Muslim rules of inheritance.

Magnarella, Paul J. "The Reception of Swiss Family Law in Turkey." *Anthropological Quarterly* 46, (1973): 100–104.

A test case of adaptation of new forms in a changing culture.

Mahmassani, S. *The Philosophy of Jurisprudence in Islam*. Leiden, Netherlands: E. J. Brill, 1961.

This book could equally appropriately be cited in Chapter 6, especially in connection with the sectarian great tradition. It is cited here because it represents the full context of family law.

Family and Child Rearing

In addition to works cited and annotated in Gray's bibliography, a few works deserve special notice here.

Ammar, Hamed. *Growing Up in an Egyptian Village*. London: Routledge & Kegan Paul, Ltd., 1954.

A classic; done in the author's own village in Upper Egypt. This book is strongly influenced by the culture-and-personality school of thought in American anthropology, which, in the late 1940s and early 1950s, was infused with psychoanalytic concepts.

Granqvist, Hilma. *Birth and Childhood Among the Arabs*. Helsingfors, Finland: Söderström & Co., 1947.

Granqvist, Hilma. *Child Problems Among the Arabs*. Helsingfors: Söderström & Co., 1950.

This pair of books is part of the series of monographs, already referred to, on Granqvist's field work in Artas, near Bethlehem, in 1926–1931. Not oriented in terms of behavioral science theories, Granqvist observed keenly, reported in great detail, and had a strong sense of empathy with the people, especially the women, of Artas.

Kendall, Katherine W. *Personality Development in an Iranian Village: An Analysis of Socialization Practices and Development of the Woman's Role*. Ph.D. dissertation, University of Washington, 1968.

Unique as a study in Iran. The title reflects the emphases of the approach. Near the conclusion (p. 205) Kendall refers to the hospitable yet reserved and suspicious adults, and the quarrelsome individuals that nevertheless submit meekly to external authority, that she feels are typically produced in this milieu.

Prothro, E. Terry. *Child Rearing in the Lebanon*. Cambridge, Mass.: Harvard Middle East Monographs, no. 6, 1961.

Analysis of interviews with Sunni Muslim, Eastern Orthodox, and Armenian rural and urban mothers and some of their children. This work systematically compares these data with Western data and notes differences and similarities among the three Lebanese sects.

Prothro, E. Terry, and Lutfy N. Diab. *Changing Family Patterns in the Arab East*. Beirut: American University of Beirut, 1974.

A study (using interviews and public records) of Sunni Muslims in the cities of Amman, Beirut, Damascus, and Tripoli (Lebanon) and in the villages of Artas and Buarij, which had been studied by Granqvist and Fuller in the 1920s and 1930s. Changes through time and differences (or similarities) among the communities are emphasized. The data relate chiefly to marriage decisions and arrangements and the status of women, but not to child rearing.

Williams, Judith R. *The Youth of Haouch el Harimi, a Lebanese Village.* Cambridge, Mass.: Harvard Middle Eastern Monographs, 20, 1968.

Emphasis on gender definitions and differentiations especially among adolescents. Its data thus add important perspectives on a topic that is more usually considered in terms of infancy and childhood.

EIGHT

CONCLUSION

PERIL, REFUGE, AND CONSTRAINT

This book has proposed the hypothesis that a peril-and-refuge mentality is characteristically brought by Middle Eastern people into their community relations. Middle Eastern communities are based on the categories of identity that were discussed in Chapter Two. Relationships between communities are often distant at best and openly hostile at worst. Relationships within communities can certainly be supportive and trusting. However, they can also be reserved and wary, and realignments and resortings of community memberships are normal and expected. As a result, individuals generally hestitate to make full commitments to group ventures and are always inclined to hedge their bets. In other words, there is an important element of constraint in intracommunity, as well as extracommunity, relations.

I have suggested that this is a sociocultural feedback system that has been perpetuated since early Florescent times. If this is true, then it has obviously been a viable enough system to survive the competition of other systems that there may have been. Is the peril-and-refuge mentality now, at last, being transformed into something different by the accumulated changes of the Islamic Machine Age? There are a few indications of what may be incipient trends in this direction, but I have not read or seen anything that is a convincing demonstration of there yet being any such trends that are substantial. In fact, much of the information that has been used in order to propose the idea of the peril-and-refuge mentality derives from observations made well within the Machine-Age Islamic period itself. Peril and refuge is a theme of human beings' relationships and of their attitudes toward, and expectations of, one another. Most of the literature (scholarly, journalistic, and propagandistic) that emphasizes the "modernization" of the Middle East does not bear very much on this subject, but when human relations *are* put at the forefront of such considerations, the continuing importance of the peril-and-refuge mentality is likely to be evident. An example is Millward's essay (1971) on modernization in Iran that begins by discussing two opposed Iranian personality stereotypes: the gharbzadegan and the sunnat-parastan ("westernizers" and "traditionalists").

If the peril-and-refuge mentality has persisted for a long time, perhaps it has done so because in a less-than-ideal world, and under Middle Eastern circumstances, it is the best possible modality of interaction. It is the expression of what is essentially a system of trade-offs between autonomy and alliance, set in a natural environment that offers limited abundance and continual uncertainty. What components of "modernization" can significantly alter these conditions?

Whether Middle Eastern people in substantial numbers see their problems in these terms, I do not know. It is clear, however, that substantial numbers of them are now dissatisfied with various conditions of their lives that I would identify as communal constraints. In particular, these constraints appear in the relations between the two genders and between land of government and land of dissidence, as well as in inequable access to the resources of existence. The constraints in themselves seem to inhibit innovative experimentation, yet it is only in those innovations that become established as norms that the dissatisfactions can eventually be mitigated.

CONSTRAINT AND POWER

Given the land of government/land of dissidence mentality, people who have governmental power are also constrained in the undertaking of cultural innovations. True, there are dramatic declarations of intent and purpose, such as the Shah of Iran's "White Revolution," but whether the intentions are realized will depend on the manner of the plan's implementation. Cultural revolutions —revolutions in normative values and the behavioral patterns associated with them—have been known to fail even when promoted by enormously powerful governments. A case in point was the Soviet Union's stringent efforts to revolutionize the status of Muslim women in Soviet Central Asia in the 1920s, efforts that resulted not only in enormous distress but also in the government's retrenchment of its project (Massell 1974).

Power can obviously move people, but power alone, exercised without sufficient understanding of the motivations and values of those being moved, may have results that diverge greatly from those envisaged. For better or worse, the generally autocratic nature of Middle Eastern governments means that government-initiated changes are undertaken autocratically. So far, the effects are varied. For example, with respect to the governments of nine Arabic-speaking countries, it has been suggested that during the

middle third of the twentieth century, their economic modernization policies have not relieved the great poverty of many of their
citizens (Amin 1974). The reasons are many, of course—one of
them being that poverty is interrelated with a complex of cultural
patterns, values, and expectations. In Turkey, however, considerably more positive effects of government-sponsored changes have
been noted (Magnarella 1974).

Many Middle Eastern officials belong to the professional middle or upper classes. They are often people who have been heavily
influenced by Western cultural life styles, and some of them are
reported even to have rejected many of the non-Western patterns of
their own cultures. Alienated though these people may have become from many aspects of their traditional culture, they are still
members of the society of which those traditional patterns are important components. Consequently, they continually face various
dilemmas in living, and these have been vividly analyzed in the
case of bilingual/bicultural individuals in the Maghrib (Gallagher
1966). In addition to this sort of problem, many officials continue to
be enmeshed in the networks of defensive maneuver that have
been analyzed by Waterbury in Morocco and Zonis in Iran (see
Chapter Two). This is the internal structure of the land of government, where the peril-and-refuge mentality is clearly apparent.

Dupree, referring to Afghanistan as one case out of many in
the Middle East, says that the state is attempting to create a nation
out of various ethnic and linguistic groups. But he asks how many
such governments can *replace* (his emphasis) the relationships involved in, and necessary for, group survival (Dupree 1974, p. 658).
Group survival, in the terms that I have used in this book, is
achieved by trade-offs between peril and refuge. Since Middle Eastern governments are themselves part of that system, how indeed
can they replace it?

The reduction of distance between the central government,
now offering social services, and the village-dwelling majorities is
one trend that some observers see as a way out of some of the
traditional impasses. Reduction of "distance" actually means several things: improved highways and transportation facilities, modernized communications technology, and less autonomy in the
regulation of local affairs. Yet even with "social services" at their
best, but without change in the traditional patterns of the exercise
of power, such distance reduction may only intensify the constraints of peril and refuge. Bureaucrats playing power games
among themselves, and relating to each other and to laymen in
styles that make manifest the superordinate-subordinate quality
that they assume to be inherent in human relationships (see
Beeman 1972), remain significantly removed from those they
theoretically serve. For the time being, at any rate, the traditional
trade-offs continue, and the status quo of tension is maintained.

For instance, in regard to the pastoral-nomadic tribes of Iran, Salzman suggests that if the tribes realize benefits from the state's economic and social programs, they will be the more inclined to accept the state's authority (Salzman 1971, p. 335). But when an Iranian peasant leader assumes an *innovative* mediator role in the effort to do something about defects in the implementation of land reform and the operations of new agricultural cooperatives, he is neglected by the officials of the state (Löffler 1971, p. 1087). In short, with the peril-and-refuge mentality still intact, perpetuation of reactions like those fictionalized by Taieb Salih in "The Doum Tree of Wad Hamid" seems likely. The mentality itself appears to be perpetuated in incidents like that at Shebika, Tunisia, where the desperate peasants finally went on strike against quarrying any more stones for a government building they neither needed nor wanted (Duvignaud 1970).

Yet there are overwhelming problems that governments must face and cope with. Many Middle Eastern governments recognize the imminent danger posed by their rapidly increasing populations, for example. The danger is that their populations will increase at greater rates than will their developing economies' abilities to improve their peoples' standards of material living. Exactly how they can significantly lessen their rates of population increase is not entirely clear, but serious thought is being given to the matter (National Academy of Sciences 1974, pp. 24–39) at the same time that in some of the countries, national family-planning programs are now in operation. There seems to be some official awareness that improved family planning alone will not achieve the desired result, one reason for this being that people accustomed to having large numbers of children must themselves perceive the benefits of having fewer children if they are going to change their behavior in this direction. How can they be helped to perceive this by governments that, traditionally, they do not trust?

Laila Shukry el-Hamamsy has discussed the many reasons why it is difficult for Egyptian peasants to envisage such benefits and therefore to act accordingly. El-Hamamsy (1972, pp. 355–356) concludes that in order for the peasants to change their behavior significantly, many other changes must occur in conjunction:

> Peasant society must develop economically and socially in such a way that the world begins to appear less threatening. It must appear to the peasant as a place where greater control is possible over the forces around him; where existence other than at a subsistence level seems feasible; where health and nutrition levels are higher and children have a greater chance of survival; where kin and children are no longer the only source of security; where women are given the opportunity to play other than family roles and to

develop a new concept of self in which personal achievement has an important place and where motherhood is not viewed as the all-important goal and the only means to achieve status; where children demand more attention and greater economic, social, and psychological investment from parents so that they constitute both a cost and a benefit; and where education brings enlightenment and exciting new opportunities for individual effort to lead to achievement.

It is of considerable interest that Dr. el-Hamamsy itemizes a number of constraints at all levels of the culture—those very constraints that characterize the peril-and-refuge mentality in the relations among the groups and aggregates in the system. She says, in effect, that they must all be broken through and overcome.

CONSTRAINTS OVERCOME?

How can such constraining patterns be overcome? Anthropologists are inclined to be ambivalent about cultural change. On the one hand, they sympathize with the reluctance of many people to radically change their life ways. The people themselves are often unable to see any alternatives to the cultural patterns that they have, while the anthropologists have seen how great the ramifications of change, once it is set in motion, can be, and how devastating its effects, often unforeseen, can be on the people involved. Consequently, there is a tendency to look upon change in negative terms or to take the position that significant changes in the values and norms of human relationships are difficult, if not impossible, unless they are accompanied by sociocultural revolution.

Anthropologists are not likely to wish such revolutions on the members of the small, relatively autonomous, technologically fragile cultures that they have traditionally studied. This attitude, often reinforced by the structural-functional orientation, which beautifully accounts for stability and continuity but not for change, is often carried over to studies of the larger-scale agrarian cultures of the world such as the Middle East.

On the other hand, where anthropologists see traditional or continuing cultural patterns as perpetuators of social injustice or of various destructive activities, they are inclined to be very much in favor of cultural change. As a result, there are anthropologists who are highly sympathetic toward peasant revolts and workers' movements, whatever the ramifications of the changes sought by them might entail.

It is difficult to reconcile these two points of view, and I think it is better to recognize the difficulty, and admit to the inconsistencies involved, than to try to cover up the problem. My own ambivalence should be evident in the foregoing material. I have presented the hypothesized peril-and-refuge mentality as a possible key to a very long lasting system of trade-offs between alliance and nonalliance. I have suggested that it may have been, and may still be, the most viable system that is possible, given the environment and the cultural-historical accumulations of the area. And I have suggested that various elements in the system will impede the processes of change—these impediments including people's inability to see alternative pathways of life or their reluctance to risk taking them. At the same time, given my own biases that I outlined in the Preface, there are elements in the system that I (and others) see as destructive and that therefore should be changed. One of these is high fertility rates, whose long-term and normative reduction I think can be achieved only with radical changes in the roles and expectations of the female and male genders. Furthermore, despite all the barriers that exist between land of government and land of dissidence, I am inclined to think that such changes can be initiated only by government action and with government encouragement. This doubtless means some coercion and the legislating of change—processes that are often ineffective, if not undesirable in other ways also.

While the anthropologist's ambivalence concerning cultural change seems to have impaled him on both horns of a dilemma, change proceeds in the Middle East anyway. Whatever the long- or short-term results may be, most Middle Eastern governments have committed themselves to mass education and technological development. There is greater political participation than there was in the quite recent past, and among many people there is active awareness of modes of behavior that are alternatives to the traditional ones. It may well be that some of the constraints that I mentioned as barriers to change will be (or are already being) overcome by changed attitudes that have perhaps not been documented with sufficient specificity.

One such new attitude may be innovativeness as opposed to fatalism. Fatalism is supposedly typical of Middle Easterners and is often linked with Islam. Though often mentioned, it has not, until recently, been studied with enough precision to warrant discussion as a cultural pattern. However, Paydarfar's survey of pastoralists, villagers, and urbanites living around and in the city of Shiraz, Iran, included some scaled items designed to measure it. On the whole, it appeared to be far less common among the urbanites than among the pastoralists and villagers, and this is interesting in view of the fact that the three aggregates did not differ particularly in their religious practices and attitudes (Paydarfar 1974, pp. 121–124). However, Paydarfar is not able to account for the diminished frequency of fatalistic responses among the urbanites except insofar as suggesting that they are more exposed to modernization and that modernization is best indicated by innovativeness.

Magnarella, in his study of a Turkish town, also touches on this subject. He, too, finds that religiosity and fatalism are not concomitant. He thinks that "fatalism ... is less a barrier to change than an ex post facto rationalization" that helps people adjust to obstacles they feel they cannot overcome. "However," Magnarella continues, "once presented with convincing evidence that they can affect their destinies, they often act with surprising spontaneity" (1974, p. 156). He thinks that the establishment of the Turkish republic and the common Turk's acquisition of voting power in 1950 did much to heighten the Turk's sense of being able to do something about the world he lives in.

This, of course, is the wisdom of hindsight. Innovation and spontaneity are particularly difficult to predict or to account for in terms of our existing theories of sociocultural behavior. Nevertheless, as the Paydarfar and Magnarella studies indicate, they are present, and perhaps growing, among many Middle Eastern people. They may well facilitate significant changes in many of the cultural patterns that have been emphasized in this book.

REFERENCES

Amin, Galal A. *The Modernization of Poverty: A Study in the Political Economy of Growth in Nine Arab Countries 1945–1970.* Leiden, Netherlands: E. J. Brill, 1974.

Beeman, William O. "Style and Strategy in Iranian Interaction: The Relative Status Dimension." Revised version of paper presented at 71st Annual Meeting of American Anthropological Association, November 29–December 3, 1972.

Dupree, Louis. *Afghanistan.* Princeton, N.J.: Princeton University Press, 1974.

Duvignaud, Jean. *Change at Shebika: Report from a North African Village.* New York: Pantheon, 1970.

Gallagher, Charles F. "Language and Identity." *In State and Society in Independent North Africa,* edited by L. Carl Brown, pp. 73–96. Washington, D.C.: Middle East Institute, 1966.

el-Hamamsy, Laila Shukry. "Belief Systems and Family Planning in Peasant Societies." In *Are Our Descendants Doomed? Technological Change and Population Growth,* edited by Harrison Brown and Edward Hutchings, Jr., pp. 335–357. New York: Viking, 1972. (Discussion by Alan W. Horton, pp. 358–361.)

Löffler, Reinhold. "The Representative Mediator and the New Peasant." *American Anthropologist* 73, no. 5 (1971): 1077–1091.

Magnarella, Paul J. *Tradition and Change in a Turkish Town.* New York: Wiley, 1974.

Massell, Gregory J. *The Surrogate Proletariat: Moslem Women and Revolutionary Strategies in Soviet Central Asia: 1919–1929.* Princeton, N.J.: Princeton University Press, 1974.

Millward, William G. "Traditional Values and Social Change in Iran." **237**
    Iranian Studies 4 (1971): 2–35.

National Academy of Sciences. *In Search of Population Policy: Views
    from the Developing World.* Washington, D.C.: Middle East Seminar
    on Population Policy, 1974, pp. 24–39.

Paydarfar, Ali A. *Social Change in a Southern Province of Iran.* Chapel
    Hill: University of North Carolina, Institute for Research in Social
    Science, Comparative Urban Studies, Monograph no. 1, 1974.

Salzman, Philip C. "National Integration of the Tribes in Modern Iran."
    The Middle East Journal 25 (1971): 325–336.

BIBLIOGRAPHICAL NOTE

Paul Magnarella's *Tradition and Change in a Turkish Town* (1974)
is one of the best anthropological community studies in the Middle East that has so far been published. Like Khuri's *From Village
to Suburb*, it is the product of using both standardized, formal
data-gathering techniques and intensive participant observation.
The data are therefore particularly rich. What especially recommends this study, however, it its presentation of traditional and
changing cultural patterns as a functioning whole and its specific
linkages of the town and its inhabitants to the larger society to
which it belongs and which is the source of all of the important
changes. Traditional patterns, as they are adapted to changing conditions, and innovations introduced from elsewhere are examined
in detail. As a result, there are none of the generalities about modernization that typify so many treatments of the subject. The many
processes that are involved are seen in the immediacy of their effects on everyday lives.

   On the whole, the reader receives a positive impression of the
effects of change, including the increased involvement of the government in people's lives. However, Magnarella draws his book to
a close with the case of a man caught in the "culture of discontent" caused by inability to achieve new aspirations. The book
ends with a warning to the societies of the world that, in modernizing, they must reject the modern Western emphases on individual self-interest, materialism, conspicuous production, acquisition, and consumption. He hopes that these societies, including
Turkey, can create a "more human self-image and social ethic"
from some of the values that they have already. This is a very different version of modernization from that which has so often, since
World War II, been promoted.

INDEX